# ECO-CITY DIMENSIONS

---

## Healthy Communities
## Healthy Planet

Edited by

Mark Roseland

NEW SOCIETY PUBLISHERS

**Canadian Cataloguing in Publication Data:**
A catalog record for this publication is available from the National
Library of Canada and the Library of Congress.

Cover design by David Lester.

Printed in Canada on acid-free, partially recycled
(20 percent post-consumer) paper using soy-based inks
by Best Book Manufacturers.

Inquiries regarding requests to reprint all or part of *Eco-City Dimensions*
should be addressed to New Society Publishers
at the address below.

Paperback ISBN: 0-86571-353-7
Hardback ISBN: 0-86571-352-9

To order directly from the publishers, please add $3.00 to the price of
the first copy, and $1.00 for each additional copy
(plus GST in Canada). Send check or money order to:

New Society Publishers,
P.O. Box 189, Gabriola Island, BC V0R 1X0, Canada.

New Society Publishers aims to publish books for fundamental social
change through nonviolent action. We focus especially on sustainable living, progressive leadership, and educational and parenting resources.
Our full list of books can be browsed on the world wide web at:
http://www.swifty.com/nsp/

**NEW SOCIETY PUBLISHERS**
Gabriola Island, BC, Canada and New Haven, CT, U.S.A.

**ON MAY 14, 1995 IN LONDON, ENGLAND, A MOCK TRAFFIC
ACCIDENT TURNS INTO A FIVE-HOUR STREET PARTY.**

An old car drove up the street to one of the busiest intersections in London:
High Street, Camden. It entered the five-way intersection at a slow pace, to
be smashed into by another car in similar condition coming the other way.
Both drivers, obviously upset, got out and started to abuse each other, much
to the annoyance of other drivers who were blockaded by the altercation.
The two drivers got so irate at each other that they both removed sledge
hammers from their trunks and proceeded to smash up each other's cars,
much to the disbelief of the drivers now in a traffic jam. But this was only
the beginning, as the altercation was a theatrical move to block the road
and to signify to hundreds of people — who then poured into the street
from the tube station — that the street was reclaimed and the party could
now begin. All cars entering the intersection got gridlocked. Shoppers and
market-goers joined the street party which lasted five hours. The smashed
cars became the focus for all to vent their anger on, and were attacked
throughout the party. The police directed traffic — what else could they do?

Reclaim the Streets is a British "disorganization" that has grown
out of the recent anti-roads movement in London and the U.K.
Photo: Nick Cobbing.
Text: adapted from N. Moxham, "Car Rage or Car Rave?" *Adbusters*,
Spring 1996 (33), reprinted from *Earth First!* Yule 1995.

# Table of Contents

# Preface

*Mark Roseland*

This book is not just about cities. It's about where and how we live, whether in villages, towns, suburbs, or mega-cities. It's about what some people call "human settlements."

Whenever agricultural or forest land is cleared for other purposes, whenever roads are built or expanded, whenever a new shopping center or subdivision is created, whenever an urban area is "redeveloped" — in short, whenever the natural or the built environment is changed through human action, the health of our communities and our planet is affected. Eco-city dimensions are universal and apply at any scale, although their application must be tailored to each unique situation and respect local conditions and opportunities.

Many people who are interested in cities are "city people." They live for people-watching, window-shopping, and sipping cappuccino at sidewalk cafés while reading about architecture in the Sunday *New York Times*. Not me. Although I enjoy some city pleasures, I am a "country person" at heart. I much prefer to live in the woods, which I did for a while — longer, in fact, than Thoreau lived at Walden Pond.

I became interested in cities not because I love cities, but rather because I began to understand them. In particular, I understand two things now that I didn't realize before. First, if we want our children to have the option of a rural lifestyle, we have to remake our cities into eco-cities. Otherwise our cities will consume the countryside, depriving future generations of the land and resources required to maintain rural lifestyles. "Country people" have at least as much at stake here as "city people."

Secondly, for the first time in history, half of the world's population is now living in cities. The ways these urban areas are developed will largely determine our success or failure in overcoming environmental challenges and achieving a sustainable future for our planet. The stakes don't get any higher than this for anyone.

◎

The authors represented in these pages come from a variety of countries and backgrounds. Some of the chapters draw substantially on research and are heavily referenced, others are written more from the basis of experience, and most combine these elements. Mixing these styles and orientations is risky, but it is precisely this mix which is producing the most lively and innovative dialogue and debate in this field worldwide (see, for example, journals such as *The Urban Ecologist* (U.S.), *Alternatives Journal: Environmental Thought, Policy, and Action* (Canada), *Local Environment* (U.K./international), and the internet discussion group ECOCITY).

It was not my intention for this book to be comprehensive: there are plenty of topics that need attention from an eco-city perspective that will have to wait for another book. In the meantime, this collection clearly demonstrates that a cohesive vision for human settlements is beginning to emerge and that creative, transferable solutions to seemingly intractable social and environmental challenges are being initiated by citizen organizations and municipal officials around the world. This volume hastens the day when our cities and towns step forward to embrace the image of themselves as eco-cities and use that image to build their future. Make no mistake about it, the transition has begun.

Perhaps I'll become a "city person" yet.

*Vancouver, British Columbia*
*July, 1996*

# Acknowledgments

The idea for this book started about two years ago when Ray Tomalty, an associate editor of the journal *Alternatives*, invited me to be guest editor for their special issue on "Green Communities" (April/May 1996). *Alternatives* is Canada's journal of environmental thought, policy, and action, and I was honored and delighted to accept their invitation.

In the process of compiling that issue, I mentioned to the editor of *Alternatives*, Bob Gibson, that we had received more good material than we could publish in the limited space available. Bob suggested I think about turning the issue into a book. I proposed this to Chris Plant at New Society Publishers, which has a great booklist focused on ecological sustainability and social justice, and discovered they were keen on the project. However, while there was more than enough material for a journal, there was less than enough for a book. I invited several authors who had not been involved in the *Alternatives* issue to contribute chapters, and to my pleasant surprise they all agreed.

Each of these contributors has my unreserved respect and admiration. Writing is hard work, and anyone talented enough to do this could be doing something less demanding and making real money. These pages are evidence of untold hours of unpaid labor and of genuine dedication to the emerging eco-city vision.

The staff at *Alternatives* has been tremendous. Although we have yet to meet (we are separated geographically by hundreds of miles), we were able by e-mail, telephone, and fax to produce an excellent issue. I'm particularly grateful to Nancy Doucet, Susanna Reid, and Marcia Ruby, as well as to Bob Gibson and Ray Tomalty.

The *Alternatives* "Green Communities" issue was made possible by funding from the Social Sciences and Humanities Research Council (SSHRC) of Canada, The Samuel and Saidye Bronfman Foundation, The Helen McCrea Peacock Foundation, the Waterloo Public Interest Research Group, and the Faculty of Environmental Studies at the University of Waterloo. The chapters in this anthology by Peter Newman and Trevor Hancock, as well as an earlier version of the chapter by Todd Saunders, first appeared in that issue and are reprinted here with permission from the authors and from *Alternatives*.

*Eco-city Dimensions* is made possible by people dedicated to making the world a better place, and hoping they won't lose their shirts in the process. Chris and Judith Plant and the staff at New Society have been supportive as well as professional, and I look forward to working with them again. Heather Wornell also provided valuable editorial assistance.

Writing makes demands on both authors and their families. I am utterly grateful to Susan Day, who not only shouldered much of the load but also, in one of my more anxious moments, talked me out of calling my chapter "Eco-city Dementia," and to Sean Rigby, who may someday insist it would have been better that way. If this effort helps the eco-city vision take hold in his lifetime, he can call it whatever he wants.

# About the Authors

## The Editor:

**Mark Roseland** is the author of the widely-acclaimed *Toward Sustainable Communities: A Resource Book for Municipal and Local Governments.* He is Associate Director of the Community Economic Development Centre at Simon Fraser University and is a professor in SFU's Department of Geography. In 1990, as Research Director for the City of Vancouver's "Clouds of Change" Task Force, he orchestrated a comprehensive municipal response to global atmospheric change and local air quality problems. A former editor of *RAIN* Magazine, he is now North American editor of the new international journal *Local Environment.* He lectures internationally and advises communities and governments on sustainability policy and planning.

## The Contributors:

**Donald Alexander** is a visiting professor in the School of Resource and Environmental Management at Simon Fraser University, and a Director of the Social Change Institute in Vancouver, British Columbia.

**David Burman** is a researcher with expertise in grassroots community economic development initiatives as a supportive strategy for the promotion of community health.

**Robert Gibson** is Editor of *Alternatives Journal: Environmental Thought, Policy, and Action,* and a professor in the Department of Environment and Resource Studies at the University of Waterloo, Ontario.

**John Grant** is a research assistant in the Resources Research Unit of the School of Urban and Regional Studies at Sheffield Hallam University in the United Kingdom.

**Trevor Hancock** has been one of the pioneers in the international movement for healthy cities/communities. He has a long-standing interest in ecological politics, and is a health promotion consultant affiliated with the Faculty of Environmental Studies at York University in Ontario.

**Jon Kellett** is a Senior Lecturer in Urban and Regional Planning in the School of Urban and Regional Studies at Sheffield Hallam University in the United Kingdom.

**Elizabeth Kline** worked with the Massachusetts Executive Office of Environmental Affairs for 12 years before becoming Director of the Consortium for Regional Sustainability at Tufts University.

**Melinda Laituri**, a geographer formerly at the University of Auckland, New Zealand, is a professor of Earth Resources at Colorado State University in Fort Collins, Colorado.

**Jennie Moore** is Coordinator of Vancouver's Eco-city Network, and a consultant on ecological sustainability for local governments and community organizations.

**Nigel Mortimer** is Principal Lecturer in Resource Economics Research and Head of the Resources Research unit in the School of Urban and Regional Studies at Sheffield Hallam University in the United Kingdom.

**Peter Newman** is Director of the Institute for Science and Technology Policy and a professor of City Policy at Murdoch University in Western Australia.

**William Rees** is Professor and Director of the School of Community and Regional Planning at the University of British Columbia.

**Todd Saunders** works on ecologically based projects with Gaia Architects and with Arkitektgruppen CUBUS in Bergen, Norway.

**Nancy Skinner** is Executive Director of Local Solutions to Global Pollution and a former City Council member in Berkeley, California. She serves on the Advisory Board of Urban Ecology, and coordinates the Cities for Climate Protection campaign of the International Council for Local Environmental Initiatives.

**Ray Tomalty** is an Associate Editor of *Alternatives Journal: Environmental Thought, Policy, and Action,* and teaches in the Environmental Studies Program of Innis College at the University of Toronto, Ontario.

**Kelly Vodden**, a founder of London (Ontario) Environmental and Economic Development Cooperative, is a researcher associated with the Community Economic Development Centre at Simon Fraser University in Vancouver.

**Lyle Walker** is a recent graduate of the School of Community and Regional Planning at the University of British Columbia. He has a research interest in the transportation and housing aspects of sustainability.

# Introduction

# Dimensions of the Future
## An Eco-city Overview

Mark Roseland

W hat would you say connects the following
ideas?

Streets for people, not cars. Destinations easily accessible by
foot, bike, and public transit. Health as wellness rather than as
absence of disease. Restoration of damaged wetlands and other
habitats. Affordable housing for all. Food produced and consumed locally. Renewable sources of energy. Less pollution
and more recycling. A vibrant local economy that does not
harm the environment. Public awareness and involvement in
decision-making. Social justice for women, people of colour
and the disabled. Consideration of future generations.

This chapter will argue that these apparently disconnected ideas
all hang upon a single framework that can be called "eco-city."
The term "eco-city" is relatively new, but it is based upon concepts
that have been around for a long time. We begin with a look at
eco-city origins, then examine roots and wings — other paradigms
or movements which strongly influenced the development of the
eco-city concept. From this broad base we explore the growing
interest in how these ideas can be applied at the local level and a

consideration of the links between various dimensions of the eco-city vision.

Each of these dimensions hangs upon a framework for the future of our planet and, in particular, the health of our communities. This chapter provides the reader with a guide to this new framework and these dimensions.

## Eco-city Origins

In 1975, Richard Register and a few friends founded Urban Ecology in Berkeley, California, as a nonprofit organization to "rebuild cities in balance with nature." (The first time I met Register, in 1979, he proudly showed me his car, a large, gutted older-model automobile filled with dirt and planted with vegetables — a garden on wheels! Register was also involved in a "car wars" campaign which gave "tickets" to cars for consuming nonrenewable fossil fuels, producing pollution, endangering civic life, uglifying the landscape, and so on.) Since then, the organization has participated with others in Berkeley to build a "Slow Street," to bring back part of a creek culverted and covered eighty years earlier, to plant and harvest fruit trees on streets, to design and build solar greenhouses, to pass energy ordinances, to establish a bus line, to promote bicycle and pedestrian alternatives to automobiles, to delay and possibly stop construction of a local freeway, and to hold conferences on these and other subjects (Register 1994).

Urban Ecology started to gather real momentum with the publication of Register's *Eco-city Berkeley* (1987), a visionary book about how Berkeley could be ecologically rebuilt over the next several decades [1], and *The Urban Ecologist,* the organization's new journal. The momentum accelerated when Urban Ecology organized the First International Eco-city Conference, held in Berkeley in 1990. This conference convened over 700 people from around the world to discuss urban problems and submit proposals toward the goal of shaping cities upon ecological principles. Among the outcomes were the Second International Eco-city Conference (held in Adelaide, Australia in 1992) and the Third International Eco-city Conference (held in Yoff, Senegal in 1996).

Shortly before the Second Eco-city Conference, David Engwicht, an Australian community activist, published *Towards an Eco-City* (1992), later reissued in North America as *Reclaiming Our Cities and Towns* (1993). In it, Engwicht illustrates how city planners and engineers have, in the name of "progress," virtually eliminated effective human exchange by building more roads, thus taking commerce out of the cities into strip malls, gutting our communities, and increasing traffic fatalities. The seeds of ecological revolution are being planted everywhere, writes Engwicht, and the most important frontier in this ecological revolution will be our cities, for they are the ultimate expressions of our science, our religion, and our culture. A city, for Engwicht, is "an invention for maximizing exchange and minimizing travel." By that he means exchanges of all sorts: goods, money, ideas, emotions, genetic material, etc. He points the way toward "eco-cities" where people can move via foot, bicycles, and mass transit and interact freely without fear of traffic and toxins.

Urban Ecology, now more than twenty years old, states that its mission is to create ecological cities by following these ten principles (Urban Ecology 1996):

> revise land use priorities to create compact, diverse, green, safe, pleasant, and vital mixed-use communities near transit nodes and other transportation facilities;
> revise transportation priorities to favor foot, bicycle, cart, and transit over autos, and to emphasize "access by proximity;"
> restore damaged urban environments, especially creeks, shore lines, ridgelines, and wetlands;
> create decent, affordable, safe, convenient, and racially and economically mixed housing;
> nurture social justice and create improved opportunities for women, people of color and the disabled;
> support local agriculture, urban greening projects, and community gardening;
> promote recycling, innovative appropriate technology, and resource conservation while reducing pollution and hazardous wastes;
> work with businesses to support ecologically sound economic activity while discouraging pollution, waste, and the use and production of hazardous materials;
> promote voluntary simplicity and discourage excessive consumption of material goods;
> increase awareness of the local environment and bioregion through activist and educational projects that increase public awareness of ecological sustainability issues.

## Roots and Wings

Register, Engwicht, and Urban Ecology certainly deserve credit for popularizing the term "eco-city" in the last decade,[2] but the eco-city concept is strongly influenced by other movements that were developing over the same period, and by a long line of thinkers and writers whose ideas were precursors to these concepts many decades ago.[3]

A survey of several paradigms or movements that have been floating around for the last twenty or so years may help readers understand the dimensions of eco-city concepts. These include, among others, healthy communities, appropriate technology, community economic development, social ecology, the green movement, bioregionalism, native world views, and sustainable development.[4] To attempt such a broad survey in a short space necessitates overgeneralization, but I believe the view that emerges from this survey is worth that risk. [5]

**Healthy Communities** Public health has been among the traditional responsibilities of local government. A century ago, municipalities were instrumental in improving public health by preventing the spread of disease through slum clearance, community planning, water treatment, and the provision of certain health services. These early interventions were based on the view of health as the absence of disease, and disease prevention as the main challenge for local government.

In the last two decades a new, broader conception of public health has been developed and adopted by municipal governments in Europe and North America. Although the name "healthy communities" implies a focus on medical care, the Ottawa Charter for Health Promotion (WHO 1986) recognizes that "the fundamental conditions and resources for health are peace, shelter, education, food, income, a stable eco-system, sustainable resources, social justice, and equity."

Local governments play a big role in all these areas through their impact on public hygiene (waste disposal and water systems), food handling and other public health regulations, recreational facilities, education, transportation, economic development, and land use planning. In Europe the World Health Organization has directed the successful creation of a 30-city network known as the Healthy Cities Project. In Canada, there have been approximately 100 active healthy community projects, and interest has been growing in Seattle and other U.S. cities.

**Appropriate Technology**[6] E.F. Schumacher in 1973 coined the term "intermediate technology" to signify "technology of production by the masses, making use of the best of modern knowledge and experience, conducive to decentralisation, compatible with the laws of ecology, gentle in its use of scarce resources, and designed to serve the human person instead of making him [*sic*] the servant of machines" (Schumacher 1973). The central tenet of appropriate technology (AT) is that a technology should be designed to fit into and be compatible with its local setting. Examples of current projects which are generally classified as AT include passive solar design, active solar collectors for heating and cooling; small windmills to provide electricity; roof-top gardens and hydroponic greenhouses; permaculture; and worker-managed craft industries. There is general agreement, however, that the main goal of the AT movement is to enhance the self-reliance of people on a local level.

Characteristics of self-reliant communities which AT can help facilitate include: 1) low resource usage coupled with extensive recycling; 2) preference for renewable over nonrenewable resources; 3) emphasis on environmental harmony; 4) emphasis on small-scale industries; and 5) a high degree of social cohesion and sense of community (see, e.g., Darrow 1981; Olkowski 1979; Mollison 1978, 1979; RAIN 1981). Communities that could be said to be practising AT include the Amish of Lancaster County, Pennsylvania and the Mennonites of southern Ontario (Foster 1987).

**Community Economic Development**. The concept of community economic development (CED), like some others here, suffers from an abundance of interpretation. At their finest, however, the distinguishing features of community economic development are characterized by the following working definition from the Community Economic Development Centre at Simon Fraser University (1996):

> Community Economic Development is a process by which communities can initiate and generate their own solutions to their common economic problems and thereby build long-term community capacity and foster the integration of economic, social and environmental objectives.[7]

Other observers describe CED in less flattering terms, arguing that in response to external funding priorities, community development organizations have lost their original focus on the creation of local employment opportunities and local control and generation of capital in low-income communities (Surpin and Bettridge 1986). Examples of CED range from small business counseling and import substitution ("buy local") programs to worker cooperatives, community development corporations, and community land trusts. Boothroyd (1991) argues that "[w]hether CED is practiced in hinterland resource towns, urban ghettos, obsolescent manufacturing cities, or Native communities' reserves, the general objective is the same: to take some measure of control of the local economy back from the markets and the state."

**Social Ecology**[8] Social ecology focuses its critique on domination and hierarchy *per se:* the struggle for the liberation of women, of workers, of blacks, of native peoples, of gays and lesbians, of nature (the ecology movement), is ultimately all part of the struggle against domination and hierarchy. Social ecology is the study of both human and natural ecosystems, and in particular of the social relations that affect the relation of society as a whole with nature. Social ecology advances a holistic worldview, appropriate technology, reconstruction of damaged ecosystems, and creative human enterprise. It combines considerations of equity and social justice with energy efficiency and appropriate technology. Social ecology goes beyond environmentalism, insisting that the issue at hand for humanity is not simply protecting nature but rather creating an ecological society in harmony with nature. The primary social unit of a proposed ecological society is the ecocommunity, a human-scale, sustainable settlement based on ecological balance, community self-reliance, and participatory democracy.

Social ecology envisions a confederation of community assemblies, working together to foster meaningful communication, cooperation, and public service in the everyday practices of civic life, and a "municipalist" concept of citizenship cutting across class and economic barriers to address dangers such as global ecological breakdown or the threat of nuclear war. Cooperation and coordination within and between communities is considered able to transcend the destructive trends of centralized politics and state power. The city can function, social ecology asserts, as "an ecological and ethical arena for vibrant political culture and a highly committed citizenry" (Bookchin 1987).

**The Green Movement** The Greens believe in the "four pillars" of ecology, social responsibility, grassroots democracy, and nonviolence (Capra and Spretnak 1984).[9] These pillars translate into principles of community self-reliance, improving the quality of life, harmony with nature, decentralization, and diversity.[10] From these principles, the Greens question many cherished assumptions about the rights of land ownership, the permanence of institutions, the meaning of progress, and the traditional patterns of authority within society. The Greens recognize that their movement will have to take different forms in different countries (Capra and Spretnak 1984). Starting in the mid-1970s in New Zealand (where it was called the Values Party), France (Les Vertes), and West Germany (Die Grünen), the Green movement soon spread to many other developed countries in Europe and North America. In countries with proportional representation, such as the former West Germany, Green politicians have been elected to seats in the Bundestag. In North America, however, Greens admit their involvement in federal political campaigns is primarily a way to educate the populace and build the movement. Local campaigns may be considered more serious bids for power, as when the New Haven, Connecticut Greens ran a slate of Green candidates for city council (Tokar 1987). Most North Americans still think Green simply means being pro-environment, but for Germans being Green means being feminist, supporting civil liberties, working for solidarity with Third World peoples, and standing for an end to the arms race (Swift 1987).

**Bioregionalism** The central idea of bioregionalism is *place*. Bioregionalism comes from *bio*, the Greek word for life, as in "biology" and "biography," and *regio*, Latin for territory to be ruled. Together they mean "a life-territory, a place defined by its life forms, its topography and its biota, rather than by human dictates; a region governed by nature, not legislature" (Sale 1985). A bioregion is considered to be the right size for human-scale organization: often defined as a river basin or a watershed, it is a natural framework for economic and political decentralization and self-determination.

Bioregional practice is oriented toward resistance against the continuing destruction of natural systems, such as forests and rivers; and toward the renewal of natural systems based on a thorough knowledge of how natural systems work and the development of techniques appropriate to specific sites (Dodge 1981).

While bioregionalism as a movement is relatively new, its precursors date back at least a century.[11] Like social ecology, it is rooted in classical anarchism. The implications of bioregional social organization are clearly for local political control by communities on their own behalf combined with broader allegiance to an institutional structure that governs according to an ecological ethic. Bioregionalism considers people as part of a life-place, as dependent on natural systems as are native plants or animals. By virtue of the emphasis it places on natural systems, perhaps, bioregionalism sometimes appears weak in terms of human systems; however, some "Green City" ideas (e.g., Berg 1989) are rooted in bioregionalism. Recent volumes edited by bioregionalist Doug Aberley for New Society's Bioregional Series explain how to do bioregional mapping for local empowerment (1993) and cover the history and theory of ecologically sound planning (1994).

**Native World View**[12] Although the subject of considerable debate, many observers (see, e.g., McNeeley and Pitt 1985) argue that sustainable patterns of resource use and management have for centuries been reflected in the belief and behaviour systems of indigenous cultures. These systems traditionally have been based in a world view that does not separate humans from their environment (Callicott 1982):

> The Western tradition pictures nature as material, mechanical, and devoid of spirit..., while the American Indian tradition pictures nature throughout as an extended family or society of living, ensouled beings. The former picture invites unrestrained exploitation of non-human nature, while the latter provides the foundations for ethical restraint in relation to non-human nature.

The World Commission on Environment and Development (WCED, see below) recognized how much industrialized cultures have to learn about sustainability from traditional peoples, and at the same time, how vulnerable the latter are to encroachment by the former (WCED 1987). A native chief speaking at a symposium on sustainable development at the University of British Columbia suggested that mainstream Canadian society should look at "Nuu-chah-nulth history, culture, and traditions and practices, and find out how they managed to survive for thousands of years before European contact" (Smith 1989).

**Sustainable Development** In December 1983, amidst growing concern over declining ecological trends and the seeming incompatibility of economic and environmental perspectives, the UN Secretary-General responded to a United Nations General Assembly resolution by appointing Gro Harlem Brundtland of Norway as chairman of an independent World Commission on Environment and Development. For the next few years the Brundtland Commission, as it became known, studied the issues and listened to people at public hearings on five continents, gathering over 10,000 pages of transcripts and written submissions from hundreds of organizations and individuals. In April 1987 the commission released its report, *Our Common Future*. At the core of the report is the principle of "sustainable development." The commission's embrace of sustainable development as an underlying principle gave political credibility to a concept many others had worked on over the previous decade. The commission defined sustainable development as meeting "the needs of the present without compromising the ability of future generations to meet their own needs" (WCED 1987). This simple, vague definition was also the foundation for *Agenda 21,* the document that emerged from the United Nations Conference on Environment and Development (the "Earth Summit" held in 1992 in Brazil) as a sustainable development action plan for the 21st century.

## Bringing It Home

Those of us who turned to these paradigms or movements for direction in applying these concepts to the communities where we work and live have found much inspiration but relatively little guidance. Only recently has there been rapidly growing interest in the practical application of these ideas at the local level.

In the last few years a literature has appeared that begins to support this practical application of ideas. Even more than the paradigms discussed above, this new literature reflects a somewhat bewildering variety of orientations and terminology. The authors include architects, academics and activists, and the terminology includes everything from "neotraditional town planning" and "pedestrian pockets" to "reurbanization," "post-industrial suburbs," and "sustainable cities."

To help the reader navigate this new literature, I have organized it into four broad categories which reflect the backgrounds, world views, or orientations of the various authors: Designers, Practitioners,

Visionaries, and Activists.[13]

The Designers category includes the literature on the Costs of Sprawl and Sustainability by Design. These authors are, for the most part, architects, planners, consultants, and related professionals. In general, they are oriented toward sustainable "developments," i.e., new subdivisions, within a social structure essentially unchanged from what we have become accustomed to over the last several decades (post-World War II). They are, for the most part, not concerned with global sustainability issues such as atmospheric change or social equity.

At the other end of the spectrum are the authors writing about Green Cities, Eco-cities, and Ecocommunities, whom together I call the Activists. These authors are, for the most part, writers and community activists who consider themselves bioregionalists, social ecologists, and various other kinds of environmentalists. Their writings are generally oriented toward community change within the context of a society that is recognizing its anti-ecological ways and embarking on a more sustainable course. The "ecotopian" social structure envisioned by these authors differs significantly from the present industrial-bureaucratic structure, which these writers consider is unlikely or unable to change fundamentally toward biophysical and social sustainability.

In between these poles are the Practitioners and the Visionaries. The Practitioners category includes the literature on Sustainable Urban Development, Sustainable Cities and Local Sustainability Initiatives. These authors represent ecologically informed and inspired practitioners: politicians, local government professionals (e.g., planners and staff of local or provincial/state offices of environmental management, energy efficiency, etc.), occasional academics, and, increasingly, citizens and community organizations. They generally define communities as municipalities, and this literature is often directed toward public sector decision-makers.

The Visionaries category includes the Sustainable Communities and Community Self-Reliance literature. These authors can be described as agriculturists, economists, architects, planning theorists, and appropriate technologists. They generally define communities of association (e.g., women of colour) and of interest (e.g., social justice) as well as of place (e.g., municipalities). This literature is often directed toward professionals, academics and other citizens concerned with issues such as energy conservation, appropriate technology, and community economic development.

While there are discernable differences in analysis, emphasis, and strategy between the variations discussed above, the "eco-city" theme is broad enough to encompass any and all of them (see Figure 1).[14]

| Sustainable Development | Healthy Communities | Community Economic Development |
|---|---|---|
| Sustainable Urban Development | **ECO-CITIES** | Appropriate Technology |
| Sustainable Communities, Sustainable Cities | | Social Ecology |
| Bioregionalism | Native World Views | Green Movement, Green Cities/Communities |

**Figure 1: Eco-city Dimensions**
The "eco-cities" theme does not stand alone but is situated in a complex array of relevant variations; the figure quite deliberately has no arrows, no lines, and no borders, and should be imagined as a hologram.

The wording of titles in many of the publications discussed here, such as *Toward Sustainable Communities* (Roseland 1992a), *Towards an Eco-city* (Engwicht 1992) and *Building Sustainable Communities* (Nozick 1992), is significant. Eco-cities, or sustainable communities, represent a goal, a direction for community development — not simply a marketing slogan. Indeed, many of these authors would argue that the only modern communities that are remotely sustainable at present are some aboriginal communities that have existed for centuries (although other communities have recently undertaken impressive initiatives toward modern sustainability).

It is at present safe to say that there is no (and perhaps should not be any) single accepted definition of "eco-cities" or of "sustainable communities."[15] Inherent in much of the literature is the recognition that communities must be involved in defining sustainability from a local perspective. The challenge is how to encourage local democracy within a framework of global sustainability.

There are by now numerous examples of citizen and community initiatives which demonstrate that creative, transferable solutions to seemingly intractable social and environmental challenges are being initiated by citizen organizations and municipal officials in cities and towns around the world (e.g., see Roseland 1992a). While many of these examples are impressive in scope or design, most have been adopted piecemeal rather than as part of a broader framework. In other words, the elements of eco-cities are being put in place, but not, as yet, the necessary synthesis.

The emerging eco-city vision offers this synthesis. I have argued that a set of what may at first appear to be disconnected ideas about the future of our communites and our planet is, upon closer inspection, a broader framework. This is reflected in the new applied literature of the Designers, Practitioners, Visionaries, and Activists, and it is rooted in a set of ideas that reaches back many years and spans many disciplines. A cohesive vision for human settlements is beginning to emerge.

The eco-city vision links ecological sustainability with social justice and the pursuit of sustainable livelihoods. It is a vision that acknowledges the ecological limits to growth, promotes ecological and cultural diversity and a vibrant community life, and supports a community-based, sustainable economy that is directed toward fulfilling real human needs, rather than just simply expanding.

Building eco-cities requires access to decision-making processes to ensure that economic and political institutions promote activities that are ecologically sustainable and socially just. It requires that these institutions respect our needs as whole human beings and citizens, not just as producers, consumers, and voters. It requires attention to issues of social equity and liveability, and to truly democratic decision-making processes that ensure the full participation of all. Effective and acceptable local solutions require local decisions, which in turn require the extensive knowledge and participation of the people most affected by those decisions, in their homes, their workplaces, and their communities.

The most direct and effective means of encouraging local democracy within a framework of global sustainability is to redevelop, retrofit, redesign and rebuild our cities and towns — in other words, to make them into eco-cities. When our communities are healthy, our planet will be healthy, too.

# Part One

# Eco-city Planning

Our exploration of eco-city dimensions moves now to the theory and practice of eco-city planning. **Peter Newman**, from Murdoch University in Western Australia, is perhaps best known internationally for coining the term "automobile dependency" (Newman and Kenworthy 1989). He is a prolific writer and has served on the local Council in his home town of Fremantle. Acknowledging the rich philosophical tradition of city visionaries and activists, Newman asserts that it is an opportune time to grasp innovative organic solutions to the problems of our cities today — solutions that incorporate nature and the local community at the heart of their rationale. Newman traces the eco-city movement as far back as ancient Greece, and warns that while its ideas have been influential, little is likely to be won without struggle. The battles are fierce, and change will depend on local initiatives. In order to regain the principles of the green, organic city as we move into a new millennium, there are three important ideas that seem to require rediscovery as part of town planning: the positive qualities of density in walking-based centers and sub-centers linked by transit; the positive qualities of mixed land use; and the positive qualities of natural processes and localized community processes in the city.

**Robert Gibson, Donald Alexander,** and **Ray Tomalty,** academics who are or have been associated with the Canadian journal Alternatives, examine the concept of ecosystem planning as a green alternative to conventional urban planning practice. They identify ten principles for eco-system planning (based on their study of thirteen Canadian and two U.S. cases), and offer five steps for implementing ecosystem planning. The central characteristic and strength of the ecosystem planning model, they argue, is the integration of data and analysis in a way that allows effective attention to whole systems within natural boundaries. Ecosystems and communities can then be linked in planning as they are in reality.

# 2

# Greening the City
## The Ecological and Human Dimensions of the City Can Be Part of Town Planning

Peter Newman

Our problems with cities today stem from ideas that not only squeeze the ecological out of town planning, but also frustrate human creativity and expression. Making our cities more livable entails making them both greener and more human. Fortunately, we can reassert ecology and creativity together in many ways — by simply being aware of the local ecology and planting as many trees as possible, as well as by seeking processes that allow the application of ecosystem theory in city development (see Newman 1975). Greening the city may seem to be a largely new idea, but incorporation of the ecological and human into city planning has been a rich philosophical tradition. History suggests, though, that while its proponents have been, and can again be, influential, little is likely to be won without a struggle.

## Modernism and the Industrial City

The modern city is an expression of the industrial revolution. The mechanistic approach to life that flowed from the industrial revolution also became part of town planning. The profession was made into a "science" of plot ratios, setbacks, percentages of open space, standardized road patterns and building forms, and endless other mechanisms for controlling land development by both governments and developers. Thus each new suburb is rolled out as though it came from a factory, no matter what the local ecology happens to be and with little consideration for, or concession to, human creativity. Nature is restricted to a bit of required open space, usually a degraded piece of leftover land that soon needs cleaning up with lawns and disciplined trees. The human side of the city is limited to individual expressions in private spaces and has little potential for enactment in the public spaces of our planned cities.

These identical, mechanical suburbs are now becoming universal. Once, you could only find them in North America and Australasia; now they appear in Europe, Asia, Latin America, and Africa as well. Despite each new suburb claiming to offer "a unique lifestyle" or "fresh country living," they are all absorbed into a monotonous megalopolis that sprawls in every direction, devouring natural bush and farmland and filling the air with automobile emissions.

There is a need to get behind the ideas that have led us to this form of building cities. Such mechanistic approaches derive from applying technological thinking to all areas of life (Ellul 1964). It is described today in rather deprecatory terms as "modernist." This mechanistic era is ending in most areas of human endeavor as post-modern critiques destroy its assumptions. These include the ideas that all human beings are the same and can be programmed into lifestyles just as machines can be driven or programmed; that nature is not important in itself and can be modified to suit our needs; and that efficiency is achieved through large-scale mass processes whether they be industrial production, urban infrastructure or governance (Cook 1990).

The questioning of modernism began in the creative community (in art, literature, architecture, etc.), but in the past twenty years the doubts have been picked up by the environmental movement which saw the impact of the industrial mechanized mindset on forests, rivers, soils, and anything else that was natural and diverse.

The creative and the environmental are inseparable parts of the critique of modernism since neither can be mechanized without losing its core character. The two are obviously linked when it comes to cities. Until very recently, however, the post-modernist critique has not been applied much to cities, probably because the environmental movement has not focused on cities until recently. Around the world now, the environmental movement has its eyes firmly on the city and is asking: how can it be greened?

## The Organic City

Today there is a global movement to green the city. The movement, known variously as urban ecology, eco-cities, sustainable cities, and ecological cities, is seeking deeper and more satisfying answers to the urban issues of our day than can be provided by better technology or more efficient government (Stren, White, and Whitney 1992; Haughton and Hunter 1994). This involves a paradigm shift, but not one that is entirely new. Today's "greening the city" efforts build on a long tradition, namely the "organic" city approach to town planning.

When any of us travels to Europe, the Middle East, or other places with pre-modern settlements, certain important qualities become immediately obvious to us. These are often summarized by the word "organic," which brings together not only their human and green texture, but also the processes that allowed them to arise from within the community rather than from above through imposition. These qualities are as follows:

First, the buildings are nonuniform, but part of a pattern; they appear to grow out of the landscape, and in many places are hard to distinguish from it. Second, the streets are filled with people walking and all major local destinations are within a short walk. The keys to this are density and mixed land use, which grow from the need to have sufficient people living nearby and sufficient work, shops, schools, etc., within walking distance. Each combination of land use is a living and evolving part of the city's peculiar history and culture, but all have the qualities of a pedestrian place. As Kostoff says, "[U]rbanism is precisely the science of relationships. And these relationships must be determined according to how much a person walking through the city can take in at a glance" (1991: 83).

Finally, nature is not lost in this city. Water and trees can be central to its streets and public spaces. Waste is recycled. Resources are used frugally. And most of all, there are productive rural land uses immediately adjacent to the city that are integrated closely into its functioning.

These are the "urban villages" of history, and although some of their characteristics can be found in modern cities, they have largely been obliterated. It is romantic to suggest that they can just be copied to replace our modern suburbs, but we can learn from these principles to see how our current technology and urban processes can help us to green future urban development. Furthermore, even though the industrial revolution started the process that has substantially obliterated this "organic" form of the city, the specific problems created by the industrial revolution itself have not always been negative to the green city.

## Greening the Industrial Revolution City

The industrial revolution brought about a rapid growth in cities as economies shifted from rural to urban industrial production. As more people and industry filled the old "walking cities" of Europe, they became impossible to live in. The wastes in the streets and the pressure for more and more housing in the confined walking dimension of five kilometres or so led to a new kind of city — the "transit city." New transport technology meant that by using trams and trains you could link a series of urban villages like pearls along a string. This solution meant that walking-scale areas could be retained once a new form of linkage was created, and it meant that natural areas could be retained in the corridors between developments. North American and Australian cities were built this way in the late 19th and early 20th centuries. Many European cities such as Stockholm and Zurich have retained this basic urban form.

City governments came to build this type of city because of the idea of town planning, which arose from the ferment of city change 100 years ago. An integration of the human and the green, this new movement included the social reformers (i.e., people committed to greater human health and moral welfare) and the environmentalists (i.e., people committed to a city more sensitive to nature and traditional city forms) (see Hall 1987 and Girouard 1985). Thus the transit city solution expressed a combination of human and green values, and reflected a new kind of technology. Many cities benefited from this solution, but all had to battle through the changes it required.

A new profession of town planning was born that integrated the guiding ideas for city layout. Histories of these urban changes from around 1880 to 1940 show that the struggles to provide answers for a new kind of city involved groups of reformers in local areas who stressed the need for organic values in the city. Since then, the mechanistic, modernist vision of cities has become more and more dominant, particularly in North America and Australasia. Now, as 100 years ago, we find green city ideas hard to locate amidst bureaucratic processes that squeeze out the organic life forces. We need to rediscover the origins and basic concepts of the "organic" city and recognize that many modern-day environmentalists are committed to winning back a more human and ecological city, and are able to understand modern needs and wants. They are, in fact, part of a long and important tradition in city building that is being neglected at the peril of the citizens.

## The Green City Movement

The lineage of those who have contributed to ideas on cities goes back to ancient Greek philosophy and Judeo-Christian theology. The Greek *polis* was a place for people to meet and be part of a more diverse and enriching community than found in separated and self-sufficient families. The Jewish city had organic principles at its heart. Zechariah (probably the first traffic calmer) said the following in 500 BC regarding his vision of Jerusalem:

> I will return to Jerusalem, my holy city, and live there. It will be known as the faithful city. Once again old men and women, so old that they use a stick when they walk, will be sitting in the city squares. And the streets will be full of boys and girls playing. (Zechariah 8:3-5)

More recently, the lineage of struggles for the green city in modern times has continued through those who stood for the organic city as opposed to the mechanical city, the human and green city as opposed to the dehumanized and artificial industrial/modernist city. The great initiators included John Ruskin (1819-1900), William Morris (1834-1896), Ebenezer Howard (1850-1928), Patrick Geddes (1854-1932), and Lewis Mumford (1895-1990). In our own time, they have been succeeded by Jane Jacobs, Ian McHarg, K. R. Schneider, Christopher Alexander, Michael Hough, R. B. Gratz, and others, all of whom express a common thread of "organic" thinking: they believe in the need for diversity, human scale, sensitivity to history and nature, community-based processes, and creative artistic expression in the city (see Jacobs 1961, McHarg 1969, Schneider 1979, Alexander 1979, Hough 1984, Gratz 1989).

Today the organic city movement has a new vision and is networked across the world. Some of its goals are to stop freeways and provide a new vision for transit-oriented urban villages, including pedestrian scale developments, traffic calming, and bicycle facilities (STPP 1994, Urban Ecology); to provide neo-traditional planning that emphasizes real streets where people can meet and kids can play, streets that lead over a short distance to shops, schools, and other activity sites (Calthorpe 1993, Katz 1994); and to bring environmental thinking into city planning through water sensitive design, waste recycling, community permaculture, and other green innovations, as well as through a strong emphasis on community-scale technologies and processes (Roseland 1992a, Newman and Mouritz 1996).

The battles for these human and ecological qualities in the city are just as fierce as they were in the 1890s when an urban paradigm shift occurred of a similar nature to the one we are now facing (Newman, Kenworthy, and Robinson 1992). The processes of change are gaining momentum at every level but, in the end, whether they live or die will depend on initiatives taken in local communities.

In order to regain the principles of the green, organic city as we move into a new millennium, there are three important ideas that require rediscovery as part of town planning: the positive qualities of density in walking-based centers and sub-centers linked by transit; the positive qualities of mixed land use; and the positive qualities of natural processes and localized community processes in the city.

## Rediscovering Density

The urban village is primarily human in scale because walking or cycling are the best ways to get anywhere. Human activity on the street of an urban village is part of day-to-day life because of the short distances involved. For this to be feasible, densities must be at least 30 to 40 people per hectare, preferably higher. Such densities are also necessary for anything like a reasonable transit service to be viable.

One of the hardest battles in cities will be over achieving such density. There are good and bad reasons why people fear density. The good reasons are that we haven't done much good design using organic high density. The 1960s flats in many North American and Australian cities are about as organic as plastic flowers. But there are also some wonderful examples of good high density that can be a guide for the future. In Canada, the West End of Vancouver and many parts of Toronto and Montreal are examples of organic, high density, walking environments. In the U.S., the Brooklyn "brown-stones" and the San Francisco "painted ladies" are testaments to high density elegance, human scale, and urbanity. In Australia, Fremantle, Subiaco in Perth, much of inner Melbourne; and Balmain, Glebe, and Paddington in Sydney show that we once knew how to do it.

There is no reason why we can't rehabilitate the notion of dense housing and provide guidance and encouragement for its use. And there are already government programs seeking to do just that, including the new "Better Cities" urban villages in Australia.

The bad reasons for fearing density are those that suggest it is something inherently evil. There has been a lot of fear that density is synonymous with health problems and social ills. One part of the 19th century town planning movement (primarily in England) associated all of the environmental and social ills of industrial cities with density. This view was reflected in the Town and Country Planning Association's slogan, "Nothing gained by overcrowding." They therefore put all of their efforts into designing new low density "garden suburbs" and "New Towns." What they lost was the human scale, as little remained accessible by walking.

Milton Keynes is typical of the totally planned "garden city" New Town with low density, heavily zoned urban parts that are set in a sea of water-hungry grassy open spaces. No one ever seems to be visible in Milton Keynes. The carefully designed walkways and cycle paths are largely unused while the roads and car parks are full. Milton Keynes has been compared to a Dutch New Town called Almere. Almere is a typical example of a European tradition of building at a density that enables walking and cycling to be the central functions (Roberts 1992). Data on these two cities are presented in Table 1.

Both cities are said to have been influenced by the garden city tradition, but only Almere has anything like the density recommended by Ebenezer Howard 100 years ago. The British town planning profession (after Howard) believed they could have a green city without the density needed for pedestrian qualities. They were wrong, and the differences in Table 1 show so quite clearly. Notice particularly the impact on children in the two cities.

The "nothing gained by overcrowding" abhorrence of density tradition was exported to other cities, mostly in the Anglo-Saxon world, by the town planning profession (King 1978). It is rarely questioned, even though the claims of social and environmental problems associated with density have been shown to be false. Crime, suicide, and health problems are more easily correlated with low density, though in general they are more obviously associated with poverty and poor infrastructure and services (Newman and Hogan 1981).

| Modal Split | MILTON KEYNES | ALMERE |
|---|---|---|
| Car | 59% | 35% |
| Public Transport | 17% | 17% |
| Bicycle | 6% } 24% | 28% } 48% |
| Walk | 18% | 20% |
| Av. Travel Distance | 7.2km | 6.9km (much less for non-work) |
| Trips <3km | 45% | 85% |
| Density | 20 dwellings/ha | 35-40dw/ha |
| Form | 'scattered', separated use. | 'organic', mixed use. |
| Proportion who see a car as 'essential' | 70% | 50% |
| Households with children < 12 years who are always supervised outside home | 52% | 16% |
| who are never supervised outside home | 8% | 48% |

Table 1: Comparison of characteristics of Milton Keynes (UK) and Almere (Netherlands) in travel and land use. Both are small New Towns.
Source: Roberts (1992).

Town planning needs to find centers to define as urban villages throughout the modern car-based cities we have constructed. It needs to ensure that transit systems are built to the center of each of these villages. And it needs to allow all of the creative forces of its urban citizenry who want to live, work, and walk in these urban villages, to be channeled into the rebuilding of a human scale village. People need to become involved in designing, building, and landscaping such villages, and filling them with all kinds of urban activity.

This is the approach adopted by Jan Gehl in his studies of how to make central cities more human and it is the approach of the New Urbanists (Gehl 1994). The technology for dense, solar-oriented, urban villages is available to assist this process and town planning can ensure that it occurs in an equitable, aesthetic, and sustainable way (Woodroffe 1994).

## Rediscovering Mixed Land Use

One of the other obvious differences between organic and

modern cities is the degree of mixed land use. Old cities and even late 19th century transit suburbs are highly mixed. For the past 50 years, however, town planning has been un-mixing cities by the use of rigid zoning that separates single uses into each differently coloured part of the city's town plan. The rationale was to prevent pollution from industry from getting into residential or other areas, but that was largely an excuse since controlling industrial impacts has always been best achieved with simple health regulations and environmental controls. If industries cannot meet standards, then they must go further away, but the majority of land uses can be completely compatible. Separated zoning was just another case of mechanistic thinking that could not accommodate any flexibility in land use.

The result is a city with less diversity in local areas and more traffic, as well as reduced safety and diminished attractiveness of local streets. The data on Milton Keynes and Almere show this. It should be emphasized that residents of Almere preferred this kind of mixed land use neighborhood, as do residents of Fremantle. There, residents recognized the value of living closer to services, and they use one third of the gasoline per capita compared with residents of rigidly zoned, low density modern suburbs (Campbell and Newman 1989).

It is feasible to remake cities with a greater mixture of uses; zoning schemes based on mixed-use goals are not difficult. This has been shown in Fremantle's "inner city" zone and in places like the city of Vancouver (MacGill and Dawkins 1988). It is technologically easy since pollution controls and noise-buffered building designs can be realized in ways that enable most work functions to be integrated back into the city, including those we formerly called "noxious." Also, the Internet allows much information or service-oriented work to be done in local tele-cottages and at home, although there are often social problems that stem from the greater isolation of strictly home-based work. Nevertheless, the reality is that more and more home-based businesses are starting up, and unfortunately, most town planning schemes still don't allow it.

## Rediscovering Natural and Localized Community Processes

The final organic element of the new green city is more related to process. First, we need to recognize more clearly the role of natural processes in the city, and second, we need to recognize how local community processes can be used to shape the city.

Natural processes, including water systems, soil and air, as well as flora and fauna, are all part of the city. They provide free ecological services and when abused they tend to get back at us. Currently we are seeing attempts to turn drains back into creeks, to find ways that nutrients and organic wastes can be reused in the urban system rather than just flowing through it, to find out the limits to the air's assimilative and cleansing capacity, and to understand the similar capacities of rivers, lakes, and estuaries on which cities are built.

By understanding better the local ecology and how the human ecology of the city interacts with it, we can make our cities more organic. Such processes are well underway, particularly when it comes to bringing water back into the city in a more natural way through completely functional systems for managing stormwater that are also celebrations of water in the city.

Local community processes have always been seen as necessary for supporting local government functions. Unfortunately, this wisdom has rarely been applied in any significant way for the important urban ecological functions of energy use, water supply, sewage systems, recycling, and public transport. In the late 1800s, when organic solutions in the transit city were being created, local governments managed most of these things. But in this century these services have been centralized into larger and larger-scale city-wide systems, which are usually justified by claims of greater efficiency due to economies of scale.

Today, the pendulum is swinging back. This is partly because the development of community-based technologies in recent decades has made it feasible to provide local services efficiently. But there is also a broader trend towards decentralized and smaller-scale operations. Modern industry has discovered that the efficiencies of large-scale systems are usually lost because the human element is disregarded. In the business world, many large corporations have been restructured so they can be more easily managed though largely autonomous units that are locally responsive. And advocates of appropriate technology have won recognition that quality can be associated with small-scale, locally responsive systems, rather than with the giantist fetishes of our 20th century engineers.

In order to have space for locally managed urban services, especially eco-services such as water and waste management, there will need to be a trade-off with density increases for pedestrian village qualities. It is not hard to see that densities should increase around transit lines and in centers of activity, but adjacent to these there may be low density areas of parkland combined with community permaculture, water recycling, and waste management systems.

None of this will be done just for ecological purposes. A localized organic approach is also better for social and economic reasons (Gratz 1989). In her books on cities, Jane Jacobs says that grand economic schemes do little for cities and that the real vitality comes from the intricate, diverse relationships that flourish in urban communities where people meet casually in streets and social gatherings. She concludes that the "science of city planning and art of city design, in real life and in real cities, must become the science and art of catalyzing and nourishing those close-grained working relationships" (Jacobs 1961). This has been confirmed in recent years by studies on innovation and the role of "local milieus" (Willoughby 1994).

There is much to gain from enlightened experiments in locally managed urban services that can help us to see whether such organic processes can work in the 21st century city. The shift in power structures, like other aspects of city greening, will not happen easily, but the process is certainly worth fighting for.

## Conclusions

Greening the city is a process that is high on the agenda of cities around the world. It is not a new phenomenon. On the contrary, there has been a long history of city visionaries and activists who have seen the organic qualities of the human and the ecological as essential parts of how we should live. But there is a new edge to the need for greening the city, not only because of the obvious maladies of today's cities, but also because the mechanistic approach that has dominated city building for this century is now seriously under question.

Rather than despairing, we should be grasping the opportunity to pursue innovative organic solutions such as dense urban villages with walking qualities and transit linkages as their primary design characteristic, mixed land use as the basis of zoning, and urban processes that incorporate nature and the local community at the heart of their rationale. The lineage of green urbanists gives us hope that the new burst of recognition will not be wasted, but will leave a legacy that future generations will appreciate.

# 3

# Putting Cities in Their Place
## Ecosystem-based Planning for Canadian Urban Regions

Robert B. Gibson, Donald H.M. Alexander, and Ray Tomalty

In Hans Christian Andersen's marvelously subversive story, "The Emperor's New Clothes," a child in the crowd is the one to point out the ruler's nakedness. All the adults have been silenced by lack of confidence and habitual deference to authority.

A rough parallel is evident in our responses to the problems of cities. There is much to be praised about Canadian cities and we should not be surprised that they continue to attract people from around the world. But in Canada as elsewhere, cities are showing ecological and social strains as more people and more material demands exceed the limits of a finite natural world, and as global pressures for rapid technological change and economic adjustment undermine the basic functions of community.

Probably every Canadian city can boast of exemplary programs and projects that address some aspects or symptoms of these problems. But typically these are the piecemeal initiatives of government agencies with fragmented mandates and developers with narrow interests. Neither is equipped to see, much less address, the bigger picture.

Ordinary citizens are usually the first to point out that established emperors of urban planning and development are failing, that communities are dissolving, environmental quality is being degraded, and ugliness is spreading. Since this is not what the authorities have been promising, deference to authority is in decline.

Promoters of public and private sector development projects now often face a skeptical, if not angry, citizenry. And this distrust of developers has been accompanied by equally evident cynicism about conventional forms of regulatory intervention. Citizens' groups as well as industrial interests have condemned governments' existing decision-making processes for land-use planning and approvals for being too fragmented, expensive, and time consuming; insufficiently sensitive to environmental and social factors; excessively rigid and rule-bound; too slow, reactive, and arbitrary; and apparently unable to ensure, even to promise, attractive, vibrant, and sustainable settlements. More of the same is not expected to help. In any event, governments facing deficits and opposition to higher taxes no longer have the option of simply expanding in response to new problems.

The clear message is that a new way of addressing urban problems is needed and that it will have to be more efficiently integrated, more sensitive to ecology and community, more respectful of uncertainties, and more open to citizen involvement than what now prevails.

Elaborating and applying such an alternative is much easier said than done. Cities are enormously complex and although we may be overcoming our traditional deference to authority, there is not yet much shared confidence in our ability to replace the established structures and processes.

There are, however, promising signs of movement in this direction. Authorities in many settled regions of Canada, including some major urban areas, have begun to experiment with new land use planning processes. From the Georgia Basin Initiative in British Columbia to the St. Croix Estuary Project in New Brunswick, there are now many serious Canadian efforts to develop and use a more open and integrated approach to land use planning and decision making and to define the areas of application largely on ecological rather than traditional administrative grounds.[1] Although these initiatives differ in many particulars, many have exhibited insights and creativity rarely seen in conventional urban planning. An illuminating example began in a most unlikely way on the blighted Toronto waterfront.

## How to Look at a Waterfront and See a Bioregion

The Toronto waterfront is a place of great aesthetic, economic, and social potential. It has a protected harbor, colorful history, attractive islands and beaches, and a location adjacent to a major commercial center in a culturally diverse city. But by the mid-eighties it had become an increasing embarrassment. Pollution had closed the beaches; expressways and condominium towers blocked public access; contaminated and abandoned industrial lands degraded the harbor area; and rehabilitation efforts were frustrated by jurisdictional squabbling among federal, provincial, regional, and municipal authorities.

In 1988 the federal government responded in the usual, apparently unimaginative way by creating a Royal Commission with an apparently narrow, though somewhat fuzzy, mandate. The Royal Commission on the Future of the Toronto Waterfront (RCFTW) was to examine matters related to "the use, enjoyment, and development" of the area under federal jurisdiction, and to address a number of specific issues that particularly embarrassed the federal government.

Fortunately, the appointed commissioner had the confidence and credibility to take a larger view. David Crombie had been a Conservative federal cabinet minister prior to heading the commission, and earlier he had been "the tiny, perfect mayor" of Toronto.

Crombie and his staff initiated broad public discussion of waterfront issues and quickly saw that the conventional, fragmented, waterfront-specific approach would not work. This enlightenment is reported in two extraordinary paragraphs near the beginning of the commission's final report (RCFTW 1992: 2-3):

> It soon became evident to the commission, as it had been to some others, that waterfront problems were both broader and deeper than the list of issues included in the commission's federal mandate. They stemmed from historical forces related to the way society and the economy had evolved over the past 200 years, and to the impact each had on the waterfront and on the local and regional environment of which the waterfront is a part.

> The public, ahead of governments, was aware of the nature of the problem. In the commission's first sets of hearings, dozens of deputants delivered the same message: by all means sort out the issues of Harborfront and the Harbor Commissioners, but help us find out how to make our lake publicly accessible, fishable, drinkable, and swimmable. This cannot happen while the rivers that empty into the lake are contaminated, the air that connects to it is dirty, the groundwaters polluted, and the soils through which they pass contaminated.

And so the commission, with support from the provincial government, expanded its scope from the waterfront to the watershed, or more accurately, to the group of adjacent watersheds formed by rivers that rise in the Oak Ridges Moraine and flow down into Lake Ontario along a 300 kilometre stretch of shoreline that includes Toronto. This larger area, which the commission called the Greater Toronto bioregion (RCFTW 1992: 21 ff.), is home to four million people as well as innumerable other creatures in complex social, as well as ecological, relations. If there was to be any hope of improvement here, the commission reasoned, it would have to be built on respect for the essential interrelationships of economic, social, and environmental well-being. Accordingly, the commission worked to develop new administrative mechanisms that could respect these interrelationships.

The commission advocated a variety of steps to strengthen and integrate the land use and environmental planning tools and practices of existing government authorities. But it did not expect these reforms to establish government agencies as effective and efficient solvers of urban planning problems. The recommended changes in law and policy were meant to reinforce the public hand in implementation of a quite different way of planning. The commission became a proponent of the ecosystem approach to planning — an approach that begins with an ecologically-bounded area, stresses the integration of social, economic, and environmental factors, and seeks to involve all the relevant interests and power holders in identifying desirable futures, evaluating alternative pathways and implementing preferred solutions.

Much of the commission's practical application of this approach was focused on specific projects, including establishment of a continuous waterfront trail along Lake Ontario from Burlington to Newcastle, rehabilitation initiatives for contaminated industrial lands and degraded natural habitat in the lower reaches of the Don River, and waterfront plans for several lakefront municipalities. But the commission also sketched out its vision for larger areas, including the whole Don River watershed.

Consistently, throughout this work, the commission sought to build solutions across agency mandates and administrative boundaries. It promoted and used informal cooperative processes, attempting to get beyond piecemeal action and jurisdictional conflicts by bringing together all the relevant parties and pushing them to work out their mutual problems together. And it insisted on careful attention to implications for ecology and community.

By 1991, when the commission submitted its final report, several rehabilitation and renewal projects were already underway and the province had established the Waterfront Regeneration Trust as a more permanent vehicle for Crombie and his staff. The province had also moved to strengthen overall planning guidance and to encourage watershed-based approaches. Inspired in part by Crombie's example, ecosystem-based planning initiatives were beginning to proliferate across the province.

A new provincial government has since undone some of the larger planning reforms. Some observers attribute the trust's more specific successes more to Crombie's personal skills than to participant acceptance of a more enlightened approach to land use decision making. And the predominant practice of land use planning in the Greater Toronto bioregion and other parts of the province still shows only occasional and fragmentary recognition of ecosystem planning ideas.

Nevertheless, the work of the Crombie Commission has been significant. Along with his colleagues in comparable bodies in Vancouver, Saskatoon, Montreal, and several other Canadian centers[2], Crombie brought the idea of ecosystem planning into the world of actual decision-making in urban Canada. Before Crombie, the notion of ecosystem planning was little known outside professional and citizen planning circles and did not seem likely to play a major role in guiding practical efforts to reunite economy, community, and ecology. Now it is a real possibility that has begun to be tested in practice, and we can see more clearly what the crucial principles are, and what difficulties have yet to be overcome.

## How Ecosystem Planning Differs from Conventional Planning

The crucial, defining principles of the ecosystem approach to planning are perhaps most clearly revealed in comparison with those of the approach to planning that typifies conventional practice today.

Conventional urban planning rests on a faith in growth. It assumes that expansion of economic activity, population, infrastructure, etc. is inherently beneficial and that any negative aspects can be minimized well enough through marginal adjustments. The ecosystem approach does not share this faith. Although it often involves enthusiastic promotion of certain economic activities, ecosystem planning also recognizes that other kinds of growth are overwhelming the resilience of communities and ecosystems, bringing seriously adverse social, economic, and biophysical effects for which there are no easy correctives or adequate compensations. Therefore, while conventional planning concentrates on nudging and accommodating prevailing trends, ecosystem planning is about choosing and pursuing a desirable future.

Ecosystem planning is founded on acceptance of human dependence on and responsibility for nature. This entails respect for ecological complexities, limits, and uncertainties, which in turn requires an emphasis on setting long term goals, giving attention to the future effects of planning decisions, and favoring planning mechanisms that are flexible enough to respond to unanticipated problems and opportunities.

Tensions between ecological and economic objectives can arise in ecosystem planning. But ultimately, ecological well-being is considered an essential basis for social and economic gains and community well-being. The development goals of ecosystem planning therefore include ecosystem health and integrity objectives along with objectives for social, economic, and political improvement, recognizing that these are mutually interdependent.

This recasting of human/non-human relations and the recognition that social and ecological goals are interdependent has some particular implications for land use planning. These implications can be stated as planning principles that are central to the ecosystem approach and distinguish it from conventional planning practices. The following seven principles are drawn chiefly from the work of the Crombie Commission and related practical experiments in southern Ontario, but they also reflect the characteristics of many other alternative planning initiatives in urban areas across Canada.

**Principle 1: Base planning units on natural boundaries.** Conventional planning uses a hierarchy of smaller-to-larger planning units with boundaries that rarely recognize ecological factors. The ecosystem approach replaces this politically-oriented hierarchy of planning units with nested units that are established at least in part to respect ecological functions and follow natural boundaries.

**Principle 2: Design with nature.** Traditionally, planners have seen "raw" land as a blank slate ready for human manipulation and use. They have not hesitated to replace complex ecological processes with engineered, often linear, systems. In ecosystem planning, human activity is part of the environment and the limits of resource availability and ecosystem resilience must be respected. Accordingly, new ecological planning and design approaches favor more creative solutions based on the biological productivity of natural systems, cycling of resources, or demand management to reduce need for new services.

**Principle 3: Consider global and cumulative effects.** Because it assumes that 'business as usual' will bring a generally benign future, conventional planning focuses on short-term and local adjustments. In ecosystem planning a desirable future is something we will have to work hard to achieve. Moreover, local successes will not be secure without larger regional and global improvements. Ecosystem planning therefore adopts a much longer and broader perspective that includes attention to off-site, cross-boundary, inter-generational, and cumulative effects.

**Principle 4: Encourage interjurisdictional decision making.** Conventional land use planning is commonly carried out by many separate planning and management authorities acting largely in isolation from each other. The ecosystem approach attempts to overcome this fragmentation by encouraging new planning units, agencies, and methods that promote integrated, inter-jurisdictional decision-making.

**Principle 5: Ensure consultation and facilitate cooperation and partnering.** Unlike conventional planning, in which land use decisions are often made in a technocratic manner after discharging any legal obligation for perfunctory public involvement, the ecosystem approach actively seeks to involve the widest range of stakeholders effectively and openly in the planning process.

**Principle 6: Initiate long term monitoring, feedback, and adaptation of plans.** Ecosystem planning and similar approaches are exercises in social learning. There can be no final answers. The process must be cyclical and iterative, always under review and dedicated to learning from experience. Monitoring mechanisms are included in the ecosystem approach to allow communities to assess progress in implementing their plans, to track the response of community health and ecosystem integrity indicators, and to provide a reliable basis for adapting plans to changing conditions. In conventional land use and environmental planning, few resources are expended to assess what happens to communities and ecosystems as plan implementation unfolds.

**Principle 7: Adopt an interdisciplinary approach to information.** Social, demographic, and economic information has been emphasized in traditional planning, with few attempts to assess ecological capacity or to assess how efforts to satisfy anticipated socio-economic demands may affect ecological functions. The ecosystem approach entails a greater scale of information gathering, more integration of information and greater cooperation among information providers, both amateur and expert. It also recognizes that information will not eliminate uncertainty in planning and that relevant information may only become available as the plan unfolds.

These seven principles summarize the ecosystem approach as it has been applied so far in land use planning involving Canadian urban centers. They may be seen as the first generation rules for defining and applying the ecosystem approach. But we now have many years and a considerable diversity of ecosystem planning experience in Canada. In our review of this experience, we found a number of common problems which suggest needs for supplementing the seven initial principles. It is now possible to go a little further and include three additional principles based on this experience and on lessons from related efforts to foster more enlightened attention to community and ecological interests.

## Three additional principles for ecosystem planning

The first problem arises from the combination of ignorance and continuing damage. Planning that follows the principles set out above is designed to recognize the complexities of ecosystems and communities. It also requires careful assessment of the potential effects of proposed initiatives, and fosters learning from experience. But it cannot quickly overcome the weakness of our current understanding of ecosystems and communities — how they work, where the limits to their resilience lie, and what to do when ecosystem integrity collapses or when communities lose their spark.

Because we know so little about these things, the precautionary principle should prevail. We should attempt always to err toward the path of least potential damage and we should avoid development options that are both risky and irreversible.

At the same time, we must recognize that avoiding more damage is no longer enough. Many urban ecosystems are already seriously degraded or subject to unsustainable pressure, and many communities have lost their most valued qualities or are crumbling in the face of unbearable pressures. Moreover, Canadian urban areas now draw heavily from ecological and community resources elsewhere; they are, in effect, appropriating carrying capacity from parts of the rest of the country and the rest of the world in ways and to an extent that is neither sustainable nor equitable (Wackernagel and Rees 1995).

Ecosystem planning must therefore go beyond caution and efforts to minimize the negative effects of growth. It must pursue those kinds of development that reduce overall stresses, return to reliance on regional carrying capacity, and make positive contributions to ecosystem and community sustainability. Thus,

**Principle 8: Adopt a precautionary but positive approach to development that aims not just to avoid further damage but also to reduce stresses and enhance the integrity of ecosystems and communities.** The second problem follows from the first. If ecosystem planning is to contribute to the sustainability of both ecosystems and communities, it must see this as essentially a single task. The challenge is not to find the most fair and reasonable balance among ecological, social, and economic objectives. It is to recognize that they are linked and must be pursued together.

This is not easy. In the abstract and in the long term, it is clear that the essential relation is mutual interdependence. But the prevailing political and economic winds are pressing individuals, corporations, and government agencies to concentrate on their own narrow interests and to focus on the short term. In the short term, narrowly-defined ecological, social, and economic objectives are easily seen as competing priorities — immediate jobs versus the environment, increased competitiveness versus internalization of social and environmental costs, greater attractiveness to investors or taxes to support social programs.

These are realities, and sometimes trade-offs must be made. However, ecosystem planning's greatest promise is in illustrating and fostering the essential unity of the ecological, social, and economic. Unlike more fragmented agencies and interests, ecosystem planning bodies are in a good position to identify and support economic activities that restore and enhance communities and ecosystems. As well, by setting long term objectives, requiring examination of broad planning alternatives, and emphasizing sustainability criteria in evaluations of these alternatives, the process of ecosystem planning can encourage more far-sighted integration.

While such efforts are unlikely to be enough by themselves, they should help to counter the trend to narrower and shorter vision. Thus,

**Principle 9: Ensure that land use planning integrates (rather than merely "balances") environmental, social, and economic objectives.** Finally, there is the problem of authority. Ecosystem planning is an integrative process working beyond the administrative mandates and boundaries of existing authorities, usually without a firm base of established institutional power. This can be a strength. Ecosystem planning bodies have often been able to foster multi-interest cooperation in part because they have not been seen as a direct threat to the power and autonomy of the interests they bring together. At the same time, experience suggests that ecosystem planning bodies need to have, or be supported by, sufficient authority to ensure implementation of planning agreements.

This is not just a matter of persuading the relevant government or governments to provide the necessary minimum of financial resources and top-down enforcement power to the new body. Getting things done through ecosystem planning depends heavily on broad support in the affected community. Integrating ecological, social, and economic concerns in land use decisions requires changes in attitudes, institutional structures, and behavior. These cannot be imposed. No single agency has a sufficiently comprehensive mandate and, in any event, resistance is too easy. Willing cooperation is crucial.

Realistically, this willingness must rest on more or less self-interested motivations as well as broader enlightenment. The usually recognized motivations in land use decision-making include desire for increased property value, concern about liability and litigation, reliance on good public image, fear of health effects or job loss, worry about crime, and hope for new commercial or professional or social opportunities. All these affect who comes to the table and whether they are inclined to bend for the collective benefit. Where these motivations are insufficient, they can be strengthened by new regulations, tax reform, publicity campaigns, and other tools. However, many of these lie outside the immediate reach of ecosystem planning initiatives. They are part of the larger political realm.

The same is true of broader enlightenment. Much can be accomplished through ecosystem planning work that gives people practical, direct experience in working together to design and apply new approaches. But such learning and working together is not always easy. While we all may be social creatures and inherently capable of cooperative effort, democracy is an acquired skill. It needs to be nurtured in practice and the opportunities for practice in ecosystem planning are insufficient by themselves.

Democratic capabilities are also not enough. Cooperative integration of ecological and community considerations requires people who have retained or developed a sense of community and commitment to a place. Here again, ecosystem planning can make a contribution but is best seen as just one part of a larger set of initiatives.

Advances in planning must therefore be linked to concurrent, broader changes in social attitudes and values that are democratic, community-oriented and environmentally responsible. Like ecosystem planning, these broader changes require involvement of people in various forms of social learning. Thus,

**Principle 10: Link ecosystem planning with other aspects of democratic change, social learning, community building, and environmental enlightenment.**

## Implement Ecosystem Planning

Urban centers wrestling with new administrative and environmental challenges now have good reasons for beginning a transition to ecosystem planning. It is increasingly evident that the old assumptions and processes of development planning are failing to avoid damages or minimize costs and conflicts. The pioneering work of Crombie and others has begun to demonstrate that ecosystem planning offers a feasible and attractive alternative. And although the new approach involves fundamental change, its implementation can proceed along lines that do not stray far from familiar planning territory.

The basic five-step framework for ecosystem planning set out below follows the general outlines of conventional land use planning and environmental assessment processes.[3]

**Step 1: Scope the planning process and set initial goals.** Identify current problems and issues; identify all relevant stakeholders; and involve them along with members of the general public in drawing up an initial list of goals and priorities.

**Step 2: Define and survey the planning region.** Settle on the various parameters to be measured; gather the relevant data; and resolve the issue of the region's boundaries.

**Step 3: Model and analyze the region.** Delineate the three main systems (biophysical, infrastructural, and urban form) and their interrelationships; identify needs and trends, starting with demography; and begin to determine the optimal location for different types of land uses, based on criteria of suitability, efficiency, and compatibility.

**Step 4: Develop a structure plan.** Formulate detailed goals and objectives in relation to the three systems; formulate rival scenarios, with assessments of their effects on the agreed-upon goals and objectives; reduce the scenarios to two or three structure plan options through negotiation; and submit them to careful environmental assessment, public debate and a selection process.

**Step 5: Refine and implement the chosen option, monitor the regional environment, and revise the plan.** Develop detailed plans and zoning designations through consultation and negotiation; establish requirements and procedures for planning, reviewing, and approving individual projects under the plan, and for interim plan amendments; monitor effects and overall changes; and, after a specified period of implementation, undertake a comprehensive plan review.

In practice no planning process works in such a rational one-step-after-another way. Nor should it. Realistic implementation needs to involve much iterative movement back and forth among the steps, consolidation of some items and re-emphasis of others. Not everything can be done at once. Information will remain imperfect. And in any event, ecosystem planning in any framework can never stand alone. It must, for example, accommodate relations with provincial highway planning, municipal funding practice, environmental law enforcement, and a host of other activities and decisions of adjacent municipal and regional authorities. Moreover, it must retain flexibility to respond to the unexpected pressures and opportunities of an uncertain world.

But so long as these complexities are respected, the five-step framework gives ordinary urban authorities, citizens, and other interests a workable model for applying an approach to planning that contrasts sharply with conventional practice.

## What the Ecosystem Planning Model Offers

The central characteristic and strength of the ecosystem planning model is the integration of data and analysis in a way that allows effective attention to whole systems within natural boundaries. Ecosystems and communities can then be linked in planning as they are in reality.

In the model, defining long term ecological, community, and development goals is crucial. This is because ecosystem planning is a vehicle for getting to a desirable future and such a future is unlikely to be achieved without deliberate, collective effort. The goals are not given. Defining and selecting them are matters of public deliberation and public choice. So are elaboration, assessment, and choice among alternative plans for pursuing these objectives. The planning is positive in that it focuses on what citizens want, rather than just on what they fear. It is also empowering in that it allows people to choose their future, rather than simply adjust to what comes.

The emphasis on overall objectives and results allows planning to be both firm and flexible. The selected plan is meant to be followed. Enforceable requirements provide stronger protection for ecosystems and communities and greater certainty for proponents of development projects. They reduce administrative waste by cutting duplication and ensuring more focused regulatory activity. And they eliminate many environmental rehabilitation costs by avoiding damages that would require costly repairs or compensation.

At the same time, the model allows both for site-specific adjust-ments and for continuous learning. Within the general framework of the plan, participants can set and enforce special rules that respect the particular conditions of individual sites. Amendment and review provisions, including monitoring and plan renewal requirements, allow flexibility and demand regular rethinking. Innovation is also encouraged by the mandatory consideration of alternatives and the emphasis on objectives to be reached rather than standards to be followed.

At all stages — from setting objectives to monitoring the effects of plan implementation — the model emphasizes broad involvement of authorities, experts, and citizens. Relevant interests are encouraged to be participating partners rather than separate authorities, regulatees, and citizens with their own mandates, demands, and fears. While longtime antagonists are not expected suddenly to become cheerfully cooperative, the model favors consensus over conflict, inclusion over imposition, and collaboration over mere consultation. The participative process recognizes that acceptability is crucial because the kinds of significant change implied in adoption of ecosystem planning are unlikely to be implementable without the agreement of most parties.

The model fosters better communication among municipalities and among municipal and provincial and watershed agencies, improving mutual awareness, providing a better information base, and facilitating cooperation. This promises to make all of these bodies more effective and efficient, more evidently valuable and less vulnerable to elimination in times of fiscal pressure.

The model also aims to encourage and strengthen the positive role of citizens in planning. Instead of trying to exclude citizens with narrow, backyard-protection concerns, the ecosystem planning model sees these concerns as powerful initial incentives for citizens to join in an exercise that leads all participants to relate their own immediate (backyard, local, corporate, or agency) interests to desired regional outcomes. The "design your own future" and "monitor your own community" elements also encourage citizens to abandon the fortress mentality and pursue more positive opportunities. Finally, the social action and hands-on involvement elements of the model demonstrate the seriousness of the new approach's commitment to actual acceptance of citizens as effective participants, rather than as targets for consultative gestures.

The model must still include legislated authority for the regional planning body. It requires mechanisms for concluding conflicts that consensual procedures cannot resolve, and it must have effective enforcement tools to ensure compliance. But it represents a large step away from planning by top-down edicts.

## Conclusion

Ecosystem planning is a rejection of 'business as usual.' It asserts ecology and community as the foundation for planning objectives and planning processes. Accordingly, it treats economic growth not as something that is naturally and necessarily beneficial, but as something that is desirable only if it is fostered and directed in ways that ensure it serves the interests of citizens who are dependent on ecology and community.

Current interest in ecosystem planning rests in part on evidence that the conventional planning process is not working and no amount of tinkering will resolve the evident problems. But the ecosystem approach also offers a great positive advantage. It promises to help the citizens of a region to build a greater whole by integrating their sense of community and place and by choosing their mutual future, rather than having a future imposed on them. While this choosing is necessarily constrained by limitations of knowledge and requirements for general consensus, it is nonetheless an exercise in both individual empowerment and community building that enriches the links between citizens and their environment.

Even highly imperfect steps in this direction should make valuable contributions to sustainability and the quality of life.

"THE ROAD TO HELL IS PAVED WITH GOOD INTENTIONS"

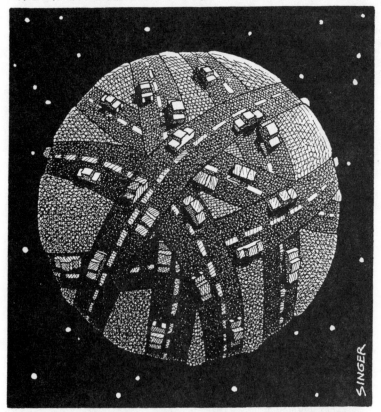

THE ROAD TO HELL IS **PAVED.**

40

# Part Two

# Healthy Communities
# Healthy Planet

*From eco-city planning we turn our attention to exploring the link between healthy communities and a healthy planet. Nearly half of the world's people will live in urban areas by the end of the century, posing a major challenge to the maintenance of human and ecosystem health. **Trevor Hancock** has been one of the pioneers in the international healthy cities/communities movement. Linking the concepts of health and sustainability, Hancock argues that decision-making for our communities should be based on a holistic approach which requires planners and others who can think and work across traditional disciplinary boundaries. It also has significant implications for the structure and functioning of local government. Hancock argues that we need a more truly democratic way of creating healthy and sustainable communities, and that this is ultimately a matter of social and political will.*

*__David Burman__ introduces Local Employment Trading Systems (LETS), grass-roots initiatives of community economic development that have emerged in response to shrinking outside resources, as a supportive strategy for promotion of community health. A pharmacist by training, Burman is now involved in a major research study on the health impacts of LETS. Burman proposes that LETSystems have the potential to enhance some health promotion programs and may be necessary for the existence of others, but there are some indications that LETS may have a more fundamental role to play in supporting the determinants of health. Burman argues that LETS addresses the basic issues of health promotion such as empowerment, social inequities, and economic and environmental sustainability, as well the more traditional ones such as enhancing access to community health services.*

# Healthy Sustainable Communities
## Concept, Fledgling Practice, and Implications for Governance

### Trevor Hancock

The 21st century will be the dawn of the urban millennium — for the first time more than half the human species will be urban. Inevitably, one of our major challenges will be to maintain and improve the health, well-being, and quality of life of the earth's increasingly urban population while also maintaining and improving ecosystem health. This means providing future generations — especially in the developing world — with at least an equal opportunity to have as high a quality of life and to achieve their maximum potential as we now have in the industrialized world, and doing so through means that are sustainable.

What is required, I will argue here, is a form of sustainable development that differs from the usual.[1] While "sustainable development" has mainly been interpreted as meaning environmentally sustainable economic development, the required development is not simply economic and the need for sustainability is not limited to the natural environment and natural resources.[2] As the Canadian Public Health Association, for example, has recognized, (CPHA 1991: 3) if sustainability is viewed from a human and ecosystem perspective, economics plays only a supporting role:

> Human development and the achievement of human potential require a form of economic activity that is socially and envi-

ronmentally sustainable in this and future generations.

The UN describes human development as an approach that "enables all individuals to enlarge their human capabilities to the full and to put those capabilities to their best use in all fields — economic, social, cultural, and political" (UNDP 1994: 4). Economic activity is merely a means to that end and not the end in itself. Moreover, if economic activity is to assist in the achievement of human development, it must be indefinitely sustainable, environmentally *and* socially.

## Conceptual Model for Planning

For communities, a shift from economic development to human development will bring significant changes in design and operation. This is because human development is centered on a view of development as an integration of health/social well-being, environmental quality/ecosystem health, and economic activity.[3]

One way of depicting this is illustrated in Figure 1, a conceptual model that links community, environment, and economy (adapted from Hancock 1993). At the center of the model is *health,* or perhaps more properly, human development, at the conjunction of three equivalent and overlapping rings — community conviviality, envi-

### Figure 1

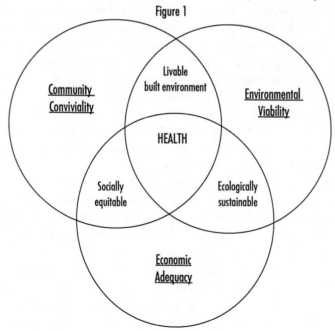

ronmental viability, and economic prosperity.

**Community conviviality** is concerned with the web of social relations — the social equivalent of the ecological concept of the web of life — and embraces such concepts as social cohesion, "the civic community," and "social solidarity" (Putnam 1993). **Environmental viability** refers to the condition of the community's environment, including local air, water, and soil quality and the integrity of the ecosystems (local, regional, and global) on which the community depends.[4] **Economic adequacy** refers to having a sufficient level of economic activity to ensure that basic needs for all are met. It is based in part on the recognition that above $5,000 per capita of gross domestic product, there is little relationship between life expectancy (as a proxy measure of overall health status) and economic development (Wilkinson 1994). Thus our health and well-being will not be severely harmed if we operate on the Gandhian basis of "enough for each person's need, but not for each person's greed."

The model recognizes that in order to ensure well-being and human development, the benefits of economic activity must be distributed in a way that is *socially equitable*. There is now a considerable body of work which suggests that the degree of equity within a society matters as much as the level of wealth in the society.[5] Equity is also related to social cohesion, for as the French philosopher Raymond Aron has reportedly remarked, "When inequality becomes too great, the idea of community becomes impossible."

In addition to being socially equitable, economic activity must be indefinitely *ecologically sustainable*. The community's impact on local, regional, or global ecosystems must not irreparably harm future generations or distant populations by depleting natural resources, polluting the environment, or otherwise impairing ecosystem health (e.g., through greenhouse gas emissions).[6]

Finally, the community requires a *livable built environment*. This refers to the quality and nature of the built environment, including housing, roads, and other transportation systems, other urban infrastructure, and urban design and land use, and their impact on safety and on personal and social well-being.

Together, these six qualities form a set of criteria for community decision making that are markedly different from the economic development criteria usually applied. One application is in policy analysis. I have worked with a couple of communities in Canada to apply the six criteria in urban policy development. We have asked, "What would a transportation policy (or a housing policy, etc.) be like if it had to support conviviality, equity, economic vitality, ecological sustainability, environmental quality, and livability?" Immediately this reveals the need for an integrated approach to urban policy and planning. Environmental, social, economic, health, and land use planning have to be considered together in a holistic approach to planning "whole communities."

An integrated or holistic approach is required because the criteria involved sit in the conjunction of overlapping spheres; they cannot be addressed adequately by planners isolated in separate social, economic, and environmental specialties. A case in Glasgow, Scotland, provides an example of the advantages of overcoming traditional planning divisions. In response to a concern with respiratory disease in children living in damp, cold housing, a program of energy conservation was initiated, using special funds from the European Union and the United Kingdom. Not only was the energy efficiency and housing quality greatly improved, but the residents now had more discretionary income because of the considerable reduction in energy costs. Moreover, since local businesses were engaged and local people were trained and employed, there was also a community economic development benefit (see Lyons 1996).

Initiating a more integrated approach demands significant changes. As Christopher Alexander (1987) and his colleagues have noted:

> This quality of wholeness does not exist in towns being built today — and indeed this quality could not exist at present because there isn't any discipline which actively sets out to create it.

They suggest that the task of creating wholeness can only be dealt with as a *process* and not by design alone. This of course has profound implications both for the training of planners and for the governance of communities.

The issue with respect to the training of planners is quite straightforward: we need to train planners and others who can think and work across traditional disciplinary boundaries, specialists in holistic thinking and working.[7] I am fortunate to teach part-time in a faculty that was established on the basis of a transdisciplinary philosophy. I firmly believe that we need to restructure much of our academic training along such lines. But such holistic planners will need to work within very different government structures if their skills and perspectives are to be effectively utilized.

## Implications for Government and Governance

From a decade of experience working with the concept of healthy communities, I have learned that the implications for government and governance are profound.[8] We need a shift in our values as a society such that economic growth and development is no longer the overriding social and political objective, but merely one objective that has to be balanced with other objectives such as sustainability, equity, liveability, social cohesion, and environmental quality. And we need processes and structures that will enable us to do this.

The attempt to create healthy and sustainable communities has a number of implications for the structure and functioning of at least six aspects of local government (from Hancock 1995).

## The Purpose of Government

Faced as we are with major challenges to the ecological and social sustainability of our way of life, we should re-examine the question, "What is the central purpose of government and governance?" I have suggested above that the central purpose of governance — and, more narrowly, of formal governments — should be enhancing the human development of the population. While this may be implicit in the structures of governments, with their functions relating to health, education, social welfare, environmental protection, and so on, it is rarely explicit. Too often it seems that the central purpose of government is very much aligned with that of business, i.e., economic development. But economic activity must be understood as a means, not as the end. If the means — economic activity as it is currently practised — threatens the end — human development — then we must change the means, not the end.

## The Approach to Government

If we are going to create healthy and sustainable communities we have to develop a holistic approach to government and governance, beginning with the recognition that everything is connected to everything else. We cannot sit contentedly in our disciplinary and departmental silos any longer, because individual sectors can no longer respond to and meet peoples' needs. Instead we have to begin to work intersectorally and collaboratively to achieve our common purpose.

We have a problem: not only are our governments not structured for a holistic approach, but as mentioned earlier, we lack the concept of wholeness and people skilled in taking a holistic approach. If we are going to take a holistic approach to governance, we will need new skills (and perhaps new holistic disciplines), as well as new processes, new styles, and new structures. The "roundtables" that have developed at the national, provincial, and local levels provide examples of the approach needed. The Premier's Council in Ontario, now regrettably abolished, was another innovative approach that deserves to be emulated elsewhere.

## The Level at which Government Occurs

The nation state is being pulled apart by two opposing forces. The first of those forces is "supranationalism." As a result of the General Agreement on Tariffs and Trade, the European Union, the North American Free Trade Agreement, and similar multinational agreements, decision making is increasingly being drawn up to the supranational level. At the same time, and perhaps in reaction to that, we are seeing the growth of the opposing forces of parochialism or localism, in which people want to establish their local identity and exert more local control. Bosnia, Quebec, Scotland, and the former U.S.S.R. all provide examples.

The same two opposing forces that are pulling apart the nation state may be being replicated at the municipal level. First, if we take the notion of ecological sustainability seriously, we need to consider not only the city or town but also the bioregion of which it is a part. For example, the recent Royal Commission on the Future of the Toronto Waterfront took the position that it is not possible to consider the waterfront in isolation; it must be addressed in the context of the entire bioregion (RCFTW 1992). Thus bioregionalism parallels supranationalism.

At the same time — as in the case for the nation state — the municipality is also being pulled apart by decentralist forces. This shift reflects the need that people feel at the neighborhood and community level to have more influence over the decisions that affect their health, well-being, and quality of life. So the level at which local government occurs is moving both upwards to the bioregional level and downwards to the neighborhood level in response, at least in part, to the concepts associated with the healthy and sustainable community.

## The Style of Government

A section of the mid-term report on the World Health Organization Europe Healthy Cities Project discusses the need to move to a new management style more consistent with the approach of health promotion (Tsouros 1990). It is a style that emphasizes "power with" rather than "power over," negotiation rather than directives, process rather than structure, collegiality rather than hierarchy, collaboration rather than competition, a holistic rather than a sectoral approach, both/and rather than either/or and win-win rather than win-lose strategies.

This new style is emerging in many organizations and is not so much a product of the healthy communities approach as it is consistent with the approach. Without such a change in style, in my view, it will be very difficult to attain a healthy and sustainable community.

## The Structure of Government

On the principle that form follows function, changes in the process of governance such as those described here will require changes in the structure of government.[9] The problem is that our present system of government is essentially based in the 19th century, both literally and metaphorically. Departments of public health, public works, parks, planning, and other municipal responsibilities originated in the 19th century. They are organized on the 19th century models of disciplinarity in separate sectors. Yet most if not all of the issues we will face in the 21st century (health, safety, sustainability, equity, mobility, food, energy, etc.) cut clear across these 19th century departments. Since the current structure is no longer capable of responding adequately to the challenges we must face, we will have to create new structures.[10] Possible models include the City of Toronto's Healthy City Office, which is a corporate rather than a departmental body, and the Healthy Community Advisory Commission in Parksville, B.C. (City of Parksville 1993).

## The Democratic Process of Governance

The healthy community approach is rooted in the concept of health promotion, which is "the process of enabling people to increase control over and improve their health" (WHO 1986). This results in a strong emphasis on greater community involvement in influencing all the many factors that affect community members' lives, their health and well-being — in short, more democracy. This is well illustrated by the fact that a 1993 training workshop for cities from six recently democratized countries of central and eastern Europe was sponsored in part by the Danish Democracy Fund, which recognized that creating a healthier city is essentially an exercise in democracy.

Concern with democracy is also to be found with respect to sustainability. As Ronald Doering, former executive director of the National Round Table on Environment and Economy, has noted:

> Sustainability planning must be community-led and consensus-based because the central issue is will, not expertise. We can't protect ecosystems, let alone restore them, unless ways and means can be found to integrate the work of all the communities within the region. We must experiment with ways that involve citizens more directly and deliberately into policy-making at all levels. Ultimately it all comes down to social and political will.

Doering also argues that some of the most important problems to be overcome are "barriers to citizen participation in decision making because, being consensus-based, the central issue for sustainability is democracy" (1994).

The many means of introducing greater democracy in the creation of healthy and sustainable communities include initiatives to "co-design" communities, based on partnerships between professionals such as architects and planners and the community (see, for example, Towers 1995, King 1988, and Wates and Knevitt 1987). Beyond design exercises, democracy can be enhanced by more co-ownership, co-control and co-management in cities, neighborhoods, and housing developments (as well as in workplaces and many other settings), in which owners and tenants (or employees and workers, or staff and students) collaborate for the common good.[11]

## Conclusion

In the 21st century the health and well-being of the planet and its human and nonhuman populations will be decided to a significant degree by cities and their citizens. As Jane Jacobs argues, cities are the basis for the economic wealth of nations (1984). If we do not succeed in creating cities that are environmentally and socially sustainable, the prospects for human development are grim. Fortunately, there is some evidence that the task is being taken seriously in many cities and towns; there are many small, local examples of action that are moving us in the right direction.

But when we begin to talk about creating a more healthy and sustainable community, we come inescapably to question our current systems of governance and our structures of government, and to talk about how we can have a more truly democratic way of creating healthy and sustainable communities. Ultimately, this comes down to social and political will. Do we have the social and political will to re-order the priorities of our societies and communities, to shift our values, to aspire to higher objectives than economic growth and consumer happiness? Are governments — who are our representatives, not our masters, we should remember — prepared to give up central control and share power and resources with communities? Indeed, are they willing to enable those communities to acquire the resources and skills they need?

If we do not change, then I fear we are doomed. But if we do, I believe we can indeed create healthy and sustainable communities that maximize socially just human development in the 21st century.

# Enhancing Community Health Promotion with Local Currencies
## The Local Employment and Trading System (LETS)

### David Burman

We are in an era of sweeping, interlinked global trends in communications, trade, technology, and culture. Free trade agreements permit the free movement of capital anywhere, while constraining the power of governments. Nation states are becoming less and less powerful, and increasingly irrelevant, as transnational corporations (TNCs) control the rules for global trade, and as individuals bypass taxation by carrying out economic transactions on the Internet.

The enormity and global scale of these changes can lead to despair at the local level. It seems that regardless of which government is elected, fiscal policies are similar. We have witnessed a Canadian Minister of Finance address a federal budget more to a foreign investment house than to the electorate. Once-powerful unions are agreeing to unheard of concessions in order to survive as a workforce (Salutin 1996). But underlying the decline in local political and labor power is a concentration of wealth and power that would have made the fascists of the 1930s envious.

These trends can only have a profound effect on the personal, social, and environmental conditions that favor health and well being, which are the determinants of health generally considered to be the backbone of health promotion as outlined in the Ottawa Charter of 1986.[1] The many initiatives in place for community health promotion and healthy communities depend to a great extent on healthy economies: there must be adequate financial resources to sustain them. But in an age of cutbacks, even expenditures that would be cost effective in the long term are shrinking (Della Costa 1995). Therefore, as the effects of global economic restructuring begin to be felt in all parts of the world, some economists (Daly and Cobb 1989; Rotstein and Duncan 1991) and health promotion advocates are seeking innovative ways of sustaining local economies.

In this chapter, I introduce Local Employment Trading Systems (LETS),[2] which are grass-roots initiatives for community economic development that have emerged in response to shrinking outside resources experienced by communities affected by the global economy, as a supportive strategy for community-based health promotion. I propose that LETS have the potential to enhance some health promotion programs and may be necessary for the existence of others, but there are some indications that LETS may have a more fundamental role to play in supporting the determinants of health. I am proposing that LETS addresses the basic issues of health promotion such as empowerment, social inequities, and economic and environmental sustainability, as well the more traditional ones such as enhancing access to community health services.[3]

## The Global Economic Problem

Although the relationship of poverty to health has been well documented (City of Toronto, 1991; Mechanic, 1989), it is not always recognized that fiscal restraint imposes limits on the abilities of governments and public health departments to deal with the escalating inequities with which they are confronted. While the number of people in poverty increases, governments, stymied by the lack of funds and mounting costs involved with servicing debt, are cutting back on essential programs at the very time they are most needed.

Perhaps even more problematic, as wealth and power are increasingly concentrated in the hands of transnational corporations, local and regional governments are being pressured to disregard environmental or labor regulations in order to attract investment in an environment of enhanced mobility of capital. Spurred by global economic restructuring, many first world communities are now experiencing the net outflow of resources that has been the lot of indigenous communities under colonialism (Adams 1987; Daly and Cobb 1989; Dobson 1993: 40). The effects of this global economic restructuring may be as fundamental and wide ranging as the changes experienced during the industrial revolution (Drucker 1993). The uncertainty of the economic climate is underscored by Rotstein and Duncan (1991) who caution that the current international money market, in which states have no national controls on the money supply, is in danger of "catastrophic banking crisis at any time" (Rotstein and Duncan 1991:422).

Although individuals, community organizations, or governments may have varying access to money depending on the boom and bust cycles of capitalism, the overall trend is for wealth to flow always toward those who charge interest and away from those who pay it.[4] The greater the concentration of wealth, the faster the flow, unless progressive taxation or other means of redistribution are enacted. But free trade agreements and electronic technology allow corporations to move capital out of the control of such redistribution, and even externally controlled investment in communities has been shown to be detrimental (Galtung 1986). At the community level, this means that large numbers of highly skilled workers are unemployed, while the existing demand for their skills remains unmet because of restricted access to the money to pay for their use.

In times of such economic constraints, when attempts at full employment or a comprehensive safety net fail, people have turned to the informal or underground economies. But, as Williams (1996b) points out, the social inequities of the formal economy are often replicated in the informal. With greater access to resources and marketable skills, the employed and relatively affluent are more active in the informal economy and tend to do more rewarding and higher paying work within it than do the poor and unemployed.

## Acting Locally: Local Employment Trading Systems

With access to local capital increasingly impeded by external interests, communities are in urgent need of a means of caring for their members that does not depend on an infusion of external capital (Galtung 1986; Meyer 1986). A solution would be to develop local economies that "protect the economic and social space of individuals and communities from the growing uncertainty of the currency and capital markets that tie all countries to the vicissitudes of this single global process" (Rotstein and Duncan 1991:415). The most widely used local economic entity is LETS — Local Employment Trading Systems (Williams 1996b) which are simple accounting systems that function like local currencies. Seen by many as a solution to the problem of reproducing the inequities of the informal sector (Offe and Heinze 1992; Willams 1994), such initiatives may have important implications for the ability of communities to "take control of the determinants of health" (WHO 1984) and thereby improve the health of their members.

LETS was first developed on Vancouver Island by Michael Linton in early 1983 in response to the disastrous local effects of the recession of 1982. In its first four years of existence the first LETS recorded $350,000 of trading in local accounting units which Linton labelled "green dollars" after his vision of the environmental and social benefits that would follow general use of the system (Linton 1989). Since then, LETS have been spreading throughout the English speaking world, and have recently spread into continental Europe. There are currently between 500 and 1,000 LETS in existence, about 25 of them in Canada.[5] In 1994, LETS were being established at the rate of one per week in the U.K. (Seyfang 1994).

## The Structure of LETS

Straddling the regular and irregular economies (Ferman 1990), LETS are based on a paradigm of money that appears entirely different from the normal economy. This approach to money "contains elements of neo-classical conservatism, neo-Ricardian liberalism and is strongly relevant to Marxist socialism," but is inherently associated with none (Seyfang 1994: 21). Quoting LETS developer Michael Linton, Seyfang (1994: 15) describes LETS as "capitalism that Karl would have loved." The LETS paradigm holds three basic underlying assumptions:

1.   Money can be issued by local individuals and businesses. Green dollars are a personal money system which are issued at the point of acknowledgment of purchase of a product or service. With the purchaser's permission, green dollars are moved from the buyer's account into that of the vendor, thereby putting that amount of community currency into circulation.[6]

2.   Money is not "real." Green dollars are not commoditized, but exist only insofar as products or services exist for trade within the community. Green dollars cannot be invested outside the community

since they can only be exchanged among account holders, nor can interest be earned for their storage. The total amount of green dollar currency in circulation (the total of positive and negative account balances) should always be zero.[7]

3. Local currency is abundant. Because they are issued when, where, and by whom they are needed, there is no limit on the number of green dollars circulating in the community at any one time. Skills, knowledge, and materials that sit idle for lack of money can be put to productive work (Greco 1994). Public projects and services that are delayed for lack of funds can also be put into action.[8]

LETS are based on the assumption that money is nothing more than a means of measuring the value of goods or services, just as a centimeter is a means of measuring length (Linton 1989). These nonconvertible, quasi-currencies are backed entirely by locally produced goods and services. The local exchange units, called green dollars, valued at par with the national currency, exist only as accounts and are created by the trading transaction itself, since all accounts start at zero.

Because local currencies exist entirely within their communities of origin, Rotstein and Duncan (1991) argue that they present a solution to the dilemma of how to satisfy the need of the state to control inflation without severely constricting employment at the local level — by separating the medium-of-exchange function from the storage-of-wealth function of money. Because green dollars are abundant and accessible to all, such systems should be able to eliminate poverty and unemployment while augmenting current self-help initiatives through multilateral networks of exchange (Dauncey 1988, Linton 1989, Racey 1990; Williams 1996a).[9]

Because LETS is a community currency, the community can decide on its structure, the variants of which are described below. All LETS operate by members holding accounts. Account holders will have a positive or negative balance depending on their level of trade. Systems work on a value-added principle, with a non-commoditized system of measurement of value. Therefore, there is no interest accrued or owed on account balances. Transactions are accounted for by the recipient (purchaser) of the service or product, who authorizes the transfer of an agreed-upon amount of accounting points from his or her account into that of the provider (seller), usually by telephoning the transaction into a central phone line, or by writing a green dollar cheque that the seller must then send or take to the LETS adminstrator. Accounting in most systems is done by a central administrator, with transactions usually entered into a readily available computer program. Monthly statements of trading activity and balance are sent to all members.

Since LETS are by agreement nonprofit and are controlled entirely by the community in which they operate, they facilitate the circulation of skills, services, and goods within the community while greatly reducing the need for federal currency. Participation in LETS does not depend on personal philosophy, values, or ideology. Linton (1989) maintains that although individuals and businesses participate because they perceive it to be in their economic interest to do so, the act of participation facilitates the reassessment of commonly held beliefs concerning the nature of wealth and money, thus empowering participants and the community itself to achieve greater economic self-reliance.[10]

Although there is some controversy as to whether the purpose of LETS is to build community,[11] all agree that communities are strengthened by its use. Since communities are socially constructed, and therefore are actively generated "through local networks and identities," LETS facilitate community-building by creating a "formal, structured framework within which social networks can develop through the medium of multilateral reciprocal exchange" (Williams 1996: 6). LETS use the language of the gift economy in their accounting, so that a negative balance represents a commitment to give something back to the community, and a credit is considered an acknowledgment for a gift or service to the community through the individual recipient.

## LETS and Determinants of Health

There are many intriguing parallels between the principles of LETS and those of health promotion. Empirical questions remain, however, regarding the extent to which the principles are practicable in and by communities, especially in an urban setting. Unfortunately, due to the recent emergence of LETS, there is very little research data in existence. Therefore, this analysis is mostly theoretical, supported with what empirical evidence is available.[12]

The concept of health promotion that focuses on community control of the determinants of health is sufficiently broad that a wide range of strategies, such as anti-poverty and community economic development, can be subsumed under this rubric (Rootman 1993).

Based on Achieving Health for All (Epp 1986) and The Ottawa Charter for Health Promotion (WHO Europe, 1986), the models of healthy communities proposed by Labonté (1993) and Hancock (1993) are useful in this analysis because they are ecological and incorporate the notion of environmental sustainability into the concept of community (environment being interpreted broadly to include the social, economic, and political). According to its proponents, LETS have the potential to make a positive impact on the health of communities precisely by creating the conditions for sustainability. Indeed, Dobson (1993: 40) argues that without the type of community economic development that LETS entail, the structural problems of money described above render communities that adhere to "old paradigm" money inherently unsustainable.

The perception is often expressed, that the gap between the imagined ideal of a healthy community and our present reality is very great, and indeed, there are few formulated strategies on how to create the necessary bridges. LETS have the potential to be the bridge that health promotion planners are looking for at several levels. The following are some of the areas in which LETS could address the challenges, mechanisms, and strategies outlined in the Framework for Health Promotion (Epp 1986) as elucidated by the models presented by Hancock (1993) and Labonté (1993).

## Links to Health Promotion and Sustainable Communities

There are six distinct links between health promotion and sustainable communities that warrant exploration. These include social equity, empowerment, enhancement of community health services, fostering of public participation, creation of a sustainable economic environment, and maintenance of a viable natural environment.

**Convivial Community / Equitable Social Environment** One key concept in health promotion that applies to LETS is social inequity (Draper 1989, Lemkow 1989) and empowerment (e.g., Labonté 1994). The most pressing of the inequities potentially addressed by LETS is poverty, the relationship of which to health has been extensively documented (City of Toronto 1991, Mechanic 1989). The degree to which individuals can meet their basic personal needs through LETS depends entirely on the extent to which these goods and services are available within the system — not on the degree to which individuals are able to obtain money from employment or transfer payments. LETS ought to be able to allow individuals to participate economically without the dependency generated by either charity or social assistance. Seyfang (1994) found that local business participation is necessary for LETS to reach their economic potential. In a variant of LETS developed in Ithaca, N.Y., many businesses and a credit union are part of the system, enabling at least one person to live entirely in local currency (Glover 1995).

A concern has been expressed that LETS might be less available to those most in need. If it is the ideologically committed, affluent, middle class who join, and not those who are most in need of what it has to offer, the potential of LETS will remain unfulfilled. Indeed, there is some evidence that the earlier systems — those started before 1990 — had disproportionately high concentrations of middle class "greens" (Seyfang 1994; Williams 1996b). Since LETS fall easily within the purview of green economics (Ekins 1986), it is not surprising that innovation of this kind should come from there.

With maturity, however, many systems are becoming more inclusive, and systems of more recent origin, at least in the U.K., tend to be started more for reasons of economic need than for ideological motives (Williams 1996a). Although the percentage of economic activity in local currency is still very small — about two per cent (Jackson 1993; Willams, 1995a), many participants perceive a direct economic benefit. There is evidence that LETS attract predominantly low income people,[13] and are perceived to be an economic benefit (Williams 1996b). In Toronto, LETS have enabled at least two individuals who were formerly dependent on welfare to thrive without direct state subsidies, and several low income associations have joined.

The need for access to inexpensive, nutritious food has been a preoccupation of the Toronto system almost since its inception. Since 1994, a food coop has been allowing payments of 15 per cent in green dollars and an organic retailer has been selling seconds for 100 per cent green dollars. Recently, the Toronto system has formed an association with an organic farmer and has been working with Foodshare, a project to provide affordable, mostly locally grown, fruit and vegetables to low income people. Shelter, too, is becoming available as people advertise rooms for rent for partial payment in green dollars.

**Empowerment**  Another issue to be considered in health promotion is how individuals with disabling health problems, the elderly, visible minorities, and others who are often marginalized from the mainstream, commodity-money economy can be empowered. The social environment of abundance engendered by a self-issued currency ought to enhance individuals' coping ability by rewarding informal care-giving and generosity within the community, addressing the issue of mutual aid (Epp, 1986). This is empowering for all individuals, regardless of ability. If basic needs can be provided through the system, thus removing many economic burdens, disabled persons and others who are marginalized economically would be able to function more freely and independently in a less competitive, more caring environment.

Several disabled groups, most notably ex-psychiatric "survivors" have formed micro-businesses either within LETS, or have joined LETS, to enable them to use their skills and benefit economically (Sheppard 1995). In Toronto, a courier service run by a "survivor" group is a vital part of the LETS community. In the states of Florida and Missouri, state run "time dollar" systems that serve mainly seniors and function similarly to LETS, report a threefold increase in voluntarism when their time is acknowledged.

**Enhancing Community Health Services** Established LETS could have a positive effect on the effectiveness of community-based health care and on the access of individuals to it in several ways. The kinds of care-giving activities traditionally done by women that are currently often unacknowledged and unpaid can be used to earn green dollars. The recognition and reward for these services at once removes the exploitative aspects of "women's work," increases the availability of service in the community, and recognizes and rewards the individual workers. This aspect of community need is being addressed in Toronto by The Womyn's Project, an initiative to recruit and support "economically marginalized and culturally diverse women and communities and use LETS for their empowerment" (project statement, May 1996).

When care-giving is decentralized into the community, there is less pressure for social service agencies to be preoccupied with the most basic needs of their clients. While the danger exists that LETS would be used as an excuse by costcutting governments to cut back further on services, experience has demonstrated that within a LETS economy providers are able to direct their skills more effectively to meet the special needs of their clients while increasing their own satisfaction, thereby preventing professional burnout (e.g., Marbach 1978). For example, in the original LETS in Courtenay, B.C., a hospital nutritionist was able to hold well-attended preventive care workshops that did not fit within her job description, paid partly in green dollars, to meet client need. Teen nutrition proved especially popular.

LETS increase access to professional care for services ineligible for coverage under provincial plans. Access to dental care is the most commonly cited issue. However, people have found they also had access to alternative health care and preventive maintenance services that in the provincially funded system are available only to the relatively wealthy. In fact "alternative" health practitioners are often among the first to be attracted to LETS. In the Toronto system, the wide range of participating practitioners includes chiropractors, chiropodists, dentists, massage therapists, naturopaths, psychologists, and psychotherapists. Conceivably, the need for tertiary care facilities such as hospitals would be much reduced by the availability of preventive health care as well as the health-enhancing social and economic environment of a LETS economy.

**Fostering Public Participation**   There is some evidence that by changing the social environment, public participation is enhanced (Gardell 1976; Seligman 1991). LETS membership facilitates members' participation in the economic life of the community. The community focus of LETS enhances the chances for social interaction as well. Community markets, trade fairs, potluck suppers, and community swaps are part of almost all LETS. In Great Britain, LETSLink, the national information exchange, holds a week-long, LETS camp every summer.

A potential obstacle to full participation is the fear of social service beneficiaries that their benefits will be reduced or cut off if they earn green dollars. This fear is partly valid; in Britain and Canada, for instance, there is no policy regarding LETS. Australia, on the other hand, has ruled that LETS earnings "are not of a commercial nature."

**Sustainable Economic Environment**   The current economic system is considered by many to be inherently unsustainable (Daly and Cobb 1989, Roberts and Brandum 1995, Rotstein and Duncan 1991) partly because social and environmental costs are externalized (Ekins 1986; Galtung 1986). Dobson (1993) contends that the structural flaws of the commodity-money system are such that the ideal of sustainability is impossible within it, suggesting that only a community-based economic system can support the necessary economic ethic.

Unemployment, aside from impeding an individual's ability to participate in the economy, diminishes feelings of self-worth. Indeed, evidence exists that links unemployment to family violence and other anti-social behavior (Goodman 1991, Remschmidt et al 1990). A substantial literature also supports the notion that unemployment and underemployment have measurable, negative effects on individual health (Brenner and Mooney 1983; Mechanic 1989; City of Toronto 1991). Freidson (1990) presents a theoretical orientation of unalienated work that corresponds closely to the community envisioned by LETS proponents (cf. Dauncey 1988) in which the prerequisites for such work may be fulfilled within the community.

With unemployment, people also lose their social networks, leaving them at a further disadvantage in finding new work (Williams 1996a). So far, the greatest measurable effect of LETS has been the availability of a wide and varied social network (Seyfang 1994; Williams 1996a).

Local currencies like LETS are designed to keep the economy local, fostering local self-reliance and protection from the shocks of global price fluctuations. By creating currency as needed, individuals can afford to resist exploitation, simulating conditions of full employment. Since it is easier to spend green dollars than federal, work that is meaningful to the individual is more easily valued and rewarded. The social dilemma of dependency is reduced when people can participate in the economy without first having to market their skills to an employer. LETS are also a source of interest-free credit that is denied the unemployed.

**Viable Natural Environment**   In his health-environment-economy model of a healthy community, Hancock (1993) emphasizes the necessity of a sound economic underpinning of both human health and the environment, while maintaining the subservience of the economy to the other two. Both Hancock (1993) and Labonté (1993) emphasize the concept of an "adequately prosperous" community that discourages unsustainable production or consumption.

Economists and environmentalists from a wide range of theoretical perspectives see the community self-reliance aspects of LETS to be important for environmental sustainability (Seyfang 1994). Instead of using scarce public monies to entice polluting or exploiting industries in order to provide much needed employment, communities enjoying self-reliance would have greater flexibility in their choice of industries. Cottage industries producing high quality, handmade goods, for example, could become cost-effective and their products preferred over mass-produced goods of inferior quality and higher (federal dollar) price. The green dollar price advantage would favor the use of local suppliers, reducing transportation costs and pollution. These factors also favor the creation of work close to home, reducing commuting and the attendant costs, pollution and social disruption.

## Conclusion

By explicitly addressing the inherent structural contradiction of money in which resources flow from poor to rich, local economic systems such as LETS protect individuals and communities from the inherently inequitable global economy, without replicating the same inequities locally. LETS are a community response to a local problem of global origin. LETS theorists argue that periods of high unemployment, combined with cutbacks in the social "safety net" such as we are currently experiencing, exacerbate the inequities inherent in the structure of national currencies (Linton and Greco 1987, Dobson 1993). It has been argued, indeed, that in the environment of global economic structural changes, local currencies like LETS are necessary for community sustainability. LETS appear to address the structural problems of money simply, without threatening the national currency. People need participate only out of economic self-interest, but in so doing change the social atmosphere from one of scarcity where people must guard their possessions for fear of losing them, to one of abundance. Theorists like Thomas Berry (1988) see this change as essential for individual, community, and planetary health.

To be successful, however, LETS and other systems will need broad public support. The increasing devolution of responsibilities, with concurrent cutbacks in funding, from the federal and provincial levels to municipalities may provide an obvious avenue for increased application. Following the successful Austrian use of local currencies during the 1930s, Canadian municipalities may well issue their own money, collect taxes in local currency, and support social programs with the proceeds. The most successful would foster neighborhood systems, networked electronically through a central office. Networked local systems could evolve to a new kind of bioregional currency, but one based on the needs of community, rather than on the needs of transnational corporations and the state. In the process of restructuring the local economy, a radical rethinking of social relations and connection to place would occur. For once, communities could create for themselves a healthier more equitable world.

# GLOBAL   WARMING

# Part Three

# Green Economic Development

*Burman's discussion of LETS as a community health promotion strategy leads us to a broader exploration of eco-city economic development. **Nancy Skinner**, Executive Director of Local Solutions to Global Pollution and a former city council member in Berkeley, California, explains how Berkeley uses economic development as a path to sustainability. Berkeley supports community-based environmental businesses as part of its municipal economic development strategy, and the city government fosters the environmental economy strategy by offering technical assistance and support. Berkeley is a "recycling market development zone," promotes new businesses through public/private partnerships, incorporates job training and employment services to increase jobs for its underemployed residents, and uses zoning and other land use tools to help finance environmental improvements. Skinner describes the West Berkeley Area Plan, which preserves the industrial base and helps protect the community from plant closures and the loss of manufacturing and industrial jobs, as evidence that an eco-city development strategy can benefit a city's environment and its economy simultaneously.*

***Kelly Vodden**, a founder of London (Ontario) Environmental and Economic Development Cooperative (LEED), details one Canadian community's attempt to build community partnerships for a sustainable local economy. London's efforts were catalyzed by a pivotal conference celebrating the city's bicentennial which formed part of a process to envision the community over the coming century. A number of creative eco-city initiatives have emerged from London. Vodden describes the community partnerships which produced the city's focus on green business, community economic development, and environmental education and management for the business community.*

# 6

# Economic Development as a Path to Sustainability
## The Berkeley Experience

### Nancy Skinner

Environmental quality is often cited as a goal that stands in opposition to economic activity. In many industrialized, wealthy, western nations, the loss of jobs through industrial plant closings and company downsizing are portrayed as the indisputable consequence of improving environmental health. The notion of achieving sustainable development along with an increase in jobs and economic vitality has seemed incompatible. Is keeping a community economically vital while on the path toward sustainability actually incompatible?

Sustainable development requires more than merely "protecting" the environment: it requires economic and social changes that will ultimately reduce the need for environmental protection (Roseland 1992a). It requires economic policies which in their formulation fully incorporate environmental concerns. It requires concerns such as quality jobs, housing, education, health care, and access to resources and services to be addressed as equally critical components of economic and environmental health.

Agenda 21, the document signed by the nations attending the 1992 Earth Summit, defined sustainable development as something which must improve the quality of human life, improve the living and working environments of all people, provide adequate shelter for all, create sustainable energy, transport and construction activities, and stimulate the related human resource development and capacity-building required to achieve these goals.

That's quite a heady challenge, and one which would be extremely difficult to achieve if the only forms of economic development available were nationally-based and dependent on huge influxes of capital from multi-national financial institutions or international monetary agencies. Fortunately, achieving economic development that is compatible with sustainable development isn't impossible. Like so many other strategies that will lead us to sustainability, an economic development strategy compatible with sustainability will be decentralized, carefully planned, environmentally sensitive, locally-based, focused on creating jobs and improving quality of life in our communities.

Local governments have an important role to play both in moving the larger economy toward sustainability and in contributing to the creation of an economically vital and sustainable local community. The local government structure in the United States provides local governments with a variety of leverage points that can directly influence the local and the larger economy. For example, most local governments have broad powers over the types of businesses that are allowed to operate within their jurisdiction and can directly influence business practices through permits, business licences, inspection programs, waste management programs, and the like. Local governments are also powerful economic engines in their own right, purchasing thousands of dollars of goods and services and operating numerous types of facilities. A comprehensive, integrated, and strategic approach which combines the local government role as a service provider, its regulatory and legislative powers, and its internal economic policies can have a remarkably positive effect on moving economic development and economic activities toward improving environmental quality and achieving sustainability.

I'd like to tell the story of my own community. It's not a perfect story and we certainly haven't achieved sustainable development, yet as a community we have tried to design economic development goals and an economic development strategy which are not only compatible with, but also enhance, the goals of environmental protection and improvement of the quality of life for our citizens. The City of Berkeley's former Director of Community Development, Neil Mayer, described Berkeley's task as "wanting to show the harmony between job creation and economic development on the one hand and environmental quality on the other. We want to provide a combination of economic opportunity for our residents, fiscal benefits to the city, and improvements in environmental quality for ourselves and others around us" (Turner 1995: 3).

The brilliance of this story is a synergistic combination of luck and a deliberate effort on the part of the city, its citizens, and its businesses to try to do something other than 'business as usual.' The luck has to do with the fact that Berkeley and the San Francisco Bay Area of California have always been home to risk-takers and innovators, and are marked by a population with a remarkably high degree of environmental values. The deliberate effort is represented by the steps the city has taken, first, to recognize the value of what David Morris of the Institute for Local Self-Reliance calls the "home grown economy," and second, to utilize the power and resources of the city government to support and expand this economy.

I want to start the story by telling you about some of the businesses, policies, and programs which were the precursors to Berkeley's current economic development focus. Berkeley was fortunate to have a number of private sector and community-based businesses which for many years had been manufacturing environmental products or providing environmental services such as residential curbside and commercial collection of recyclable materials and compost processing. And as a local government, Berkeley had strong environmental legislation and policies which affected both governmental and business practices. As early as 1976 Berkeley had passed a law banning the city government's use of pesticides and we were one of the first cities in the United States to prohibit businesses from using, selling, or manufacturing ozone-destroying compounds.

In fact, these early environmental policies and the community-based businesses were the infrastructure upon which Berkeley's environmental economy, which has come to be known as the Green Valley strategy, was built.

## Supporting Community-Based Environmental Businesses

As early as 1972, a citizens' environmental group was collecting recyclables from households citywide. Later different citizens' groups went on to form profit and nonprofit businesses which operated community compost sites, reusable goods salvage yards, recycling drop-off centers, and many more. Other community-based groups formed businesses providing energy conservation products and services.

During the energy crisis of the 1970s and the garbage crisis of the 1980s the Berkeley city government began to realize the benefit of these community business activities. The city began actively supporting them and contracting with the community businesses to provide recycling, residential energy conservation, and other services. In addition, the city adopted legislation and policies such as a 50 per cent recycling goal, residential and commercial building energy-conservation retrofit ordinances, and a "Buy recycled" policy for the city's own purchases which encouraged the markets for these services.

A recent study conducted by Berkeley's community-based recycling businesses and the Centre for Neighborhood Technology estimates that these community recycling businesses recover over 83,000 tons of material per year, provide over 90 jobs, have reduced the amount of garbage the city has to collect and haul by 30 per cent, and circulate approximately $8.5 million annually through the local economy (Urban Ore Inc. and The Centre for Neighborhood Technology 1993).

By endorsing and institutionalizing community-based business activities, the City of Berkeley utilized city resources and resources that were once considered garbage, more efficiently. The city also kept useful things out of the waste stream, kept jobs and dollars within the community, and garnered the numerous environmental benefits that result from increasing energy efficiency and reducing waste.

## The Green Valley Strategy

Berkeley's interest in becoming a center for "green businesses" was motivated not only by our desire to protect the environment and, of course, increase the city's revenue base, but also to expand Berkeley's economy in a direction that was consistent with the city's values and social goals. Job retention and job growth, especially in good entry-level jobs for unemployed and underemployed residents, was an essential goal. Berkeley's environmental economy program, which has come to be known as the Green Valley, was designed to have two parallel and equally important goals: 1) job protection and creation, and 2) protecting the environment.

Fortunately for Berkeley's chosen strategy, many of the business activities that have come to be known as "green businesses" tend to produce a higher number of jobs per unit of economic activity than many other business types. The recycling industry is a prime example. Virgin materials extraction industries (like timber, mining, and drilling) and waste disposal industries (like land-filling and incineration) tend to be highly centralized, capital intensive, and provide a low number of jobs per economic unit. Recycling and reuse industries, in contrast, tend to be diverse and labor-intensive (Regional Roundtable on Recycling and Community Economic Development 1994). Results from an Institute for Local Self-Reliance study indicate that one job is created for every 15,000 tons of solid waste land-filled in a year. If a similar amount is composted, seven jobs are created. If the same amount of material is recycled, the collection and processing required would generate nine jobs. On a jobs per million tons basis, this amounts to 67 jobs for waste landfilling, 467 jobs for composting and 600 jobs for recycling (Take It Back Foundation and The Institute for Local Self-Reliance 1993).

One of the first issues Berkeley faced was how the Green Valley strategy would define an environmental or "green business." To address that concern the following criteria evolved. Targeted businesses were those which:

> provide environmental services (e.g., energy conservation services, recycling collection ,or hazardous materials remediation service);

> produce environmental goods and products (e.g., a manufacturer of goods made from recycled or secondary materials, manufacturer of nontoxic household cleaners); or

> in their management, production, and/or operations apply state of the art environmental practice (e.g., pollution prevention, hazardous and toxic material use reduction, and waste minimization).

The city realized that success could be achieved by tapping into resources existing in the community — the businesses which were alive and well and were abiding by our social and environmental standards. The strategy did not have to depend primarily on attracting businesses from elsewhere and having them relocate to Berkeley; enterprises like the community-based recycling and energy conservation businesses and others were already providing jobs and contributing to Berkeley's economy. Including them in the Green Valley strategy and strengthening their efforts to do well economically and environmentally made sense.

Staff of the city's Community and Economic Development Department began collecting information on existing businesses and community resources. The result was the creation of a database describing 125 businesses which fit the Green Valley criteria. This was very exciting news! A base upon which to build the Green Valley strategy was right here at home. The businesses on the list varied greatly in size and type and included businesses such as Cyclamen Pottery, a manufacturer of art ceramics made from recycled materials; EME Systems, a manufacturer of equipment to monitor weather; Earthsake, a retailer specializing in products made from organic cotton; and Poly Plus Battery, researching the development of rechargeable batteries for electric cars.

City staff began to think about things the city could do to help the businesses on the list succeed and thrive. Realizing that their business skills and their access to capital were limited, programs were established to provide technical assistance and to help in securing loans and low cost leases and in making arrangements for the use of city equipment, city-owned property, or facilities.

Economic development staff also turned to the nongovernmental infrastructure which supports businesses and community development, activities such as the Chamber of Commerce and other business groups, the community college, and local job training programs. Creatively tapping county, state, and federal resources, city staff obtained financial and other support for the Green Valley effort.

The development of Berkeley's environmental economy has taken a number of years and, of course, is still in progress. I will describe now some of the steps that were taken and some of the programs which were established as part of the Green Valley strategy.

## City Government Technical Assistance and Support

To foster the environmental economy strategy, Community and Economic Development Department staff first gave special attention to firms meeting the Green Valley criteria. This special attention included assistance to help the businesses find appropriate commercial or industrial sites within Berkeley's boundaries and the city's creation of a revolving loan fund for green firms.

To help all businesses and industry adopt the environmental

practices, such as pollution prevention and waste minimization, that the city advocates, Berkeley's environmental health department, which operates the business inspection programs and the toxic and hazardous materials program, was reorganized to include a technical assistance component. Inspectors that visit business sites now supply the businesses with information on pollution prevention actions like process changes and product substitutions that can reduce the need to use or store toxic and hazardous materials. Fees charged to the businesses have also been redesigned with incentives for reducing the use of toxins and hazardous materials.

This same department, working with a citizen-appointed commission, initiated an environmental business awards program. Businesses that have made the greatest progress in pollution prevention or environmental protection are given awards and honored at a citywide reception. For example, Meyer Sound, a stereo speaker manufacturer, won the award in 1992 for innovation in developing non-styrofoam packaging. Stickers were also made which announce, "We Recycle with the City of Berkeley" or "Pollution Prevention Award Winner." These are given to appropriate businesses to display on their doors or windows.

## The Recycling Market Development Zone

Another example of the technical assistance and support aspect of the city's environmental economy strategy is Berkeley's designation as a Recycling Market Development Zone. Berkeley, in cooperation with the neighboring city of Oakland, was one of the first of four local governments in the State of California to receive this designation. The intent of this California state program is to "close the loop in recycling" so that recycling is not only the collection of materials but also ensures the reuse of these materials. The development zone's purpose is to encourage the start-up and expansion of secondary materials businesses, e.g., businesses that manufacture products using recycled materials as their feedstock and businesses that repair and/or reuse materials.

The low interest loans, technical assistance, tax credits, and other incentives provided by the recycling market development zone designation were a great boost to Berkeley's environmental economy effort. In its first two years of operation, the Oakland/Berkeley recycling market development zone leveraged over $7 million in investment in recycling and reuse businesses, assisted in the creation of 130 new jobs, attracted four new businesses, and diverted over 100,000 tons of material that would have otherwise been labeled as waste and sent off to the dump (City of Oakland 1994).

## Promoting New Business Development Through Public/Private Partnerships

Contrary to Adam Smith's hands-off approach, the city of Berkeley has chosen to take an active role in shaping and supporting its dream of an environmental economy. One example is the Community Energy Services Corporation (CESC), a public/private partnership providing energy audits, lighting retrofits, and other energy conservation services to Berkeley businesses and city-owned facilities and operations.

The CESC was established in 1985 by the Berkeley city council as an independent corporation with a publicly (city council) appointed board of directors. The city council provided the CESC with seed capital and gave the CESC its first contracts to provide retrofit services for some of Berkeley's municipally owned buildings. From this initial start-up, the CESC began marketing its services to businesses and commercial property owners.

Recently the CESC expanded its operation and began working with the local utility and other financial entities to leverage financing to help businesses pay for energy conservation improvements. More than 100 private businesses have used the company's services and the corporation is generating more than a million dollars of activity annually. And the city government, which started the CESC, has directly benefited as well. To date over 75 per cent of Berkeley's municipally owned buildings and facilities have been retrofitted, saving the city budget over $100,000 a year in electrical and heating costs.[1]

Here is another perspective on the impact an activity like the CESC can have on the local economy. According to economic studies conducted by the U.S. federal Department of Energy, each 10 per cent improvement in the energy efficiency of the commercial and industrial building stock of a community like Berkeley could save the community's economy approximately $6 million a year (U.S. Department of Energy 1994, Laitner,n.d.). Rather than being sent outside the community to pay for energy production, this is money that would likely be spent inside the community for business expansion, job creation, and the purchase of products and services.

## Incorporating Job Training and Employment Services

Since one of the goals of the environmental economy strategy was to increase jobs for Berkeley's underemployed residents, the city wanted Berkeley residents to be able to take advantage of the green business opportunities. Additionally, the city wanted Green Valley businesses to have easy access to qualified workers. Working with the local community college district, adult and youth employment programs, a training curriculum was developed to prepare residents for environmental service fields and to develop skill areas identified as lacking within Berkeley's labor pool. Job training programs began to provide training in fields such as energy conservation and hazardous materials management.

Many of the staff that the Community Energy Services Corporation hires to conduct its commercial building audits and lighting retrofits are young adults trained by one of the city-sponsored youth employment training programs. This same program also trains youth how to conduct residential energy audits and then employs them to provide weatherization, insulation, and other energy conservation improvements as a free service to Berkeley's low-income households.

The city also established a "First Source" employment program to encourage businesses to hire Berkeley residents. The First Source program maintains a list of jobseekers and their skills, including residents who have participated in the new job training programs. Businesses that receive city permits or other assistance through programs like the recycling market development zone are given incentives to use the First Source program to fill their hiring needs. While providing jobs for unemployed Berkeley residents, First Source is also contributing to the reduction of pollution-generating, energy-consuming auto trips by nonresidents who would have to commute into the city.

## Use of Zoning and Other Land Use Tools

Zoning and land use policies are another powerful tool for encouraging the type of economic activity a community prefers and for minimizing the undesirable impacts of various activities. Zoning and land use policies can also be designed as economic instruments and used by a local government to help finance environmental improvements.

The City of Berkeley has creatively structured many of its developer fees, business permits, and other fees to provide an incentive for practices that meet the city's environmental and community improvement objectives. Berkeley has also creatively applied the concept of mitigations to fund environmental programs and improvements. In negotiating permits with new housing or business developers, the Office of Economic Development has established a set of mitigations for environmental detriment which then fund environmental benefits of the city's choosing. The city's negotiations during a recent development agreement resulted in the developer agreeing to comply with state of the art environmental standards and fund the construction of bike paths as a mitigation for increased traffic.

Finally, as I shall describe in the next section, zoning and land use policies can be used to protect essential economic activities while ensuring high quality environmental standards.

## A Success Story: The West Berkeley Area Plan

One key component of Berkeley's environmental economic development plan is the preservation of manufacturing and light industry in the West Berkeley industrial area. Seeking to preserve industrial businesses may seem an anathema to improving environmental quality since when we think of industry we most often think of environmental degradation. Unless the time comes when there is no demand for manufactured products and no need for industrial processes, this is an obstacle that must be overcome. One of the major challenges facing sustainable development advocates and local governments committed to restoring and maintaining environmental quality is the development of environmentally sound production and manufacturing capabilities.

The well-being of an urban area is dependent on both a healthy environment and a vibrant economy. Unemployment and related social problems detract from a community's ability to focus on environmental restoration and management. For most communities, plant closures and the loss of industrial and manufacturing jobs have not been an environmental benefit. Encouraging sustainable industry by assisting in the implementation of pollution prevention and environmentally sound practices is one of the most sound and forward-thinking urban environmental strategies.

In undertaking the planning process for West Berkeley, historically the city's industrial and manufacturing area, the challenge was to preserve these uses and prevent the area's success from pricing out manufacturing and industry. Successful mixed use areas often become attractive to developers promoting retail and office complexes which can afford higher square-foot leases and land costs, which then force out industry and manufacturing. To prevent the eroding of Berkeley's industrial base and the resulting loss of high quality industrial jobs, one of the unique features of the West Berkeley plan is its creation of a special district designed to retain light industry and manufacturing. Zoning now adopted designates specific areas for light manufacturing and industrial uses and excludes from those areas any conflicting uses.

Hammered out over a three year process involving residents, workers, industrial business owners, and city staff, a central driving premise of the plan is to maintain and expand West Berkeley's manufacturing and industrial base while maintaining and improving West Berkeley's environment. To achieve this, strict environmental quality regulations were proposed along with the zoning protections so that industrial and other development would not mean environmental degradation. And the plan called on the city not only to act as enforcer, but also to assist businesses in complying with the new environmental regulations.

Other features which the community process incorporated in the final plan included negotiating reductions with existing industries in their production, transport, and handling of toxic and hazardous materials and establishing clear limits on these activities by any new industries. Endorsing the concept of self-enforcement, the plan requires "good neighbor" agreements between existing industries, institutions, and adjacent residents and businesses.

The people involved in designing the plan understood that working to ensure that West Berkeley manufacturing and industrial jobs were filled by Berkeley residents would result in a major environmental benefit of reducing automobile commuter traffic. Thus the plan includes employer-based automobile trip reduction, improved pedestrian access, and new bikeways to make it easier to move around West Berkeley without having to drive.

## Benefits to the Community, to the Local Government, to the Businesses

Berkeley's effort to achieve an environmental economy is still in process. But recent census tract data and information compiled by the Office of Economic Development would indicate that the strategy's goal of job retention and job creation has so far been successful. Unemployment figures for 1991, 1992, and 1993 improved over previous years and 1992 showed the first increase in over a decade in both manufacturing jobs and new industrial businesses. While the city government's monitoring of environmental indicators is limited, some indicators of progress in improving environmental quality are evident. The amount of both solid and hazardous waste generated by Berkeley residents and businesses has decreased, as well as per capita water use and utility-supplied energy use.

The city government has benefited from its strategic environmental approach as well. Policies that eliminated single-sided copying and many disposable products saved the city money in supply purchases. Improving the energy efficiency of the city's buildings, street lights, and other facilities have reduced the city's utility expenditures by hundreds of thousands of dollars. Recycling, compost, and other waste reduction programs have lessened the number of city trucks having to make the daily 90-mile round-trip trek to the landfill. Effective pollution prevention policies have reduced the incidents of toxic releases and accidents involving hazardous materials both at city-owned facilities and private businesses.

The environmental programs directed to the community have saved Berkeley residents and businesses money. Increasing the disposable income of Berkeley residents and businesses can be a boon to city coffers when the extra cash is spent and returns as sales tax and other revenue. And with the environmental economy's success at decreasing unemployment, the quality of life of the entire Berkeley community is improved.

But the businesses are perhaps the real winners of the environmental economy strategy. Gil Friend, a consultant in the development of Berkeley's strategy, writes, "All businesses are affected by environmental costs — utility expenditures, waste management fees, regulatory compliance, etc. — which can be reduced (in some cases significantly reduced) by the adoption of environmental quality strategies" (Friend 1993). Among the many success stories is an aerospace coating manufacturer. Working with the environmental health department, this Berkeley industrial business saved thousands of dollars in front-end purchases and back-end toxic material storage, as well as handling and disposal fees by eliminating cadmium, mercury, and other heavy metals from their paint formula. Their action also created goodwill with neighboring residents who had been fighting the business' plans for expansion due to concerns that the business' practices were threatening the health of the residents.

## Conclusion

My opening question asked whether a community could increase its economically vitality and still be moving on the path toward sustainability. My answer to this question was based on the experience of one community. It may be legitimate to ask whether Berkeley's story is interesting but perhaps unique, even rarefied. Fortunately many other communities, including ones as diverse as Chattanooga, Tennessee; Curitiba, Brazil; and Freiburg, Germany, have engaged in similar comprehensive, strategic, and integrated approaches which combine the local government role as a service provider, its regulatory and legislative powers, and its internal economic policies. Each has achieved results that could be told in a story such as Berkeley's.[2]

Recent research would indicate that economic vitality and environmental quality are not only compatible, but that one cannot be achieved without the other. A 1994 study by the Durham, North Carolina-based Institute for Southern Studies revealed that governments need not sacrifice environmental quality for economic well being. The report of this state-by-state study showed that those states that ranked highest on the institute's environmental criteria also ranked highest using its economic criteria. Nearly all of the states that landed on the bottom of the environmental list were also at the bottom economically (Smothers 1994).

As articulated in Agenda 21, the concept of sustainable development incorporates a critical interrelationship between social equity, environmental quality, and economic vitality. The study cited above is not the only research to support this conclusion. My purpose in telling Berkeley's story is to provide an actual example of these principles in practice and to illustrate my own opinion that working at the community level provides both the best hope for and the best opportunity for solutions that can incorporate social equity, economic vitality, and environmental quality — solutions which can truly place us on the path to sustainable development. Former economic development director Neil Mayer has noted that Berkeley's Green Valley approach, while not completely satisfying the concept of sustainable development, "certainly can be a contributor. If we improve the environmental performance of all of our companies and our communities, it allows us to imagine that the growth of the economy can be consistent with good environmental quality" (Riggle 1995).

As my story of Berkeley conveys, the benefit of local, community-based solutions are many. They can be designed not only to respond to a region's unique ecological features but also to address the region's economic and human needs. Efforts at national and international levels will always be handicapped by those governments' distance from, and lack of understanding of, local human and ecological conditions.

Like Berkeley's environmental economy strategy, locally-based solutions to environmental problems can be designed to create jobs, to improve the community and to contribute to social equity. Almost all of the sustainable activities I can think of have a proportionately lower capital and higher job creation potential than their unsustainable counterparts. And locally-based solutions not only produce benefits for our communities, they also contribute to solving problems on a global scale. They are the catalysts that motivate state, national, and international action.

# 7

# Working Together for a Green Economy

## Kelly Vodden

Everyone has a stake in the "livability" of their community. Although each of us may have unique ideas about what makes a community or neighborhood livable, qualities such as safe streets, adequate employment opportunities, accessible health care, and clean air and water have widespread appeal. Many people are also concerned about maintaining this quality of life for future generations. It is this common ground that brings people from diverse interests and backgrounds together to shape the future of their communities, making successful sustainability initiatives possible.

One arena where the principles of sustainability and broadly based community participation most need to be applied is economic development. Traditional economic development practices have left a legacy of economic, social, and environmental problems around the world. Modern industrial systems are often incompatible with the ecological systems we depend upon, extracting natural resources at a rate greater than they are renewed and producing wastes that overload the capacity of air, water, and soils to assimilate them. Only recently have the far-reaching consequences of this behavior become apparent. Despite a growing awareness that the ecosystem cannot sustain consumption at even current levels, indices such as consumer spending are used to measure economic health, accounting for standard of living but not quality of life (Hawken 1993).

Contrary to conventional wisdom, this economic "progress" has not benefited all sectors of society. Insufficient jobs have been created. Efficiency and productivity gains, primarily made by substituting technology for human labor, have not been equally distributed. Nor have those who benefit chosen to replace work-time (and consumption) with leisure. Economies, more global than local, have grown beyond the control of those whose lives are most affected, and the separation of points of production and consumption conceal the true impacts of economic activity. In contrast, sustainable economic development implies management of economic demand (Roseland 1992a). It is equitable, community-based, and does not threaten the integrity of global or local ecological systems.

The idea of forming local "round tables" to integrate the social, economic, and environmental concerns of a broad range of community interests in sustainability planning was first recommended by Canada's Task Force on Environment and Economy in 1987 (BCRTEE 1994). Since this time the "round table approach" has become widely used and much has been learned about the challenges and benefits of collaborative planning and decision-making (e.g., see Roseland 1996a).

One Canadian city where the notion of achieving sustainability through multi-sectoral partnerships is being put into practice is London, Ontario. London business, labor, environmental and social justice organizations, educational institutions, and all levels of government are pooling their ideas and resources with the aim of proving that communities can have healthy economies *and* healthy ecosystems. The initiatives described below (see Table 1) demonstrate how communities can begin to create a more sustainable future and provide insights into the importance of local self-reliance and the benefits and potential pitfalls of building community partnerships.

## The Forest City

London is the regional center of southwestern Ontario, Canada, and the Lower Great Lakes region, located between the major urban areas of Toronto and Detroit. Over 320,000 people live in the city. Millions more live within a day's drive.

Proudly named the "Forest City," London has always been known as a "green" community, with its tree-lined streets, abundant parkland, and the Thames River running through the downtown core. London is home to several longstanding environmental organizations, and a growing number of individuals from all walks of life are active in local sustainability initiatives.

The city's environmental movement has a history of cooperation upon which recent initiatives have been built. Many of London's environmental organizations are located in a heritage building that has been converted to a community resource center. Organizations share notice boards, administrative services, a library, and meeting spaces. The London Round Table on the Environment and Economy was formed in 1992 and each year activities are planned by a committee consisting of members from business, First Nations, environmental organizations, municipal government, and others to celebrate Waste Reduction Week. Similarly, Earth Day is honored annually by a wide spectrum of community members.

## London's Economy

London is also known for its wealth. The headquarters of large corporations such as 3M Canada, Cuddy Foods, Canada Trust, and London Life are located here, employing thousands of residents. Other major nongovernment employers include General Motors of Canada, Ford Motor Company, and Bell Canada. The region is frequently used as a test market for new products and boasts a diversified industrial, commercial, and institutional base. Labor force participation is well above both the provincial and federal rates. Official unemployment rates are among the lowest in the province. Local industries benefit from access to the first class research capabilities and facilities of nearby post-secondary institutions. The city was well prepared for the transition to a "new economy," having developed significant expertise in sectors such as medical and telecommunications technology.

Behind this picture of economic vibrancy, however, lie some familiar but unsettling truths. In the early 1990s a significant number of jobs were lost in traditional sectors such as manufacturing and construction. Plant shutdowns, downsizing, and bankruptcies hit not only these sectors but others such as telecommunications and financial services. Despite a slight economic recovery many of these jobs will not return. Low paying hospitality and retail positions, including sales, food service, and babysitting, have taken their place. Part-time work accounts for approximately forty per cent of the employment opportunities now available, at wages that cannot support part-time workers and their families. Approximately sixty per cent of new jobs are in "sales and service," many in telemarketing and canvassing (United Way 1994). Food bank use hit an all-time high in 1996.

The gap between the rich and the poor in London often goes unnoticed along its clean-swept streets and sidewalks. The average family income in one area of the city is $130,000, while in another, where a large concentration of lone parents, people without high-school education, and new Canadians reside, many families live below the poverty line. Disadvantaged Londoners are often excluded from decision-making and community activities.

## London 200 - Looking Forward

The early 1990s was a time of reflection and change in the city. The year 1993 marked London's bicentennial and residents began a process of envisioning their community in the century to come. Sustainability emerged early on as an important part of this vision. London had grown significantly over the years and had recently annexed 64,220 acres of surrounding land to accommodate antici-pated residential, commercial, and industrial growth. Many Londoners feared that valuable agricultural and natural areas would be lost in a process of unsustainable urban growth.

The municipality launched an ambitious community involvement process entitled *Vision '96* which culminated in the completion of a new Official Community Plan in 1996. An early highlight of the visioning process was *London into the Next Century: An Agenda for the Responsible City*, a two-day conference that examined the challenges of planning a sustainable future and explored models from other communities and countries. Participants were assisted in identifying local issues and possible solutions through presentations by international sustainability experts. The conference served as a catalyst for subsequent planning processes.

*Vision '96* demonstrated that Londoners want a clean and envi-ronmentally responsible city (City of London 1994). Not only was sustainability a priority within the community at this time but provincial, national, and international leaders shared Londoners' concerns. Evidence of environmental destruction had been mount-ing, brought to the public and political consciousness by the Brundtland Report in 1987. Nor, in the midst of a recession, were policymakers confident in the economic system's ability to deliver jobs or prosperity.

The Ontario government, then governed by the New Democratic Party, introduced stringent new environmental regulations aimed at preventing waste and pollution and facilitating public participation in environmental decision-making. A provincial community economic development (CED) secretariat was formed, along with *jobsOntario Community Action,* a vehicle for promoting and supporting CED activities. Finally, the Green Communities Initiative was created, launching green CED initiatives in communities across Ontario. London was one of those communities.

### Table 1: Sustainable Economy Initiatives in London

| Organization | Main Activities |
|---|---|
| London Green Communities Initiative | Green Home and Business Checkups |
| London Environmental and Economic Development Cooperative Organizations (LEED) | Technical Assistance for Community and Environmental Entrepreneurs |
| Life*Spin | CED Training and Enterprise Development |
| London Community Small Business Centre | Entrepreneurial Training, Resource Centre, and Incubator |
| Environmental Management Resource Centre for Business (EMRCB) | Environmental Education for Business |

The London Green Communities Initiative began as a partnership between two organizations, one representing business and another, heritage and environment. Over 50 local organizations, ranging from the Chamber of Commerce to the Girl Guides, eventually became involved, with the purpose of "working in harmony to foster a healthy environment and to create a sustainable community for present and future generations." While the city had a history of cross-sectoral partnerships, the level of community cooperation achieved in this process was unprecedented.

A key component of the London Green Communities Initiative was a program to green London's industrial, commercial, and institutional sectors. The program sought to improve the sustainability of London's economy on two fronts. Development of London's green business sector was the program's first goal. Priority for new business development activities was to be given to projects that addressed the needs of London's marginalized citizens. Second, the program sought to reduce the environmental impact of other sectors of London's economy by providing environmental management assistance and education.

## Green Community Economic Development

**Environmental Entrepreneurship** The environmental or "green" industry sector is made up of enterprises that produce or sell products or services related to the protection and restoration of the natural environment. Green businesses can provide sustainable jobs and environmentally responsible business and consumer purchasing alternatives. According to the Canadian Environmental Industry Association, Canada rates third in world environmental technology exports, behind only Japan and Germany. Tough environmental regulations have contributed to this success. The environmental industry is now the fifth largest economic sector in Canada (Industry Canada 1994).

While exportable environmental technologies have been the focus of provincial and federal green industry development strategies, the city of London, through its waste management department, has been an active participant in the development of another type of green industry — reuse and recycling. The department produces a *Recycling Markets Directory* to assist waste generators with their waste reduction programs and to generate business for local recycling firms. A 100 per cent surcharge is added to landfill tipping fees for materials accepted by local recyclers, making recycling more cost-effective than disposal. The department was also instrumental in the formation of the London Environmental & Economic Development Cooperative (LEED), a nonprofit cooperative that brings community organizations and agencies together to identify green business opportunities and provide assistance to local environmental entrepreneurs.

Martin Zimmer, manager of recycling and collection for the City of London, was responsible for managing the waste problems of a growing city. Seeing opportunities for creating small businesses from recyclable materials, he wondered how best to turn these opportunities into reality. A construction materials reuse center was one example of a business idea that Zimmer believed could be viable. The department commissioned a feasibility study which confirmed this belief. Despite the public availability of study results, no one had pursued the opportunity. After several meetings, the city's economic development department had shown little interest. Large waste management firms were unwilling to take on products with limited supply and increased handling requirements, and the Waste Management Department had neither the human or financial resources to enter the field of business development.

Zimmer joined up with two recent graduates of the University of Western Ontario's School of Business Administration who were working as small business consultants in the environmental field and believed in the need for low-cost business development assistance. Together with a faculty member from the School of Business Administration, local environmentalists, the community credit union, a First Nations organization, and a representative from both the Ontario Ministry of Environment and Energy and the local labor council, they developed the LEED concept — integration of environment and economy through business development, sustainable job creation, and environmental protection.

The LEED mandate was to include research, education, and business development. Researchers would monitor London's green industry sector as well as new environmental business ideas from other areas of Canada and the world that might be applied to London. Educational programs were meant to raise public awareness about the link between the environment and the economy and the potential for both areas to prosper when integrated. Local, environmentally responsible businesses would also be promoted. Finally, business development services, including market and supplier research, feasibility studies, business plans, and financing proposals, were to be offered.

After establishing an advisory team, board of directors, and staff (funded by seed money from the province), the group began by launching a research project to determine the size and scope of London's green industry sector. What they found was over 250 firms, ranging from organic farmers to a manufacturer of reusable plastic beer cases. London is home to industry leaders in waste water technology, environmental assessment, and energy efficiency. The highest number of environmental firms in London, however, were found to be in the business of recycling, followed by environmental consulting. A database and directory was compiled. The environmental industry is now recognized as a significant contributor to the local economy.

The construction materials reuse center was the first business development project to which LEED turned its attention. By this time Goodwill Industries had indicated their interest in pursuing the idea. LEED staff met with Goodwill to offer advice on developing the business plan and obtaining funding. By 1996, with help from the community and all levels of government, the reuse center was fully operational. Suppliers were located for a woman who wanted to expand her flower shop product line to include environmental items. The organization has helped develop or assess the feasibility of enterprises that include organic farming, packaging and distribution of locally grown food products, marketing and distribution of composted municipal yard waste, recycling technologies and a bicycle delivery cooperative.

Despite these accomplishments, it soon became obvious that the LEED plan had been too ambitious. The organization went from being almost entirely government-funded to near self-sufficiency in only two years, but revenue from business services covered only the cost of providing those services and time spent responding to telephone and walk-in enquiries. Further, many of LEED's clients had secured provincial funding for feasibility studies, business plans, and implementation. With the election in 1995 of a Conservative provincial government and the funding cuts that followed, consulting revenues declined. Research and education activities, primarily financed through government grants, were also significantly reduced. The number of business ideas examined that had either not proven feasible or not proceeded due to lack of financing was not surprising, but discouraging nonetheless. Finally, volatile markets for recyclable materials increased the difficulty in establishing viable recycling enterprises. The organization continues to adapt to such challenges while pursuing the goal of developing London's green industry sector.

**Green Home Checkups** Providers of environmental products and services in London received a boost when London Green

Horizons introduced its Green Home Checkup program in the fall of 1994. The purpose of these home visits was to make recommendations for conserving waste, water, and energy in the home, as well as to stimulate the market for products and services such as energy-saving home renovations. The Checkups were the central component of the Green Communities Initiative province-wide and have contributed millions of dollars to Ontario's economy.

Jobs were created for sixteen assessors who visited over 2,600 London homes in the program's first year. The cost was shared by the Ontario government and a number of community partners. Some common retrofit measures resulting from the Checkups include basement and attic insulation upgrades, window and door sealing, and installation of energy efficient lighting. Local financial institutions have helped to encourage these investments in conservation by providing low interest personal "enviro-loans."

Companies such as Tuckey Hardware and Zerodraft, a weather stripping manufacturer, have not only benefited from new customers but have strengthened the program by providing incentives for homeowners to implement the assessors' recommendations. Tuckey Hardware, for example, offers money-saving coupons for air sealing, weatherstripping, and caulking products. Other commercial partners include suppliers of rain barrels, solar panels, and composters, as well as waste management companies who welcome the opportunity to encourage better use of residential recycling programs.

**Community Economic Development** Green industry cannot create a sustainable local economy without addressing poverty and economic injustice. Recognizing this, LEED and other community partners have worked with nonprofit community organizations and marginalized citizens to develop environmentally and socially responsible revenue-generating initiatives and to deliver training programs that provide low-income Londoners with the skills needed to become leaders in community-based economic development.

Community economic development (CED) fosters the economic, environmental, and social health of communities by employing business means to meet community needs. CED is a comprehensive vehicle for economic revitalization and can include a wide range of activities including training, housing, and food security projects, and financial, research, and technical assistance for business development. It is a strategy for achieving individual and community self-reliance through collaborative action, returning control of business enterprises, capital, labor, and other resources from the global marketplace to communities.

In London, CED projects include a joint business venture in housing weatherization formed between an association dedicated to cooperative housing development and London Green Communities. The London and District Labor Council partnered with LEED to investigate options for worker cooperatives promoting bicycling as a transportation alternative, and Life*Spin, an organization dedicated to providing information and support for individuals surviving on low incomes, launched the Green Market Basket program. The Green Market Basket provides long-term meaningful employment, builds neighborhood communication links, and brings low-cost local produce, including organically grown fruits and vegetables, to individuals and families throughout London.

While job creation and business development are key components of any CED strategy, equipping people with the necessary skills to participate in CED activities is equally important. Londoners have access to a wide variety of relevant training services, from entrepreneurial skills to English as a Second Language.

In 1995, Life*Spin launched a CED training program with the assistance of Westcoast Development, an organization with a track record of helping communities across Canada start CED programs. Almost 100 women participated in an introductory workshop and many continued on with the more intensive training program that followed. One of the program's key success factors has been Life*Spin's ability to assess and adapt to participant needs. When language became a barrier for Cambodian Canadians, for example, Life*Spin and the Cambodian Women's Committee worked together to make the necessary program improvements, including the provision of interpretive services. The two groups have since conducted a feasibility study for a Cambodian restaurant business.

Entrepreneurial training is provided by the London Community Small Business Centre, by both the college and university, and in local secondary schools. The Small Business Centre works with a number of community organizations, such as Women's Community Enterprises and Women Immigrants of London, to deliver programs that suit the needs of their constituents. The center is a focal point in the community for small business development and training. As a business incubator, the center houses up to thirty companies and has a success rate for incubated ventures of eighty per cent. Thirty companies have graduated from the center, now employing one hundred sixty-one local people.

Lack of financing for CED is a common barrier to the realization of otherwise feasible CED projects in London. One reason for this is that individuals surviving on low incomes and community groups seldom have the required collateral. In response to this barrier, LEED, Life*Spin, and two other community organizations made a proposal to the provincial government to serve as a pilot project for a community loan fund. Money raised from the community would serve as security for micro-business loans made by the local credit union. These community investments would in turn be guaranteed by the province. The proposal was accepted: the province would guarantee $600,000 in micro-loans over a five year period. However, after more than two years of work and waiting and a change in government, the promise had still not been fulfilled. Having learned several such lessons, the groups are redirecting their efforts toward establishing a loan fund that is not dependent on government support.

## Managing the Environmental Bottom Line

**Environmental Education — Business Helping Business**
While green, community-based enterprises should ultimately form the backbone of a sustainable economy, today's economy is supported by other types of business enterprises. In what is sure to be a long transition to sustainability, the environmental impacts of the traditional economy are significant and efforts to manage them can have immediate environmental benefits.

The Chamber of Commerce has taken a leadership role in managing the environmental impact of business in London. Their work began with the establishment of an environment committee. One of the committee's early projects was to conduct a membership market survey. The study was conducted in partnership with the City of London, who provided staff and office space. The results demonstrated a need for improved environmental knowledge and training, particularly within small and medium-sized enterprises. While most business managers were aware that environmental regulations affected them in some way, few had the knowledge or expertise needed to ensure compliance. The impact of progressive new legislation was diminished without the necessary assistance for businesses willing to make changes. Managers feared environmental agencies and, therefore, were reluctant to seek their assistance. Nongovernment environmental organizations were viewed with similar distrust. Consultants and environmental staff were considered too costly by many firms.

Recognizing that members were in danger of non-compliance and that opportunities for cost savings and improved environmental performance were being lost, the Chamber formed the Environmental Management Resource Centre for Business Inc. (EMRCB), which first opened its doors in 1994. EMRCB members benefit from services such as a confidential, call-in information line; library resources; *The Business Informer*, a monthly environmental information bulletin; workshops; information sessions; and training programs. The EMRCB also provides business education packages that address the concerns and solutions available to specific industrial sectors.

One of the key strengths of the environmental management program for London businesses is the environmental leadership of the business community itself. Among these leaders are Bell Canada and Home Hardware. Bell developed an aerosol can recycling facility in its London warehouse, removing toxic paint residue and recovering thousands of aluminum cans that previously ended up in a local landfill site. London's Home Hardware established the first return-to-retailer paint recycling program in Canada. The activities of the EMRCB create opportunities for business people to network and share information with others who have similar concerns and experiences. By sharing local success stories, businesses learn from and encourage one another.

**Business Checkups** While education can provide businesses with much of the information needed for implementing an environmental program, some firms need help getting started or identifying opportunities for further improvement after basic steps have been taken, such as setting up a 3Rs program. An in-depth environmental audit can be prohibitively expensive for many smaller companies. In response to this need, London Green Horizons and the EMRCB created the Green Business Checkup. The on-site "walk through" assessment is completed within a few hours and is offered at a minimal cost.

The Green Business Checkup began as a pilot project in 1995.

Assessments are now offered on an ongoing basis. The program has achieved positive results. Some institutions are slowly implementing changes, starting with recommendations such as installing energy-efficient light bulbs and improving building insulation. Even these simple, inexpensive measures result in significant energy savings. A local brewery reduced their waste by 85 per cent after an opportunity for diverting spent grains was identified. The grains are now fed to the livestock of local farmers instead of being shipped to landfill. Another company received tips on safe storage for hazardous materials, previously stored near a drain.

## The London Experience — Successes and Challenges

London's efforts to create a more sustainable economy are in its early stages. It may take a decade or more for new programs to stand the test of time. Some valuable lessons have, however, been learned and significant accomplishments made. Self-reliance and community partnerships have emerged as both the biggest challenges and the key success factors in local sustainability initiatives.

**Self-reliance** A change in government threatened the existence of many London programs in 1995, reinforcing the importance of one of the key tenets of CED — self-reliance. Strategies for sustainability have since been implemented with programs being run primarily on a cost-recovery basis. In response to cutbacks LEED has reoriented its services and promotions strategy toward small business clients while seeking new ways to finance community projects. The EMRCB is looking to expand its audience to outlying communities to increase revenues and ensure self-sufficiency.

The number of Green Home Checkups dropped with the introduction of a cost recovery fee, but the program continues to provide on a smaller scale the benefits it was created to achieve. Under the Green Communities Network, communities are banding together to solve common problems, including the lack of government funding. London utilities and suppliers who benefit from green home and business checkups have been asked to increase their financial contributions.

Londoners have also learned that self-reliance is not just about financial independence. Self-reliance also implies decision-making power. Restrictive terms set by governments initiating community involvement processes decrease the likelihood of process success. Adaptation to local circumstances is required. Government-imposed priorities have created a number of difficulties for the fledging initiatives taking place in London. Unrealistic timelines satisfy funding requirements and political deadlines but not community needs. Short- term thinking contradicts the very goals sustainability programs are meant to achieve. Community-based initiatives are not well served by top-down government management. Governments must learn to offer leadership as a partner with, not controller of, community. Communities must become adamant about setting their own terms and confident in the importance and validity of their local knowledge.

**Partnerships**   In the long term the survival of Londoners' efforts to achieve sustainability will depend largely on the strength of their community partnerships. Partnerships help to achieve community self-reliance by ensuring local resources are directed towards meeting local needs. In London, local businesses have provided significant financial and in-kind support to sustainability initiatives, and community organizations have banded together to share their skills and resources. Provincial and municipal governments have played an important role, providing both financial assistance and guidance. Students and faculty from educational institutions have provided expertise and volunteer support. Local utilities who benefit from the help in managing local demand for waste, water, and energy services have also pitched in. Londoners have shown, once again, that many hands and minds can accomplish what few cannot.

The story of community partnerships in London not only demonstrates that broad-based community involvement is necessary to achieve sustainability but that such processes must be carefully designed, managed, and governed. Genuine partnerships take time to unfold and to develop trust, mutual understanding, and agreed-upon ways of working together. Londoners launched into numerous new partnerships over a few short months in order to meet government-established timelines. As a result, some of those partnerships quickly collapsed. The damage done is still being repaired.

The most effective partnerships have proven to be ongoing working relationships based on common interests and producing mutual benefits. Too many partners can result in an unwieldy decision-making structure and communications requirements beyond the ability of the coordinating body. Such a process has the potential to collapse under its own weight. Finally, partnerships require an openness and sensitivity to each other's needs and way of doing business.

The journey to a sustainable local economy is far from over. While innovative strategies for self-reliance are being put in place and community members and organizations offer much needed support, it will be exceedingly difficult to make significant change without the assistance and regulatory backing of governments. Londoners are faced with many challenges in designing effective community partnerships, creating a new sustainable, community-based approach to local economic development, and reducing the environmental and social impacts of traditional economic activities.

Traditional economic development practices cannot be sustained by the ecosystems that support them. Environmental management must evolve into a system of production that operates within the limits of the natural world and models the efficiency of ecological systems. Tough issues of overconsumption and management of economic demand will have to be addressed; new methods of economic analysis will have to be designed that can account for social and environmental costs. Change is beginning through local initiatives such as those taking place in London, Ontario. These are necessary, albeit insufficient, first steps in moving toward sustainability, made possible by the commitment and common interest of a diverse range of citizens in the future of their community.

# Part Four

# Eco-city Housing and Community Development

---

*We turn our attention next to eco-city housing and community develop-*
*ment. **Lyle Walker**, a recent graduate of the School of Community and*
*Regional Planning at the University of British Columbia, and **William***
***Rees**, professor and Director of the School, examine the ecological*
*implications of a consumption choice that all households face, that of*
*dwelling type. They use a new tool which Rees originated, "ecological*
*footprint analysis," to translate the total ecological impact associated with*
*different housing types into the area of productive land required to*
*support associated resource consumption. Walker and Rees find that*
*occupants of detached houses have the largest housing-related ecological*
*footprints, an additional argument for higher density living in a world*
*approaching global carrying capacity. Sustainable communities should*
*strive to preserve on-site natural capital, particularly highly productive*
*ecosystems, and to minimize the ecological footprint of each development*
*and its occupants, which largely manifests itself off-site.*

*****Todd Saunders**, who helps design ecological communities in Bergen,*
*Norway, explores the idea of resident participation in relation to*
*ecological community design. Ecological communities are designed to*
*imitate the efficiency in nature, where there is a balance of inputs and*
*outputs of energies, products, and waste. Saunders offers ten*
*recommendations for community designers and others wishing to translate*
*ecological community theory into practice. He draws lessons for us from*
*the experience of northern European communities, which demonstrate that*
*well-rounded ecological communities are not only desirable, but also*
*clearly possible.*

# Urban Density and Ecological Footprints
## An Analysis of Canadian Households

Lyle A. Walker and William E. Rees

Achieving sustainability will require difficult choices about both public expenditures and personal consumption patterns. This chapter examines the ecological implications of a consumption choice that all households face, that of dwelling type, recognizing that private decisions about housing also affect public investment. We use a new tool, "ecological footprint analysis," to translate the total ecological impact associated with different housing types into the area of productive land required to support associated resource consumption.[1]

## Thinking Ecological Footprints

Urbanization and technology have increasingly alienated people both spatially and psychologically from their biological roots. How many city-dwellers have ever paused to wonder just how much of the Earth's surface is dedicated to supporting just themselves? Not very many! The fact remains, however, that humans everywhere are still dependent for their survival on numerous biophysical "goods and services" provided by terrestrial and aquatic ecosystems. High income urban societies in particular require a constant flow of material and energy from nature not only to feed themselves, but also to build and operate their factories and other capital goods, their consumer products, the service infrastructure — indeed, all the accoutrements of modern life. The waste burden has, of course, increased proportionately. In fact, since the beginning of the industrial revolution, our so-called "industrial metabolism" has grown greatly to exceed our biological demands on the ecosphere.

In recognition of the role of nature in maintaining the human economy, ecological economists have begun to recognize that ecosystems and biophysical resources can be treated as forms of "natural capital" (Costanza and Daly 1992). In economics, capital is the means of generating wealth. It is the means of production, our way of generating money income.  Thus, like other forms of capital, well-managed natural capital is capable of producing a stream of income indefinitely into the future. Indeed, all the goods and services flowing from nature can therefore be thought of as "natural income." Fish stocks and forests are forms of natural capital, and sustainable annual harvests represent natural income. The ecological dimension of sustainability requires that we live within nature's means, on the income generated by natural capital. By contrast, much of our money income at present is derived less from sustainable flows than from the liquidation of Earth's once bounteous natural wealth.

In this light, a fundamental question for sustainability is whether remaining natural capital stocks are even theoretically adequate to support the growing human population with its rising material standards through the next century (Rees 1996). William Rees and his students at the University of British Columbia have developed ecological footprint analysis as one approach to addressing this question (Rees and Wackernagel 1994, Wackernagel and Rees 1995, Rees 1996). Ecological footprinting provides an area-based estimate of the natural capital requirements of any defined human population, from an individual to an entire city or country. It starts from the premise that energy and material production and waste assimilation by nature require the services of a measurable area of land and water ecosystems. Thus, we define the ecological footprint of a given population as the total area of productive land and water required on a continuous basis to produce all the resources consumed, and to assimilate all the wastes produced, by that population, *wherever on Earth that land is located.*

Let us consider a typical household to illustrate the concept. When we build a home, we obviously physically occupy a certain amount of land. But housing consumes a lot more land than the foundation area. Besides the building site, there is the household's share of all the streets in the city and intercity highways. The forest products consumed in constructing and maintaining the house — framing timbers, wooden floors, building paper, etc. — can be translated into an equivalent area of productive forest land. We can also convert the carbon dioxide generated by the household for space heating into a land area equivalent. This would be the area of "carbon sink" forest needed to prevent these emissions from accumulating in the atmosphere and adding to the greenhouse effect. These items contribute to just the "housing" component of the household's ecological footprint. If we sum the land area equivalents of the household's entire average annual shopping basket of consumption

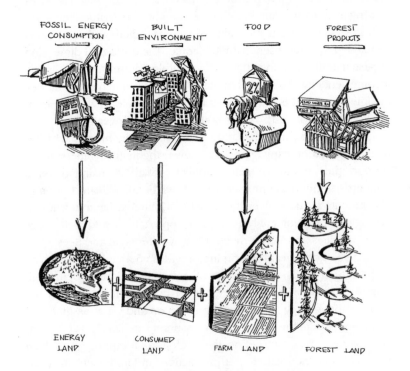

**Figure 1: Converting Consumption Into Land Area.**
The production and use of any good or service depends on various types of ecological productivity, which can be converted into a land-area equivalent. Summing the land requirements for all significant categories of consumption and waste yields the total ecological footprint for that population.
Illustration by Phil Testemale. Source: Wackernagel and Rees 1995: 67.

items, we obtain an estimate of the household's total ecological footprint (Figure 1).

We use a simple two-dimensional matrix relating consumption with land productivity to organize our ecological footprint estimates. The rows of the matrix represent five main consumption categories: 1) food, 2) housing, 3) transportation, 4) consumer goods, and 5) services. The columns of the matrix represent specific land use categories: a) fossil energy land, b) consumed land, c) food land, and d) forest land. Fossil energy land is land used to sequester carbon dioxide emissions. Consumed land includes degraded land that humans have rendered biologically unproductive, such as building sites and road surfaces. Food and forest land are cultivated or modified landscapes whose annual production of biomass (natural income) is appropriated by people. Each cell in the matrix represents the land area required to satisfy the *per capita* demand for the corresponding consumption item on a sustainable basis.

Wackernagel and Rees (1995) estimate that the ecological footprint of an average Canadian is about 4.3 hectares. Comparing this calculation with the actual *per capita* productive land available on the planet produces a startling result. If everyone on the planet consumed like an average Canadian, we would need approximately two additional Earths to support the consumption demands of the world population! These findings indicate that it is not biophysically possible using prevailing technologies to bring the world's population up to North American material standards on a sustainable basis.

## Some Pros and Cons of Footprint Analysis

The major strength of ecological footprint analysis is its conceptual simplicity. This method provides an intuitive and visually graphic tool for communicating one of the most important dimensions of the sustainability dilemma. It aggregates the ecological flows associated with consumption and translates these into appropriated land area, a familiar indicator that anyone can understand. The ecological footprint of any defined population and level of technology can then be compared with the available supply of productive land. The conclusion is unambiguous for the conditions specified because land is assuredly finite and represents an inelastic limit on material growth. In short, ecological footprinting succeeds as a communication tool because it conveys a profound message that can readily be communicated to the general public.

While acknowledging its power to communicate a fundamental message, some commentators have suggested that the footprint concept is too simplistic. It is true, of course, that footprint analysis is static, rather than dynamic, modeling and that it has no predictive capability. However, prediction was never our intent. Ecological footprinting acts as an ecological camera — each analysis provides a snapshot of our current demands on nature, a portrait of how things stand *right now* under prevailing technology and social values. We show that humanity has already exceeded carrying capacity and that some people contribute significantly more to this ecological "overshoot" than do others. Once such basic conclusions are accepted, the analysis begs such policy-relevant questions as just how large is our ecological deficit and what must be done to reduce it?[2] We believe that this in itself is an important contribution.

It is also true that eco-footprinting ignores many other factors at the heart of sustainability.[3] Of at least equal relevance are considerations of political and economic power, the responsiveness of the political process to the ecological imperative, and chronic distributional inequity which actually seems to be worsening (both within rich countries and between North and South) as the market economy becomes an increasingly global affair. In fact, our current approach does not even account for the myriad indirect effects of production/consumption such as the disruption of traditional livelihoods and the damage to public health that results from expanding economic activity. Obviously such limitations call for additional research on the issues raised, but none detracts from the fundamental message of ecological footprint analysis — that whatever the distribution of power or wealth, society will ultimately have to deal with the growing global ecological debt. (For an expanded discussion of the strengths and weaknesses of eco-footprint analysis, see Rees and Wackernagel 1996.)

## Resource Consumption Related to Dwelling Type and Density

As noted, dwelling type and density affect sustainability through differences in the consumption of energy, materials, and land for housing, transportation, and urban infrastructure. Nationwide, this represents a significant portion of total resource consumption. In 1989, housing and transportation accounted for 21 per cent and 28 per cent respectively of final energy use in Canada (Environment Canada 1991: 12-11). Housing and transportation also consume significant quantities of land. Residential land and roads, including parking lots, typically consume approximately 51 per cent and 19 per cent of land use respectively in large urban areas (Hodge 1991: 148).

Housing and transportation are also the two largest expenditure items in most households in Canada, representing about 25 per cent and 17 per cent respectively of the average household's after-tax expenditures (Statistics Canada 1993b: 35). Given the resource and financial significance of housing and transportation, these sectors represent great potential scope for reducing consumption.

## The Influence of Dwelling Type and Density on Consumption Patterns

**Dwelling Type and Resource Consumption for Housing** Lot size determines the amount of land directly occupied by a household. We consider land lying underneath the dwelling and any impervious surfaces, such as driveways, to be permanently degraded. The remainder of the lot is in the "garden" land category.

Different dwelling types have differing energy requirements for space heating and cooling which account for 64 per cent of energy consumption in B.C. homes (B.C. Energy Council 1994: 98). Dwelling type determines the proportion of walls and floors that are shared with other dwellings which affect the amount of exposed surface area for heat transfer. In addition, floor space generally decreases as density increases. Thus, as density increases, the *per capita* requirements for space conditioning in buildings decreases (Lang 1985: 18). Detached houses consume the most operating and embodied energy per unit of floor space when other factors are held constant (Burby et al. 1982).

Higher densities also facilitate the use of more efficient energy technologies, such as district energy systems which are used extensively in Scandinavia and northern Europe. Such systems pump hot water, steam, or chilled water generated at locations along the system to buildings on the network to satisfy their space heating, domestic water, or industrial process needs (MacRae 1992). In Britain, a threshold of 44 units per hectare was considered to be the minimum density required to introduce district energy systems (Owens 1986). Efficient design and building codes can further reduce energy needs. An R2000 house may use half the energy of standard detached houses, while an energy efficient Advanced House may save an additional 50 per cent.

Dwelling type, floor space, construction materials, and building height all influence gross material consumption. For example, an average Canadian home requires approximately 24 cubic metres of wood for its frame and floors (Environment Canada 1991: 10-11), significantly more than that required for a wood-frame apartment. Above four storeys, building frame materials are generally steel or reinforced concrete which have higher embodied energy contents than wood.

**Density and Energy Consumption for Transportation** The number and length of trips, the split among transportation modes, trip speed, and vehicle occupancy rates all affect total transportation energy consumption (Handy 1992: 2). The most important factor relating urban form and transport energy consumption is the separation of activities which is itself a function of density and land use mix (Owens 1986: 32). Density and distance between destinations affect the availability and feasibility of alternative transportation modes. For example, densities of 15 and 30 units per gross residential hectare have been suggested as the thresholds for cost-effective bus and rapid transit service respectively (Snohomish County Transportation Authority 1994: 21). Walking and cycling are feasible options only for short trips. Not surprisingly, automobile ownership is highest among single-family households at 94 per cent compared to 56 per cent for apartment-dwelling households (Statistics Canada 1992b). Similarly, about 77 per cent of fully-detached households have at least one auto commuter compared to only 57 per cent of apartment-dwelling families (Statistics Canada 1993a: 55).

How people travel affects energy consumption. Walking and cycling require only caloric intake from food. Transit is more energy efficient per passenger-kilometre than are automobiles at typical occupancy rates. However, there is potential for a ten-fold increase in vehicle energy efficiency by shifting to ultralight hybrid cars (Lovins and Lovins 1995).

In a study of 32 international cities, Newman and Kenworthy (1989) found an exponential decrease in *per capita* gasoline consumption with increasing density (Figure 2). Reduced auto dependency occurs above a density of 30-40 persons per urban hectare. High density European and modern Asian cities consume the least gasoline consumption while low density U.S. and Australian cities have the highest consumption. Toronto and five other Canadian cities fell within this range (Newman, Kenworthy, and Lyons 1990). It should be noted that many studies have been unable to isolate the effect of density on consumption from that of other factors, such as the socio-economic characteristics of households.

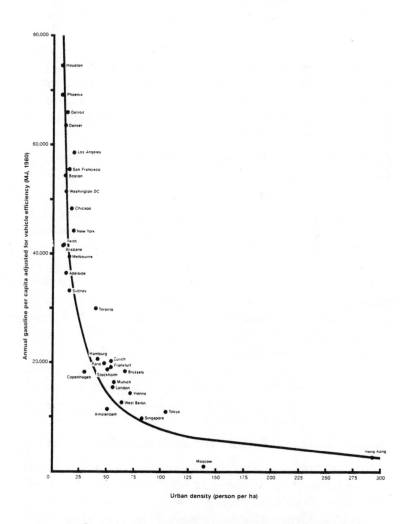

Figure 2: Urban Density Versus Gasoline Use Per Capita Adjusted for Vehicle Efficiency, Newman and Kenworthy 1989: 49. Reprinted with permission from P. Newman and J. Kenworthy, *Cities and Automobile Dependency: An International Sourcebook* (Gower Publishing Ltd., 1989), p.49.

**Density and Resource Consumption for Infrastructure**
Buildings require infrastructure such as roads, sidewalks, street lights, and water and sanitary sewers, all of which consume land, energy, and materials. Density, lot size, municipal standards, characteristics of occupancy, contiguity of development, distance to central facilities, and settlement size are the main variables affecting infrastructure costs and presumably resource consumption (Frank 1989). Gagnon (cited in D'Amour 1993) estimates that street length per dwelling unit falls from 17.5 metres for single-family bungalows to one metre for eight-storey apartments. Nevertheless, the energy savings from infrastructure at high densities are believed to be less than those associated with corresponding shifts in building type and transportation mode (Lang 1985: 31).

## Applying the Ecological Footprint Concept to Household Comparisons

To assess the housing-related ecological impacts of different housing options, we performed an ecological footprint analysis at the household level and made comparisons on a per occupant basis. Each housing type has characteristics — e.g., floor space, lot size, and number of occupants — that measurably affect consumption related to house construction and operation, and transportation.[4] Similarly there is a link between lot size and the energy, material, and land required for infrastructure. Lot size determines the frontage which in turn dictates the amount of linear infrastructure, such as residential streets, electricity, and communications cables, water and sewage lines, etc., required to service the lot. As noted, we convert fossil energy consumption into the area of carbon-sink forest required to absorb carbon dioxide emissions, taking into account electricity derived from fossil fuels.

## Mirrored Density: Reflections of a Household's Housing Choice

We used "mirrored density" as the basis for comparison among housing types. Mirrored density is the overall density that would result if all households were similarly housed. In other words, consumption estimates for each household type are based on the assumption that everyone lives in the same type of house and that the resultant density is uniform across the city. Mirrored density is preferred to actual density  because we were not interested in specific sites but rather with the general implications of dwelling type. In mixed residential areas, those households living on smaller lots effectively subsidize transportation services for households living on larger lots (i.e., higher densities make public transit more feasible). Thus data on particular housing types from real-world mixed neighborhoods would be augmented or diluted by spill-over effects from other housing types. Mirrored density avoids this problem.

Mirrored density provides a way to link dwelling type and lot size with transportation energy consumption. To make this link, we used Newman and Kenworthy's (1989: 49) graph of urban density and gasoline consumption data. We matched our mirrored densities to their gross urban density scale and took the corresponding gasoline consumption from the graph.

## Description of Housing Types

We made ecological footprint calculations for four dwelling types: single-family detached, townhouse, walk-up, and high-rise apartment. We examined detached houses on both 8,400 square foot lots and 6,000 square foot lots. For each dwelling type, the physical characteristics of the existing Canadian housing stock were assumed (Table 1). Note that occupancy decreases from about three in detached houses to 1.8 in apartments. Average floor space decreases from about 1,700 square feet in detached houses to 800 square feet in apartments.

## Comparison of Ecological Footprints

We compared the ecological footprints of the dwellings by consumption category (Figure 3). The per occupant housing-related ecological footprint of a standard detached house is about one and a half hectares. Approximately 53 per cent of the footprint is for housing, 44 per cent for transportation, and three per cent for infrastructure. The ecological footprint of the small-lot house is 92 per cent of the standard house value, mostly due to reduced energy consumption for transportation. The per occupant ecological footprint of a typical townhouse was estimated to be 78 per cent of that for a standard detached house. The smallest eco-footprints are for residents of high-rise and walk-up apartments at 60 per cent to 64 per cent respectively of the value obtained for occupants of standard detached houses. For reasons noted above (see Note 3), the ecological footprint calculations are probably underestimates. However, more refined calculations would not much affect the relative differences between dwelling types.

| Table 1: Profile of Household and Dwelling Characteristics by Housing Type | | | | | |
|---|---|---|---|---|---|
| | Standard lot Detached House | Small lot Detached House | Townhouse | Walk-up Apartment | High rise Apartment |
| Household characteristics | | | | | |
| - number of occupants | 3.0 | 3.0 | 2.3 | 1.8 | 1.8 |
| Dwelling characteristics | | | | | |
| - net floor space (m$^2$) | 159.8 | 159.8 | 120.8 | 74.3 | 74.3 |
| Building characteristics | | | | | |
| - framing material | wood | wood | wood | wood | reinforced concrete |
| Lot characteristics | | | | | |
| - net dwelling unit density (units/ha.) | 12.8 | 17.3 | 36.0 | 72.0 | 188.7 |
| - lot size/dwelling unit (m$^2$/unit) | 780.4 | 557.4 | 277.7 | 138.9 | 53.2 |
| - lot width/dwelling unit (m/unit) | 18.3 | 15.0 | 9.0 | 7.9 | 3.0 |
| Transportation characteristics | | | | | |
| - number of vehicles owned | 2.04 | 2.04 | 1.46 | 0.94 | 0.94 |

Figure 4 plots housing-related ecological footprints versus dwelling unit density. The ecological footprint per occupant falls steeply between low-density detached houses and medium-density townhouses and walk-up apartments. It declines more slowly between medium and high density high-rise apartments.

Operating energy for housing and transportation account for over 60 per cent of the housing-related ecological footprint regardless of housing type. When embodied energy use is added, this rises to 82-90 per cent. Wood and fibre consumption is the next most important component for all dwelling types except high-rise apartments. Forest land occupies five to 15 per cent of the housing-related footprint depending on dwelling type.

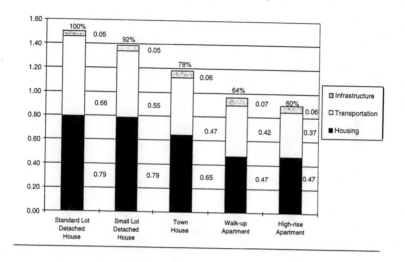

Figure 3: Comparison of Ecological Footprints per Occupant by Dwelling Type (ha/capita)

Interestingly, the smallest bit of the housing eco-footprint (four to five per cent) is the building lot and land required for infrastructure. For a household in a detached house, its housing-related ecological footprint is over 50 times its lot size. The ratio is even higher for townhouses and apartments since lot size per unit decreases faster than the ecological footprint. Here the total land appropriated for housing and related transportation needs is at least one to two orders of magnitude larger than the per occupant lot size (this increases to two to three orders of magnitude if all consumption categories [including food, clothing, etc.] are considered). It seems that the most tangible portion of a household's ecological footprint is the least significant.

## Strength of this Approach

This study illustrates an integrated approach to the analysis of the ecological demands of different housing types. In addition to housing *per se*, it also includes resource consumption associated with housing-related transportation and infrastructure requirements. For example, consider the case of single-detached houses on different lot sizes: if only the housing portion of the ecological footprint were considered, there would be a reduction of less than 0.01 hectare per

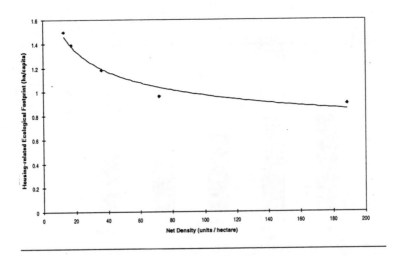

**Figure 4: Urban Density versus Ecological Footprint per Occupant and Trend Line**

occupant for the household on the small lot due to smaller lot size. However, when we include the relationship between density and travel requirements, the ecological footprint shrinks much further from the decline in transportation energy consumption. Another strength of the method is its ability to integrate the consumption of different resources. Consider the fact that buried infrastructure, such as sewers, does not directly occupy land. However, infrastructure requires embodied energy for its manufacture and installation. By converting the fossil energy used into carbon sink land, it becomes apparent that buried infrastructure does in fact "consume" land.

## Conclusions: Policy Implications for Planning

Society continues to debate the goods and bads of higher urban densities. At higher densities, the needs of a changing demographic structure and the trend towards smaller households are better met, housing is more affordable, infrastructure costs are reduced, public transit becomes feasible, the city may be more accessible and even healthier, and farmland and environmental assets can better be preserved (Rees and Wackernagel 1996, Mitlin and Satterthwaite 1994). Countering this, the market continues to demand low density housing, there is a perception that low densities provide a higher quality of life, and some analysts argue that the environmental benefits of higher density are exaggerated (Isin and Tomalty 1993).

Our finding that occupants of detached houses have the largest housing-related ecological footprints is an additional argument for higher density living in a world approaching global carrying capacity. Single-family detached houses have the largest eco-footprint and, in general, as density increases, the footprint per occupant decreases. Significantly, however, single-family detached houses comprise 57 per cent of the current housing stock in Canada and detached houses are preferred by a majority of Canadians. If we wish to reduce the ecological footprint of housing, then taxation, zoning, and related policies should provide incentives to promote higher density living. To be truly effective, a policy of increasing densities should be integrated with policies respecting land use, transportation, and urban form.

Operating energy for housing and transportation comprise over 60 per cent of a household's housing-related ecological footprint. These two areas should therefore be targeted as high leverage areas for eco-footprint reduction. This accords with Marshall Macklin Monaghan (1982: 5-2) who conclude that "transportation and space heating have been identified as the two aspects of new development which offer the greatest potential for energy conservation and are capable of being directly influenced by municipal planners. They are typically the two largest users of energy in urban areas." One reason for this is that under-pricing generally leads to the over-consumption of resources and discourages the development of alternative technologies. Accordingly, the artificially low prices for fossil fuels will be among the first to be adjusted upward by accelerating depletion taxes should governments introduce ecological fiscal reform as a conservation and sustainability measure (Rees 1995).

Strong measures to deal with the ecological crisis will remain politically unacceptable without public education to increase awareness about sustainability. Today's urban residents are generally alienated from the natural environment. They do not appreciate the volume of resources they use and wastes they generate to satisfy their consumption patterns. This research shows that, contrary to popular perceptions, the land used for residential lots and roads — most of the modern city's built-up area — comprises only a small part of the actual total land appropriation by high-income cities.

Thus, ecological footprinting can be a powerful heuristic tool in communicating the *de facto* impact of our consumer lifestyles and the potential gains from adopting alternative consumption patterns. The data also show that shifting to high density multi-family from low-density single family housing can carve as much as 40 per cent from the housing-related component of our personal ecological footprints. The implications of this measure for long-term sustainability are much easier to grasp than the corresponding value of dollars saved or calories unspent.

### Rethinking the Characteristics of Sustainable Communities

Thinking from an ecological footprint perspective suggests that sustainable communities would meet the following two criteria (among others):

1) Preserves on-site natural capital, particularly highly productive ecosystems;

2) Minimizes the ecological footprint of the development and its occupants, which largely manifests itself off-site.

Some so-called "environmentally friendly" developments may only reflect the first criterion. However, as this study shows, preserving stream corridors, wetlands, and natural areas in a low density, automobile-dependent subdivision, is a far from complete model of sustainability. Conversely, development may have a small ecological footprint while doing little to preserve on-site natural capital. Indeed, one can readily imagine a sterile, compact, medium to high density city with efficient housing, excellent public transit, and a smaller ecological footprint than the comparable North American city today. However, the livability of such a community would be greatly compromised in the absence of the amenities associated with vibrant local natural capital stocks.

### Reducing Our Housing-Related Ecological Footprints

The steep slope of the ecological footprint curve at the low density end (Figure 4) indicates that even small increases in density can greatly reduce a household's ecological footprint. To achieve these higher densities, it will be necessary to make the associated lifestyle desirable, especially for those households that have choice over dwelling type and location.[5] In this light, it is important to distinguish perceived densities from actual densities. Good design, public open space, and creative landscaping can reduce perceived density.

In general, the traditional homogeneous single-family subdivision should be discouraged. We can begin the transition by mixing medium density dwelling types with detached houses and by allowing secondary suites or 'granny flats' in single-family residential neighborhoods. Higher densities in existing urban areas without intruding on neighborhoods can be achieved by building three or four storey apartments along commercial streets, with retail on the first floor and residential suites above. As such medium density buildings are less intrusive than high-rise structures, some communities may choose to make them a mainstay of densification policy.

Extra care needs to be exercised when planning for high-rise apartments. High-rise apartments should be carefully located on desirable sites. Sites with high amenity value, particularly access to open space or waterfront areas, public facilities, shopping and restaurants, enhances the attractiveness and value of the apartment units. One of the most successful and highest-density residential areas in North America is Vancouver's West End. This area is bounded by waterfront on two sides, and by Stanley Park and downtown Vancouver on the other sides. It has very low vacancy rates and a vibrant commercial area. Most significantly, 40 per cent of households do not own automobiles.

In developing densification strategies, we need to search for synergies where multiple objectives can be achieved by a policy. As noted, a policy to harden the urban fringe preserves farmland, enhances food security, reduces the costs of infrastructure, and improves the efficiency of public transit. Similarly, housing coops, public housing, and other forms of affordable housing can be integrated with energy and water conservation policies to further enhance both affordability and sustainability. Building to at least an R2000 standard would in itself greatly reduce the ecological footprint of housing. Expanding our focus to affordable living, we would also consider transportation, the second or third largest expenditure for most households. Locating efficient medium-density housing near transit corridors and shopping would reduce the amount of travel, number of cars owned, and associated transportation costs.

There is clearly no shortage of strategies to increase densities and otherwise reduce our urban ecological footprints. However, sustainability requires more than technical means and political good intentions. Taking sustainability seriously forces a re-examination of deep social values, popular beliefs, and personal behaviors. Thus, if ordinary citizens are to "buy in" to sustainability, they must be convinced that they have more to gain than to lose by doing so. Success will undoubtedly require strong leadership and integrated strategies and plans for future development. Most important, however, will be an informed public supportive of strong policies for change, many of which seem to fly in the face of popular perceptions today.

# Ecology and Community Design
## Lessons from Northern European Ecological Communities

## Todd Saunders

In many ways, ecology and community design are in contradiction. Most designs for development inevitably require the destruction of natural ecologies. Consequently, designers often face the paradox that sometimes the most ecologically desirable decision is not to build at all (Kareoja 1993). There are solutions to this paradox. Designers can create communities that have less impact on the natural environment and are practical alternatives to conventional community design.

Unfortunately, in North America, architectural and planning theorists, not practitioners, develop most ecology and community design concepts. While these works confirm the need for an alternative approach to design, the solutions put forward often are highly theoretical, and do not address practical concerns. Although many architects and planners profess an interest in both ecology and community design, there are virtually no contemporary built examples of "ecological communities" in North America.[1]

Northern Europe, in contrast, supports a long tradition and ever-expanding practice of ecological community design, with a large palette of academic and practical research to draw upon. In 1994, I spent four months visiting 15 ecological communities in northern Europe. I examined five in detail — Ecolonia, in Alphen aan der Rijn, The Netherlands; Lebensgarten, near Steyerberg,

Germany; Frasenweg, in Kassel, Germany; Vallersund Gård, Norway; and Järna, Sweden — seeking to identify the guiding principles and main lessons we can learn from northern European ecological communities.[2]

## What are Ecological Communities?

"Ecological community" is not a common term in the field of architecture and planning, and as such requires some definition. Ecological communities share similar principles with concepts created by other researchers, which include Green Cities (Gordon 1990), Ecological Villages (Gilman and Gilman 1991), Sustainable Communities (Roseland 1992a), Eco-cities (Register 1987), and Green Communities (Roseland 1996b). I chose ecological community as a generic term since all definitions available have common features. These researchers and designers of ecological communities, who look for new ways to integrate artificial environments with natural environments, study human settlements as ecosystems. Viewed as ecosystems, human settlements should be energy efficient, produce little waste, and be self-reliant — much the same as ecosystems appearing in nature.

In accordance with the authors mentioned, and through my own personal experience, I suggest that an ecological community exists if it: 1) applies renewable energy technologies — such as solar energy, combined heat and power schemes, or wind-generated electricity rather than fossil-fuel-related energy supplies; 2) uses alternative sewage and waste water treatment systems; 3) strives to work in conjunction with natural surroundings without disrupting natural features (e.g., soils, water, natural vegetation, and habitat); 4) attempts to function like ecosystems to conserve natural resources, to be self-regulating, and to produce little waste. Furthermore, people living in ecological communities practise recycling and waste recovery as a way of life. In sum, ecological communities are designed to imitate the efficiency in nature, where there is a balance of inputs and outputs of energies, products, and waste. And, ideally, the surplus of these materials is still valuable to the community.

On the basis of my observations and the literature of built ecological communities in northern Europe, I offer ten main recommendations for community designers and others wishing to translate ecological community theory into practice. While these recommendations should help participants to avoid common mistakes on similar projects, they are not definitive. Each community will have its own specific ecosystem and its own set of residents.

**1. Monitor Input and Output of Community Resources** In their efforts to integrate artificial environments with natural environments, ecological community researchers and designers study human settlements as ecosystems, which should be energy efficient and self-reliant and produce little waste. Herbert Girardet, for example, considers a community to be ecological when it adopts a circular metabolism (Figure 1), whereby outputs of the system are equal to the inputs, thus only affecting a small area (1992). Conventional communities have a linear metabolism (Figure 2) where input has no relationship with output: the community takes what it needs with no consideration to consequences.

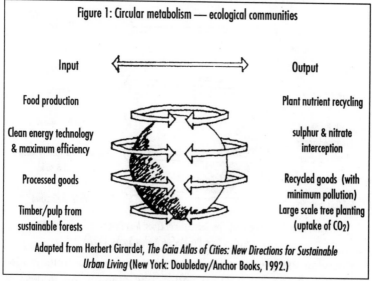

**Figure 1: Circular metabolism — ecological communities**

Input ⟷ Output

| Input | Output |
|---|---|
| Food production | Plant nutrient recycling |
| Clean energy technology & maximum efficiency | sulphur & nitrate interception |
| Processed goods | Recycled goods (with minimum pollution) |
| Timber/pulp from sustainable forests | Large scale tree planting (uptake of $CO_2$) |

Adapted from Herbert Girardet, *The Gaia Atlas of Cities: New Directions for Sustainable Urban Living* (New York: Doubleday/Anchor Books, 1992.)

Attaining the goal of an ecological community is easier when residents understand the input and output of resources. Monitoring is therefore an important educational tool that enables residents to learn how their homes and community are connected to a much larger system. In the five communities I examined in detail, residents are generally aware of the amount of waste materials, energy, and resources they create, produce, and utilize. They can point to areas of the community that need improvement or help establish a circular metabolism.

Residents at Vallersund Gård monitor the amount of energy

produced and utilized by the community's windmill. Residents at Järna are aware of the amount and quality of effluent being treated by their biological wastewater treatment ponds. They avoid flushing plastic and other artificial objects down the toilet because they have seen and learned the consequences of these actions. All the communities in this study know the estimated amount of solid waste produced by and leaving the community. As well, most of the communities monitor their water consumption levels, and know when and how they reduce their water consumption. Through an understanding of these figures residents can take action to lessen environmental impacts and save money spent on excess water, energy, and waste handling.

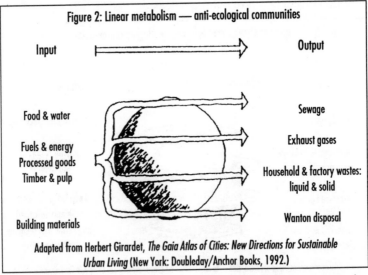

Figure 2: Linear metabolism — anti-ecological communities

Input → Output

Food & water

Fuels & energy
Processed goods
Timber & pulp

Building materials

Sewage

Exhaust gases

Household & factory wastes:
liquid & solid

Wanton disposal

Adapted from Herbert Girardet, *The Gaia Atlas of Cities: New Directions for Sustainable Urban Living* (New York: Doubleday/Anchor Books, 1992.)

Knowing the numbers for resource inputs and outputs is also crucial for change of political and public opinion. Awareness of energy savings, waste reduction, and water conservation equips residents with facts that prove the viability of their ecological community. For example, residents at the Frasenweg project reduced solid waste by 50 per cent, and were then able to convince authorities to reduce waste collection fees by the same percentage. Basically, the numbers make it easier for the public and politicians to visualize the efficiency of ecological communities.

**2. Involve the Community** Community involvement in the design and development of ecological communities is crucial, yet it is difficult to measure the quantitative and qualitative benefits. Community groups provide insight into local ecological and social opportunities and constraints that might otherwise be overlooked by architects and designers. Residents can offer first-hand solutions rather than acting as obstacles to the design of the community. In addition, residents can enhance community support for ecological concerns, and use their position as a mechanism for influencing continued environmental stewardship and motivation in the community.

In almost all the communities studied, residents have been and continue to be involved in major decisions concerning the design, management, or construction process. As a consequence, they understand their local environment. The community can create a design they are comfortable with, and change the design as their needs evolve. Because it is rooted in this understanding, the overall design reflects the needs of the community instead of preconceived design solutions imposed by outsiders.

Since the communities are able to make design, management, and construction decisions, residents respect and conserve the local environment because they have a vested interest in ecological protection. Topics of ecology are no longer abstract, but directly connected to the results of the decision-making process. With community involvement, designs are more likely to correspond to local ecological needs. Without community involvement, sustained environmental protection is unlikely (Agarwal and Narain 1989).

**3. Employ Alternative Housing Arrangements** The ecological communities studied consider the single-family detached house as anti-ecological. As a result they explore other housing forms. In the northern European ecological communities, the dominant housing includes multifamily and cooperative housing arrangements. Cooperative housing is particularly conducive to many environmental community technologies (for example, combined heat and power schemes and windmills) that would require excessive amounts of energy and capital if used for single-detached houses. Residents of cooperative housing share appliances, tools, and automobiles to minimize consumption levels. As well, residents can share maintenance activities, which reduces expenses and may increase leisure time.

Because of their higher densities, cooperative housing, cluster housing, and similar forms reduce urban sprawl as well as car dependency. Higher densities encourage pedestrian and bicycle traffic, make public transit more efficient, allow shorter travel distances to community facilities, including schools, and lower costs for services such as waste and snow removal. Tighter arrangements of housing leave more land for gardening and play areas, and for the natural treatment of wastewater and storm water. The reduced built-over space facilitates conservation of environmentally sensitive areas that may otherwise be consumed by inefficient land uses. And, along with these contributions to efficiency and environmental protection, higher density housing forms frequently increase the availability of affordable housing.

4. **Design for the Pedestrian** A community designed for the pedestrian helps conserve the surrounding environment. All the northern European communities I visited have been designed for the pedestrian, while the automobile received a lesser priority. Close comparison of these communities' site plans with those of conventional communities confirms that ecological communities devote much less land to the automobile in every case.

With fewer roads in the community, more areas can come into use for children. Streets for pedestrians become active places for meeting residents in the community. And less parking space and fewer roads make it possible to increase space for housing, parkland, and natural habitats.

While living without an automobile is almost impossible in contemporary society, residents of the northern European ecological communities attempt to reduce auto dependency and use the car as a tool. The communities studied have used various methods to reduce car dependency. All the communities have access to public transportation. In addition, the residents of Steyerberg, Germany, Vallersund Gård, Norway, and Järna, Sweden, share their cars. They reserve the designated automobiles in advance, and group all of their chores into one or two days a week, to reduce unnecessary auto trips. The booking system caters to carpooling as well.

Residents of Frasenweg in Kassel, Germany, own their cars independently, but the cars stay outside the community in a carport at the entrance. The result for Frasenweg is an auto-free community. The design of Ecolonia, The Netherlands, controls and slows traffic. The designer, Lucien Kroll, employs the Dutch *woonerf* (living yard) in which the design of the road slows traffic to ten to 15 kilometres per hour. The *woonerf* includes changes such as speedbumps and signs at the entrance reminding drivers that they are entering a controlled traffic zone.

**5. Incorporate Natural Areas into the Community** Many of the northern European ecological communities include natural areas within their boundaries, protect them from disturbance during construction, and minimize other human interference. The presence of these natural areas allows people to experience, observe, and understand the cyclic processes of nature. In turn, this understanding can foster a greater appreciation of natural areas that is not possible in the biologically sterile landscapes of conventional communities. The absence of nature lessens people's perception and appreciation of natural processes and can lead to the loss of sensual perceptions, loss of orientation, and loss of identification (Hahn and Simonis 1991). The presence of nature can, however, achieve the opposite.

In conventional communities, designers often place natural areas at the edges of the community far from where most people live. The resulting travel distance limits the number of times a person can experience a natural area, wastes energy in the form of gasoline, and often leaves people without access to an automobile at a loss. Furthermore, Hough warns that the absence of nature can put environmentalists at a disadvantage. He argues that the perception of human settlements as separate from nature has long been a central problem for the environmental movement and for environmental thinking (Hough 1990).

**6. Use Experimental Projects to Induce Gradual Change of Opinion** Many of the communities in this study are experimental and recognize that standardized solutions outlined by government agencies cannot fulfill the needs and desires for those with a commitment to ecological living (Hagenand and Rose 1989). Residents and designers of ecological communities suggest that experimental projects induce learning, encourage innovative thinking, and provide flexible opportunities to test new ideas. The general public understands models, especially working ones, better than concepts. As well, a built example is influential because lessons from experimentation can be employed and improved for future projects, thus contributing to the evolution of good design.

In a Canadian study involving extensive field research and interviews, William Perks and David Van Vliet found that experimental projects are considered essential if ecologically responsible community designs are to win acceptance from design professionals, public officials, citizens, and the private sector (Perks and Van Vliet 1993). They report that experimental projects provide real examples that persuade public and local authorities of the richness of ecologically sensitive living environments, and help create new housing markets as developers begin to show more interest in ecological communities.

cument describes the various policies to be implemented to ensure the participation and inclusion of Maori in the decision-making process. In the strategic plan, "Tanaga Whenua: the Treaty of Waitangi and Maori Residents" is identified as one of nine key action platforms.[1] The key action platform describes the policies, targets, and actions of the city council (Table 1) and includes such things as identification and response to issues related to the treaty and relevant legislation, liaison with Maori community to ensure equitable services and to consolidate the role of *Te Taumata Runanga* (Maori Perspectives Committee).

**7. Change the Role of the Community Designer**  It is becoming evident that environmental issues must become the primary responsibility for the architecture and community design profession, starting now and continuing into the future. A major difficulty, however, is that many of the solutions to environmental problems add to the numerous tasks a designer has to deal with in everyday practice. The need to assimilate so much more information before making any positive changes can easily seem overwhelming.

One response is an integrated team approach to ecological community design. Mark Alden-Branch notes that many projects are now being managed by designers who "assemble and lead teams of experts, including urban designers, material consultants, waste consultants, and others" (Alden-Branch 1993). Similarly, John Turner calls for "professional enablement" where the designer can bring together specialized skills for the community to capitalize on (see Kemeny 1989). In this manner the designer's outside knowledge can be combined with the community's insider knowledge to create a community that best suits all needs and desires.

Other designers believe that solving problems on a much smaller or intimate scale and assuming an active role in the design and construction process will make the greatest difference. Many of the designers of the northern European ecological communities (including Declan and Margrit Kennedy in Lebensgarten, Germany; Gernot Minke and Doris and Manfred Hegger in Kassel, Germany; and Erik Asmussen in Järna, Sweden) have submerged themselves in community design by becoming residents. They argue that when the design and construction processes are separated, too many good design intentions are ignored or never implemented.

Designers commonly avoid the site because if they overlook mistakes they are often held accountable for the problems that arise. The designers living in the ecological communities studied cannot avoid the site. Since the project is their home, they have a vested interest in conserving the local ecosystems and educating other residents. During site construction, designers are able to meet frequently to discuss the preservation of the site. These designers are then able to minimize the damages more easily and set precedents for others to follow. It is evident to these designers that the organization of, and their involvement in, the building process is the secret to minimizing negative effects on the natural environment.

**8. Plan in Stages and For the Long Term** Many of the ecological communities in northern Europe have adopted a comfortable pace of development consisting of a series of stages to be implemented over the years.[3] The designers and residents believe that overexertion contributes to an exhaustion of physical, emotional, and financial resources. They also believe that moving too slowly causes them to become overly theoretical without accomplishing anything of significance. Most have set flexible time limits to meet their objective of eventually establishing a fully ecological community.

It is often frustrating for designers to plan for the long term. Designers concerned about the future may want to rush their visions quickly into reality so they can test their ideas. For the community, however, the process of design and construction is perhaps more important than the final product.

During the design and construction process people build a sense of community and develop relationships. Developing in a series of stages allows residents to revisit their initial design assumptions and intentions. They can change the community plan to adapt to their increased understanding of the local ecologies, their evolving community identity, and their appreciation of the lessons gained in the initial stages. The result is a community design that more closely fits the needs and desires of the residents.

**9. Share Information** Many ecological communities have a multitude of factors in common. Designers planning to create ecological communities may not want to reinvent the wheel, given the increasing amount of research and practice concerning ecological community design available. The problem, however, is that this information is scattered and hard to obtain.

Setting up organizations to disseminate information can speed up the process of development and help communities avoid mistakes that may have already been made by other communities. By spreading information across a greater area, these organizations can help alternative design ideas permeate into mainstream design practices. It is surprising how effective information exchange can be for the success of an idea.

Among the communities I visited, many associate themselves with a larger organization. Lebensgarten, Germany, is a member of Ékodorf—Informationen (Ecological Villages/Communities—Information), an organization that publishes a magazine every two months on matters pertaining to ecological communities around Europe. Vallersund Gård in Norway belongs to the Camphill Trust for the care of mentally challenged adults, which has five other communities in Norway and upwards of 80 communities in more than 18 countries around the world.

As well, many of the northern European countries have ecological community organizations to assist the development of more ecological communities. Norway and Sweden have the Eco-community Programs and Denmark has its Green Community Projects started in 1986, 1990, and 1989 respectively. They all aim to develop strategies for participating ecological communities, and to serve as examples for other communities.

Such organizations can provide a forum where communities with similar interests learn from each other's successes as well as the inevitable failures. Institutional methods can be transferred from one community to another. Perhaps most importantly, the communities can benefit from shared support, especially in times of need. Central organizations can also represent smaller communities on a much larger scale, protect their interests, and extend their influence (Shenker 1986).

**10. Maintain a Balance** This final lesson combines all the observations above. Designers can misconceive ecological communities as single-purpose exercises and approach their task with, for example, only alternative energy systems or some other ecological feature in mind, neglecting such important aspects as community, economics, and lifestyle. Such single-purpose thinking has led the modern architecture and planning movement to create many problems. Eivor Bucht (1991: 101) suggests that many ecological communities in Scandinavia may unfortunately suffer the same result because their design was not approached in a holistic manner:

> there are many more examples of negative consequences of such a one-sided ecological design. The problem is that certain ecological criteria are allowed to dominate design and deprive it of the basic principle of good urban planning and design, comprehensive thinking. Therefore I view all ecological architecture and ecological design with scepticism.

Ecology can undoubtedly become the cornerstone of the community, but ecological responsibility is by no means a single remedy for success. Too much devotion to ecological issues may lead to neglect of the very residents who are needed for the persistence of the community. While the ecological factors are crucial, so is the human aspect, which was the reason why the community was constructed in the first place.

## Conclusions

There are two conclusions I consider essential for the transition of the concept of ecological community design from theory into practice. These final points may help bridge the gap between the subjects of ecology and community design. First, in order for ecological communities to make an impact on current environmental problems, these communities must be able to transfer to existing urban areas, in addition to rural areas. Cities can be seen as a salvation for solving ecological and community design issues, but have been viewed by the public as anti-ecological. This conclusion, it may be argued, is not surprising. The literature is filled with examples proving that cities can easily adopt stronger ecological principles (Berg 1989, Girardet 1992, Gordon 1990, Hough 1984, Register 1987, among others). They argue that the city best represents the relationship between the artificial and the natural environments, and is the place where humans consume large amounts of resources, invent new technologies, affect popular culture, and constitute the largest segment of the world's present and future populations. The actions of cities have implications well beyond their own bioregions. As well, in the city it is possible to live without an automobile, thus minimizing the environmental problems associated with the automobile. For these reasons alone, the city presents the most appropriate place to begin solving current environmental problems.

In northern European countries, particularly Denmark and Germany, more and more of the ecological projects are now in cities. Designers devise efforts to restructure existing urban environments. Under the title urban ecologists, these people assist grassroots organizations and governments in changing the living environments and environmental values of city dwellers. Projects include retro-fitting buildings with environmental technologies, lobbying for more efficient transport systems, implementing waste management programs, and converting grey areas to green spaces. In Germany, these actions have been cunningly called "gentle urban renewal." The urban ecologists have found that their activities have increased community morale, reduced waste costs, created local jobs, and improved the vitality of the respective communities.

Second, the residents and designers of these ecological communities have accomplished a revival of real and practical solutions, that act as springboards for elaboration of design ideas for the future. A return to rigorous studies that bridge the gap between theory and practice is desperately needed. The residents of these communities have discovered that by applying practical solutions, they are understanding more about themselves and their environment. When compared with conventional communities — not with perfection or the utopian dream — ecological communities and what they represent can provide designers with potential development alternatives.

In short, it is the combination of the principles of ecological communities that is decisive in the creation of viable ecological communities. Establishing well-rounded ecological communities that integrate all aspects of design is not just desirable, it is also clearly possible. The experience of the northern European ecological communities proves that it is practical and attractive to support a number of interests all in one design.

# Part Five

# Municipal Eco-city Initiatives

At this point in our exploration of eco-city dimensions we examine cases of municipal eco-city initiatives. The city council of Waitakere City, New Zealand, has designated itself as an eco-city. **Melinda Laituri**, a geographer formerly at the University of Auckland, describes the incorporation of Maori concepts of resource management into the "Green-print" for the future development and growth of Waitakere City. In the context of the United Nations' Agenda 21, with its explicit recognition of indigenous rights, Waitakere City has adopted Maori concepts of resource management for issues such as environmental preservation and water quality. Laituri discusses the cross-cultural dynamics of natural resource management in Waitakere City, the role of Agenda 21 in creating the eco-city, and the arenas in which the principles for sustainability with regard to the Maori people will be tested in the future.

**Nigel Mortimer, Jon Kellett,** and **John Grant** are all affiliated with the School of Urban and Regional Studies at Sheffield Hallam University in the United Kingdom. In chapter 11, they examine municipal initiatives for promoting the use of renewable energy. The movement toward eco-cities requires that cities reduce their dependence on finite sources of energy such as fossil fuels and nuclear power. Municipal authorities and agencies play a pivotal role in the promotion of relevant initiatives, although specific approaches adopted depend strongly on the administrative framework set at the national level. Using experience gained from a collaborative research project involving participants from across the European Union, this chapter describes the opportunities for promoting renewable energy schemes in urban areas, and summarizes the key features of the innovative policies, programs, and initiatives applied by municipal authorities and agencies to assist such developments.

# 10

# Cultural Dynamics in Waitakere City
## New Zealand

Melinda Laituri

During the 1980s, New Zealand undertook a fundamental restructuring of its economy and administration. One result of this restructuring has been the development of new administrative arrangements for resource management, culminating in the adoption of the Resource Management Act (RMA) in 1991. The primary goal of the RMA is sustainable management of natural resources at a regional scale. There are no prescriptive definitions for sustainable management in the act; rather, the act allows regional and local governments to develop strategies that reflect the unique needs and requirements of their specific locality.

In 1993 Waitakere City formally adopted Agenda 21 and became New Zealand's first eco-city, the primary goal of which is to "consider our children and their children in all that we do, and working towards achieving a sustainable city" (Strategy and Development Unit 1994: 3). Waitakere City is located on the western margin of the Auckland Region, New Zealand's largest metropolitan area. The Waitakere Ranges are situated within the city's boundaries and provide an important recreational resource as well as being the major water supply catchment for the region. However, the city is experiencing all the problems associated with rapidly growing urban areas: urban sprawl, traffic congestion, and associated pressures on natural resources.

An important component of the RMA and other associated national legislation (the Treaty of Waitangi, 1840, the Maori Land Act, 1993, and the Local Government Reform Act, 1989) and of Agenda 21 is the explicit recognition of indigenous rights. Waitakere City has adopted specific strategies to achieve the mandate of this national legislation and Agenda 21 through a participatory approach to decision-making with Maori.

## Agenda 21, New Zealand National Legislation, and Maori Values

Agenda 21 and the RMA have in common the goal of sustainable development (albeit from different perspectives) and the need for changes in current growth and development patterns to be determined and defined at the community level. These goals are not incompatible with Maori values and have implications for how decision-making structures will be and need to be changed.

In 1993, Waitakere City committed itself to implementing the goals proposed in Agenda 21 — the document that was the outcome of the Earth Summit, the United Nations conference held in Brazil in 1992. In an effort to address social inequities, Agenda 21 explicitly identifies the endangered status of indigenous people throughout the world and recommends the following:

> Adopt or strengthen appropriate policies and/or legal instruments that will protect indigenous intellectual and cultural property and the right to preserve customary and administrative systems and practices (UNCED, Agenda 21, 1992).

Agenda 21 presents an international perspective of global problems, but promotes across-the-board changes to be initiated and to occur at the local community level.

Agenda 21 and recent New Zealand legislation both echo fundamental Maori principles with regard to sustainable management, which may signal reforms with regard to the use of natural resources. However, it is important to note that these principles are discrete elements from a distinct culture and represent only part of the Maori social system. The success of this system depended on social interrelationships, patterns of reciprocity, and other culturally compatible forms of organization.

"Maori values, behavior, and social organization are the basis

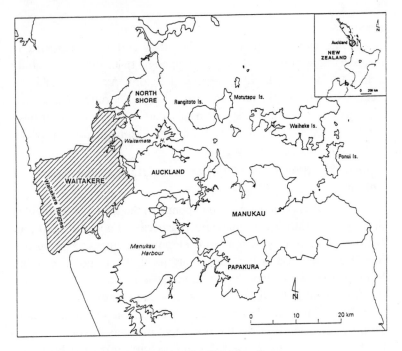

Figure 1: Location of Waitakere City

of sound social order and the common good. In this sense, common good is concerned with people's long term development and is not necessarily confined to one distinct or isolated action. It implies the well-being of all, especially the weak who benefit continually from the common good, via social, economic, and political procedures" (Manuka Henare in "Who Gets What?" New Zealand Planning Council 1990: 61-62).

There exists the potential to superimpose selected Maori values onto ideals of sustainable management — picking and choosing the most relevant aspects of Maori culture. "The argument is that, first, Maori were dispossessed of their land; now the Crown is also taking their ways of thinking" (Ballantyne and Sutherland 1994: 232).

The challenge for strategies of sustainable management are twofold: 1) that sustainable management does not represent yet another form of cooptation and colonialism of Maori into the dominant culture — that it is truly an integrated and lateral effort, and 2) that sustainable management is more than rhetoric and represents recognition, commitment, and implementation of changes to the larger socio-economic systems that direct human relations.

How, then, is Waitakere City meeting this challenge?

## Waitakere City: The Eco-City

Waitakere City is part of the Auckland Region which is also includes the cities of Manukau, North Shore, and Auckland (Figure 1). It covers approximately 39,134 hectares and is dominated by the Waitakere Ranges. The ranges provide a major recreational resource to the Auckland region as well as being the source of one third of the region's domestic water supply.

Waitakere City is the sixth largest city in New Zealand (population: 136,716) and has experienced the country's largest increase in population during the period 1986 to 1993 (Statistics NZ 1991). In 1991, 74 per cent of residents stated their ethnic group as European, 11 per cent as Maori, and the remaining identifying themselves as Pacific Islander or Other (Strategy and Development Unit 1994). In 1991, five per cent of Waitakere City's population held a qualification from university and 30 per cent held no qualification of any kind. Waitakere City ranks third among the four cities in terms of average personal income for adults at $NZ19,086 per annum (Statistics NZ 1991).

Within Waitakere City there are several regionally and nationally important ecosystems. The original podocarp-hardwood and kauri (Agathis australis) forest have been significantly altered. The predominantly tawa (Beilschmiedia tawa) forest canopy punctuated by regenerating kauri, rimu (Dacrydium cupressinum), rata (Metrosideros robusta), and totara (Podocarpus totara) cover a large part of the ranges. However, there are significant areas covered in the transient habitat of kanuka (Kunzea ericoides) and manuka (Leptospermum scoparium) scrub. As regeneration of the forest occurs, second-growth forests are supporting an increasingly diverse range of plant and animal species (Bishop 1992).

## Eco-City Strategies

The mission of Waitakere City is to become the Waitakere eco-city, *Te Taiao o Waitakere* (Figure 2). Since adopting the principles of Agenda 21, Waitakere City has developed several strategies with regard to Maori, including 1) the integration of Maori language and principles in policy documents; 2) the creation of explicit policies with regard to Maori; and 3) implementation of policy — establishment of the Maori Issues Unit, hiring of staff, and establishment of *Te Taumata Runanga* (Maori Perspectives Committee).

| Figure 2: Mission, goals, and principles ||
| Te Teiao o Waitakere | Waitakere eco-city |
| --- | --- |
| Kia mau tonunga tikanga | sustainable |
| whakahirahira | dynamic |
| tino rangatiratanga | just |
| | |
| nga tikanga | principles |
| | |
| Kia pono Kiangawari | open honest communication |
| Kia m_m_nga wawata | responsiveness |
| Ko te whanau hei titiro | accountability |
| Kia haere Kotahi | partnership |
| Kia KamaKama | innovation |
| Kia tino at_ahua | excellence |
| Kia haere t_tika i roto i te rangimarie | integrity |
| Source: Waitakere City Council, Annual Plan 1994/95: 4-5. ||

**Maori principles and language** Waitakere City has prepared several documents that include discussion of Maori principles and use of Maori language. The Waitakere City Annual Plan 1994/5 provides the mayor's introductory message and the city's mission statement in both Maori and English; however, the rest of the document is in English only. Other documents, "Environmental Issues: An Overview" and the Draft Waitakere City Greenprint, include specific discussion of Maori values. "Environmental Issues" provides an overview of *tangata whenua* (people of the land) and the principles that direct their relationship with the environment. It states:

> There is common ground in their [Maori] world view and the concerns other groups in the city have about the environment. Council has begun to look more carefully at the views of *tangata whenua* and to share the management of re-

sources...which will provide a basis for the continued shared development of environmental policy in the city (Waitakere City Council 1993a: 7).

A key goal the city council faces is how and to what extent development and management of the city's environmental policy will be shared with *tangata whenua*. The mechanisms to achieve this goal are addressed within the Draft Waitakere City Greenprint discussed below.

**Explicit policies with regard to Maori** Waitakere City's strategic plan is described in "City Futures: Stategic Directions." This document describes the various policies to be implemented to ensure the participation and inclusion of Maori in the decision-making process. In the strategic plan, "Tanaga Whenua: the Treaty of Waitangi and Maori Residents" is identified as one of nine key action platforms.[1] The key action platform describes the policies, targets, and actions of the city council (Table 1) and includes such things as identification and response to issues related to the treaty and relevant legislation, liaison with Maori community to ensure equitable services and to consolidate the role of *Te Taumata Runanga* (Maori Perspectives Committee).

The Draft Waitakere Greenprint has served to consolidate many of the ideals and goals discussed in the strategic plan and previous policy documents. It is a guide to the development of policies as mandated by Agenda 21, the Treaty of Waitangi, the Local Government Reform Act (LGRA), and the RMA. The Draft Waitakere City Greenprint identifies several key focus areas with guiding principles and economic, social and environmental issues and goals. It has significant reference to *tangata whenua* in the following key focus areas: a) council's relationship with other parties (other parties identified as the national and regional governments, *tangata whenua* and the rest of the community); b) communities (to create partnerships by providing access to information and forum for debate through consultation, dialogue and advocacy); and c) *taonga* (treasure) — to recognize the role of *kaitiaki* (guardianship) and *taonga* as the economic base for *iwi* (tibe).

**Council's relationship with other parties** Waitakere City Council recognizes a special relationship with *tangata whenua*. It is responsible for giving effect to the Treaty of Waitangi and other national legislation (RMA and LGRA) which requires that Council

**Table 1: Key Action Platform 7 — Tangata Whenua:
The Treaty of Waitangi and Maori residents**

*Overview*
- Recognition of the rights and special interests of *tangata whenua* and Maori generally has developed significantly in the last few years. Provisions of the Resource Management Act, the Local Government Amendment Act, and the Transit NZ Act require the Council to work with *tangata whenua*, and to liaise meaningfully with Maori interest groups.

*Eco-City*
- Fundamental to the eco-city concept is sustainable management of the environment in liaison with those most directly affected including *tangata whenua*.

*Policies*
- Identify and respond to the issues arising from the Treaty of Waitangi and relevant legislative obligations to Maori, as they affect the city.
- Recognize *Te Kawerau a Maki* and *Ngati Whatua* as having *tangata whenua* status within Waitakere City.
- Liaise to ensure services are equitable to the Maori community.
- Consolidate the role of the *Taumata Runanga* (Maori Perspectives Committee).
- Include in the systematic annual review of services a review of services to the Maori community.

*Targets*
- Effective communication with *tangata whenua*.
- In consultation with tangata whenua, appropriate protection of their significant sites.
- Effective response to legal obligations, including resourcing *iwi* plans.
- Equitable service to the Maori community.

*Actions*
- Continue efforts to develop effective communication between Council and Maori.
- Recognize Maori needs in staffing structure.
- Consultation with *tangata whenua* and Maori on matters of significance to Maori and the council.
- Sponsor facilities that teach *Te-Reo-Maori*.
- Provide personnel and grants for *iwi* plans.
- Carry out joint projects with key Maori agencies particularly with respect to environmental, tourism, and related projects.

Source: Waitakere City Council, "City Futures: Strategic Directions," December 1993: 64.

must explicitly have regard to Maori as partners. Waitakere City recognizes two *iwi* (tribes), *Te Kawerau a Maki* and *Ngati Whatua*, as having *tangata whenua* status within the city. However, the long coastline of the city means that the interests of other *iwi* must also be considered. Council must also recognize the special rights and interests of other Maori living or working in the city.

The Greenprint identifies the first duty of council as being the responsibility to establish processes for shared decision making, communication, and consultation with Maori to "help ensure that Maori values and interests are integrated in everything Council does" (Waitakere City Council 1994b: 20).

**Communities** To achieve the goal of shared decision making, the council has established a Maori Issues Unit and *Te Taumata Runanga* (discussed below). Other initiatives include an annual review of services to the Maori community, provision of grants for *iwi* management plans, protecting sites of significance to *iwi*, and joint projects with Maori agencies.

**Taonga** The Maori principle of *taonga* has been adopted as a key focus area in the Greenprint. *Taonga* refers to the community's greatest treasures, including forests, seas, rivers, animals, humans, and the health of the environment. The Greenprint is explicit in recognizing the holistic nature of this principle — "*taonga* does not stand alone" (Waitakere City Council 1994b: 57).

> The focus of this chapter [*taonga*] is on those things in the environment which people see and therefore value. This in only one part of environmental management — the other part concerns looking after those things which people do not directly experience but which are essential to a healthy environment (Waitakere City Council 1994b: 57).

With regard to *tangata whenua*, the Greenprint describes three aspects of *taonga*:

> > to recognize the vital role of *kaitiaki* (those selected by the tribe to act as stewards of the *taonga*) in safeguarding the health of the physical and spiritual environment, and their rights to act as *kaitiaki* under the Treaty of Waitangi (Waitekere City Council, 1994b: 59);
> > to recognize the *taonga* are the economic base for *iwi*, and that *iwi* have the preeminent role in achieving the sustainable

management of their *taonga* (Waitakere City Council, 1994b: 61);
> to protect and restore *taonga*, because this will reinforce and
strengthen the *mana* of *whanua, hapu* (sub-tribe) and *iwi* and
to achieve community recognition of the role of *iwi* and of
*kaitiaki* in the use and protection of the natural environment
(Waitakere City Council 1994b, p. 62).

How these goals will be achieved remains largely undetermined
to date; however, the fact that they are recognized in the Greenprint
represents an important step. Implementation of these goals and
policies are beginning to be addressed with the establishment of the
Maori Issues Unit and *Te Taumata Runanga*.

## Policy implementation

Policy implementation has occurred through the establishment of
the Maori Issues unit, the hiring of staff with specifically designated
responsibilities with regard to Maori issues, and the creation of the
*Te Taumata Runanga*.

**The Maori Issues Unit**  The Maori Issues Unit is a separate unit
within the functional organization of Waitakere City and was established in 1994. Its fundamental goal is to ensure that the city council
meets its moral obligation to fulfill the mandate of the Treaty of
Waitangi. The Unit's purpose is to advise, liaison, train, target,
provide information, and assist in meeting the needs and concerns
of Maori (Table 2). In general, according to Wallace Paki, Maori
Issues Coordinator, Maori are concerned with the social implications
of all aspects of council activity. The key issues identified in a
management workshop are:
> creating appropriate targeted training programs;
> achieving a base level compliance in Council's legislative
requirements;
> providing protocol and cultural advice to elected members and
management;
> ensuring that a structured approach which addresses all Maori
issues is built into the management of all projects;
> developing a strategic direction for *Te Taumata Runanga*
involvement in Council's issues; and
> improving service delivery to Maori (Maori Issues Unit 1995b).

**Staff**  The Maori Issues Unit is composed of three staff members,
with one position shared between the Maori Issues Unit and the

| Table 2: Responsibilities for environmental management for the Maori Issues Unit ||
| Issue identified in Annual Plan | Maori Unit Role |
| --- | --- |
| Treaty of Waitangi | —Advise all units on council obligations under the terms of the Treaty. Provide advice to Councillors on treaty obligations. |
| Sewage and storm water<br>Water supply<br>Solid waste<br>Roading traffic and transport<br>Parks and other leisure activities | —Advise on significant Maori issues as affected by drainage, discharge of sewage, water catchment, solid waste disposal.<br>—Liaise with iwi on Annual Plan issues as they affect iwi and provide feedback to Unit. |
| Business development and promotion | —Promote Greenprint and eco-city principles to iwi<br>—Provide information on special needs on Maori employment and training<br>—Identify tourism potential/needs and advise unit. |
| Resource management<br>Building control<br>Environmental health and safety | —Liaise with iwi on resource issues for District Plan change, land information and property information.<br>—Advise unit and iwi on RMA, Building Act 1991 as they affect Maori people.<br>Liaise with iwi on noise control, dog control, noxious weeds, pollution control, food safety, where relevant to iwi.<br>—Ensure Maori taonga, historic sites, artifacts are noted and preserved. |
| Civic | —Assist mayor and councillors with protocol, speeches.<br>—Liaise with Te Taumata Runanga. |
| District Plan | —Provide advice on issues affecting iwi. |
| Performance measurement | —Ensure annual plan objectives and other major projects as they affect Maori are managed efficiently and effectively. |
| EEO | —Participate in staff training on bicultural issues. |
| Adapted from Maori Issues Unit: Responsibilities Memo 1995a. ||

Strategy and Development Unit.

**Te Taumata Runanga** *Te Taumata Runanga* or Maori Perspectives Committee is a standing committee which has representatives of *iwi*, local *marae* and local boards. Within the functional organization of Waitakere City *Te Taumata Runanga* is a part of the Mayor and Council on par with the Chief Executive Officer. The major role of the committee is to ensure that Maori values are upheld in Council decision-making, that Council can meet obligations to the *tangata whenua* and that Council will provide effective services for Maori residents. It is the responsibility of the committee to regularize communication between Maori and Council, to ensure Council is aware of and sensitive to issues of concern to the *tangata whenua* and local Maori people, and to provide Council with a structure to facilitate input into Council's decisions that have cultural significance to Maori people. Representatives are elected for a three-year term.

An important component of the eco-city mandate and national legislation is to recognize and have regard for Maori issues. This is occurring through several activities: the inclusion of Maori values in policy documents and in the development and implementation of policy. The City Council proclaimed Waitakere City an eco-city in February of 1993; it is as yet too early to ascertain the success of these policies in addressing Maori concerns. However, there are several issues that will provide a testing arena.

## Conclusion

New Zealand is unique in some respects due to the fact that the RMA institutionalizes the concept of sustainable management. This national legislation and the adoption of Agenda 21 make Waitakere City a leader in the creation of sustainable cities. Waitakere City is still in the infancy of implementing and determining the viability of different policies for sustainable management. Recently, Waitakere City hosted an international seminar on the issue of sustainable cities to establish the need for a unified and cohesive set of policies which would allow cities to grow.

Specific issues that will provide a testing arena for the sustainable management include streams, the coast, heritage, and the countryside. Specifically, issues related to bodies of water must address the concerns of *tangata whenua* who oppose direct water-based disposal of pollutants and sewage. Maori have specific cultural expectations with regard to water, including the maintenance of unpolluted water and access to traditional fishing grounds (Strategy and Development 1993d). Coastal management issues would include not only the question of waste disposal, but also *kaitiakitanga* (stewardship), *waahi tapu* (sacred sites), *mahinga maataitai* (food resource areas), *taonga raranga* (cultural plants), and *kaimoana* (seafood) (Strategy and Development 1993a). Heritage issues involve both archaeological sites and sites of spiritual significance. Definitions of spiritual integrity need to be developed to identify and protect such areas. Heritage issues are related to development of policy with regard to the countryside.

It is necessary to identify any sites of importance to the *tangata whenua* and to ensure that their customs and traditions will be respected when policy for the future of the countryside area is developed. Little is known of the relationships of *tangata whenua* to the land in the countryside area, and if there are sites of special value, protection may be necessary (Strategy and Development Unit 1993b: 19).

The relationship of *tangata whenua* is well understood in the historic sense; what remains poorly understood is the Maori relationship to the landscape as modified by Europeans. These issues provide the basis for application of policies for sustainable management and implementation of the RMA in a dynamic situation. Waitakere City has chosen to accept the challenge of becoming an eco-city; its success or failure will need to be assessed in the next few years.

# 11

# Municipal Initiatives for Promoting the Use of Renewable Energy

## Nigel D. Mortimer, Jon E. Kellett and John F. Grant

The development of sustainable cities has been emerging as a fundamental policy aim over the past few years. The concept of the sustainable city covers a vast range of issues, many related to including the provision of energy in a sustainable manner.

Cities are energy-hungry, yet few provide for their own needs. Most import energy from surrounding areas, quite often from long distances, thus imposing the environmental impacts of energy production on other regions. In addition to this spatial separation of conventional energy supply and demand, the bulk of energy consumed in cities is provided by non-renewable sources such as coal, oil, natural gas, and uranium for nuclear power. All are depletable resources, the utilization of which not only causes a reduction in the total stock of energy available for future generations, but also results in significant environmental implications.

Studies have shown that in many cities, there is considerable scope for improving energy efficiency (Newcastle City Council 1992, and Organization for Economic Cooperation and Development 1995). Relevant measures include better thermal insulation and the use of low energy appliances. New buildings can take account of orientation, design characteristics, and choice of fabric to ensure that as much solar energy as possible is captured and utilized, and heat loss minimized. Existing buildings can be retrofitted with passive solar energy technology such as conservatories and Trombe walls to gain similar benefits. Both new and existing buildings can be fitted with active solar collectors for space and water heating, and photovoltaic cells for electricity generation.

The movement of people and goods within and between cities is a second major use of energy. A sustainable transport policy would, therefore, seek to minimize the need to travel, and shorten the length of trips, for example, by ensuring that more people live close to their place of employment. Reducing dependency on the private automobile is imperative, and encouraging the use of public transport and other forms of alternative transportation is a further vital aspect of sustainability.

Finally, cities can seek to relieve the environmental burden they place on other areas by localizing energy production, and reducing reliance on fossil fuels by substitution of renewable energy sources. The development of indigenous renewable energy sources, such as solar, wind, hydro, geothermal and biomass, is an essential part of this process. Biomass, in the form of agricultural or forestry wastes, municipal wastes or specially-grown crops, is a particularly important stored type of renewable energy which can supply space heating and cooling needs in urban areas by means of shared distribution networks, to generate electricity or to provide transport fuels.

Achieving progress in these three main policy areas depends crucially on a number of factors. First, the availability of proven, reliable technology is a vital prerequisite of progress. In all of the areas discussed, technology is sufficiently advanced to conclude that the policy aims are technically feasible. However, the existence of proven technology alone is not sufficient to ensure its utilization. A second factor to be considered is the economics of such technologies, which have to be seen to be competitive with established and conventional options in order for substitution to take place. Depending on technical maturity, the existence of temporary subsidies and financial incentives, and localized factors influencing the price of conventional and alternative systems, some of these technologies are economically feasible now, while others will only become so in the future.

Third, a variety of nontechnical considerations must also be taken into account. These considerations are equally important in determining the pace and direction of sustainable development, and include social and environmental acceptability, organizational, financial, and legal implications. All of these nontechnical issues fall within the scope of planning. Although planning in the specific sense is applied to individual developments, it also plays an integral role in merging individual developments into a cohesive whole intended to achieve a given policy goal, such as sustainability.

Finally, political will is vital if progress is to be made, and this must be supported by an appropriate institutional framework for translating both vision and will into the reality of practical action. Hence, despite the fact that technology is often internationally transferable, its implementation as part of a comprehensive policy depends on the prevailing national and local framework of economic, financial, social, environmental, legal, political and organizational conditions. Consequently, it is argued that the equal consideration of all relevant factors, rather than only technical ones, presents the main challenge to achieving sustainability in cities.

## Comparative Studies in Sustainability

It is important to examine the procedures adopted to promote sustainable development in different countries with diverse policy frameworks for a number of reasons. In particular, it enables common problems to be identified, and effective solutions to be reported. Sharing practical experience and innovative approaches is essential both within and between countries. A considerable amount of work has been conducted on case studies, especially in connection with urban energy management and the reduction of carbon dioxide emissions.

For example, the Organization for Economic Cooperation and Development (OECD) has recently published an Urban Energy Handbook which contains case studies of good practice from over 40 cities in 16 countries (OECD 1995). Similarly, the International Council for Local Environmental Initiatives (ICLEI) has produced material based on approaches for municipal and other authorities to Local Agenda 21 (Jessup, Hamm, and Fraser 1993). Additionally, case studies are often adopted in various guides for local authority action on sustainable development and global climate change (Parr 1994, and Welbank 1994). However, the usefulness of case studies is limited unless they also explain the context within which specific policies are formulated and implemented. Additionally, it is essential to formulate and describe general principles so that similar approaches can be applied elsewhere.

In the European Union (EU) and elsewhere, international projects have been established to evaluate aspects of sustainable development from this broader policy perspective. Particularly good examples of this can be found in work on renewable energy development funded by Directorate General XII of the Commission of the European Communities. Although sustainable development may not be an explicitly stated aim of such work, these projects clearly emphasize the need to formulate practical mechanisms for promoting the widespread use of renewable energy technologies (which is recognized as one essential component of sustainable development).

Although several projects have been funded, the one described herein is entitled "Development of an Integration Scheme for Renewable Energies in Municipalities, Taking into Account the Interfaces between the Municipality and Surround Region" (Contract Reference No. JOU2-CT92-0117). This project was conducted between December 1, 1992 and April 30, 1995, and was coordinated by the Centrum Neue Technologie (Centre for New Technology: CENET) in Munich, Germany. The municipality of Verona in Italy was the main contractor, and the project also involved partners from Hamburg, Germany, Storström County, Denmark, and Newcastle-upon-Tyne, Sheffield, and Southampton in the United Kingdom.

## Municipal Integration of Renewable Energy

The goals of this particular project were to: 1) investigate and describe procedures for assessing the potential of renewable energy sources to contribute to managing energy demand and supply within given municipalities, 2) determine existing and potential relationships between municipalities and their surrounding regions, in terms of the balance of energy supply and demand, and 3) evaluate strategies for increasing the use of renewable energy sources.

These goals were attained by establishing a number of tasks, defined by CENET, for every partner which included:

> providing a basic description of the municipality and surrounding region under consideration, estimating the current total energy demand and its pattern by sector and fuel type, elaborating the current structure of energy supply,

> investigating prospective energy efficiency improvements and their possible impact on future total energy demand, assessing the local potential of renewable energy resources in relation to their technical aspects, economic costs and environmental benefits,
> explaining the technical and nontechnical considerations for the practical deployment of renewable energy technologies,
> summarizing essential features of actual local energy schemes, postponed or failed projects and new proposals,
> describing the organizational structures or networks involved in local energy management and development, and
> outlining existing or possible strategies for encouraging the use of renewable energy.

Progress reports on these tasks, along with supplementary reports on particular issues, were produced by each partner during the course of the project. In addition, a final report, recording all relevant experience and establishing the basis for a general integration scheme, was prepared by CENET at the end of the project.

In addition to specific aims, a number of other important concerns were addressed. In particular, emphasis was placed on the description and explanation of methodologies applied, as well as on the results they produced. The essential features of some of these methodologies have been reported elsewhere (Newcastle City Council 1992; Grant, Kellett, and Mortimer 1994). The nature and availability of local sources of data was also key. Since data sources can vary even within the same country, it was difficult to devise common methodologies which could be adopted in other situations. Considerable progress was achieved by ensuring that standard terms and definitions were used, and by recognizing that different methods were required to obtain different degrees of detail and accuracy in results.

The following sections summarize the principal features of the strategies applied by each of the partners in the project to exemplify how each community and region met the aims and completed the tasks of the project.

## Renewable Energy Integration in Verona

As the main contractor on this project, work in Verona was undertaken by the Azienda Generale Servize Municipalizzati del Comune di Verona (General Municipal Utilities Agency: AGSM), one of four public agencies owned by the municipal authority. It is responsible for, amongst other activities, energy supply and management. AGSM operates five fossil fuel-fired co-generation plants which supply both district heating and electricity within Verona, and a hydro power scheme located in the surrounding region. AGSM also operates four district heating networks in Verona, has 45 per cent ownership in a power only plant, and is involved in a number of renewable energy developments including solar photovoltaic power schemes. AGSM does not provide all the electricity consumed in Verona; the rest is supplied by the Italian Electrical Company, ENEL, via the national grid. Private companies provide other fuels such as natural gas and petroleum products. AGSM plans to construct a municipal waste incineration plant which will produce heat and electricity in Verona.

Although AGSM is only responsible for the supply of part of the total energy demand in Verona, it could exert considerable influence on the use of renewable energy supply within the municipality and surrounding area. In particular, its operation of district heating networks, and its involvement in electricity generation could enable AGSM to encourage the dissemination of renewable energy technologies throughout the existing energy supply system. Cooperation with other municipally-owned agencies, including waste collection and public transport, provide opportunities for integrating initiatives into complementary strategies. This would be specifically relevant to developing municipal waste incineration schemes for heat and electricity production, and for promoting energy efficiency in the transport sector.

The municipality can influence private development to a certain degree through the Town Plan, which affects land use zoning. However, historical, architectural, and landscape factors must be taken into account in a large portion of the city. Restrictions on private development can be imposed by relevant national and provincial agencies in these areas. The major obstacles to renewable energy development in Verona are economic, legal, and political, rather than technical. The availability of adequate capital investment is an essential consideration, although various financial incentives and subsidies seem to exist, supported by relevant national legislation. It is recognized that greater coordination is required to promote renewable energy development, both within the municipality, and between the municipality and the surrounding region. This would potentially involve the creation of an appropriate agency to formulate relevant plans, influence regulations, provide information, offer incentives, and organize financing.

## Renewable Energy Integration in Hamburg

The direct involvement of municipal authorities in energy supply is relatively common in Germany, and in this respect, there are some similarities between Verona and Hamburg. Work on this project was undertaken by Consulectra Unternehmensberatung GmbH which is a consultancy company currently advising the Hamburgische Electricitts-Werke AG (HEW). Electricity is supplied in Hamburg by HEW, 71 per cent of which is owned by the municipality. HEW operates four nuclear power stations, five fossil fuel-fired co-generation plants, and a number of peak load power plants. The co-generation plants with additional peak load boilers feed one of the largest district heating networks in the EU. Additionally, other companies, such as the municipally-owned gas utility (HGW), have fossil fuel-fired boilers supplying the district heating network. A municipal waste incineration district heating plant has also recently been completed by a subsidiary of HEW.

HEW is engaged in renewable energy development, as well as energy efficiency improvements and demand-side management, through Energiekonzept Zukunft (Energy Concept Future). A number of wind power schemes are operating, under construction or planned in Hamburg and the surrounding region. HGW and the municipality have built individual and communal solar heating schemes, are planning new developments (consisting of heat storage and network facilities and landfill gas and biogas developments), are actively investigating the use of geothermal and biomass energy for heating and co-generation, and are constructing a pumped storage plant in the surrounding region. As part of the Euro Quebec Hydropower Hydrogen Program, HEW, HGW, and other partners are involved in a research project for producing, transporting, and using hydrogen derived from renewable energy sources in fuel cells for electricity generation. This is a promising development since hydrogen could become an important storage medium and carrier for energy from renewable sources in the future.

The most prominent aspect of renewable energy development in Hamburg is the solar photovoltaic project, which supplies electricity into the local grid and provides power for a small fleet of electric vehicles. This scheme is supported by the federal government's "1,000 Roof Program" for promoting a market in solar photovoltaic cells, to in turn encourage prices to fall in the long run. Indeed, there is strong support at the national level for renewable energy development and energy efficiency improvements in general. Both federal and municipal subsidies exist, and HEW operates credit schemes locally. One of the most successful national means for promoting renewable energy technologies has been the Einspeisegesetz ("Grid Feeding Law"), which provides substantial economic incentives.

Problems with financing can be overcome by various mechanisms. One means is to include cooperative ventures and contracting schemes which only require customers to pay for heat supplied, without involving them in investment arrangements for new infrastructure and equipment. A training center for local advisers and installers of renewable energy technology is also in place. In other cities in Germany, such as Saarbrücken, "Energy Shops" exist to provide energy efficiency and renewable energy information, demonstration, and advice. Such initiatives promote confidence among consumers to invest in these small scale technologies.

## Renewable Energy Strategy in Storström County

The importance of a supporting national policy for local renewable energy development is reiterated by the experience of another partner in the project, Storström County. This experience was reported by the county authority, Storström amt, assisted by the Roskilde University Centre. Renewable energy development has been encouraged in Denmark since 1981. Danish energy policy provides support through economic, legal, and planning measures. The National Plan for Action, entitled "Energy 2000: Plan of Action for Sustainable Development," is supplemented by other plans, laws, and regulations. A subsidy system linked to a carbon dioxide tax promotes energy efficiency. Substantial increases in the use of renewable energy sources have been achieved.

In Storström County, composed of 24 municipalities, renewable energy sources, mainly consisting of straw, wood, and waste, accounted for 18 per cent of delivered heat and electricity in 1993. Subsidies are in place for the construction of a combined heat and power plant. Each municipality devises local heating plans which are approved by national authorities and aid in increasing the profile of district heating schemes. There are now 19 district heating companies locally, some of which are owned by municipalities. These networks assist the introduction of diverse, small-scale renewable energy schemes. Solar heating has been promoted in Storström County since 1989, and there is a planning procedure for wind power development identifying areas for potential single turbines or wind farms.

Traditional common ownership arrangements also assist the spread of wind power and other renewable energy technologies in Denmark. Some private wind power companies are cooperatives, and regulations encourage local people to become members. However, due to the attraction of financial subsidies, it is necessary to limit shareholdings and the number of members. The specific benefit of local ownership means that those who bear the local environmental burden, such as visual impact, are compensated.

Cooperative ownership also extends, at present, to the main local electricity company, SEAS. Electricity production and investment plans for this and other companies are formulated by Elkraft Amba which is also a cooperative. Subsidies are available for constructing certain types of renewable energy initiatives, and their output can be economically competitive with the prices of conventional fuels and electricity, due to substantial carbon dioxide taxes. The Danish credit system can finance their construction. A number of national centers provide advice and demonstrate renewable energy technologies, and the Storström Energy Service offers training on topics such as the marketing and installation of solar heating systems.

## Renewable Energy Activities in the United Kingdom

Fundamental differences in national energy policy and the role of local authorities disallow similar approaches to the municipal use of renewable energy technologies to be adopted in the United Kingdom. Although there are many obstacles to renewable energy development in municipalities, activities in Newcastle-upon-Tyne, Sheffield, and Southampton demonstrate that progress is possible. This project was undertaken in these locations by Newcastle City Council, the Newcastle Photovoltaics Applications Centre of the University of Northumbria, Sheffield Heat and Power, the Resources Research Unit of Sheffield Hallam University, Southampton City Council, the Southampton Environment Centre and Richmond Walker Associates.

Current development of the renewable energy industry in the

United Kingdom is principally due to the Non-Fossil Fuel Obligation (NFFO). Initially established to provide subsidies for nuclear power as a result of privatization of the rest of the electricity supply industry, the NFFO now indirectly fosters the growth of electricity generation from renewable energy sources. However, the NFFO does not provide incentives for renewable energy technologies which do not produce electricity. Additionally, most of the initiatives established under the NFFO are located in rural areas and involve private companies.

However, a number of local authorities have launched significant urban energy management and development initiatives, even though such activities are not regarded as part of their normal role. This is an innovative approach, assisting in the formulation of networks of commercial developers, planners, financiers, and other key participants to promote local energy initiatives.

In some cases, local authorities have become primary shareholders in private companies created to achieve specific local objectives. Particularly relevant examples are the planning and construction of district heating schemes which, by their nature, integrate the use of a variety of heat sources, including renewable energy sources. In Newcastle-upon-Tyne, municipal waste is processed into fuel pellets, providing heat in an existing district heating network. An expanded district heating system is planned to link together major heat loads to be supplied by a combined cycle natural gas-fired heat and power plant, supplemented by other heat sources.

In Sheffield, a large municipal waste incinerator supplies the heat for an expanding district heating network. Sheffield Heat and Power operates the network, in which Sheffield City Council has a minority shareholding. To use excess steam when supply exceeds demand, an electricity co-generation plant is being added to the waste incinerator with the assistance of a NFFO license. As a result of an initiative by Southampton City Council, a local district heating plan has been established to exploit geothermal energy in Southampton. The initiative is operated by the privately-owned Southampton Geothermal Heating Company, and they plan to expand to include other heat sources such as biogas.

A solar photovoltaic cladding demonstration initiative in Newcastle-upon-Tyne is a further significant achievement. There are numerous opportunities for local authorities to become involved in such initiatives to disseminate ideas, and promote the use of renewable energy. Despite limited powers and financial resources, local authorities in the United Kingdom can assist renewable energy development in many ways. Apart from coordinating disparate activities and bringing together commercial developers and other interested parties to establish specific projects, local authorities can influence renewable energy development through the planning system. National planning guidelines are available for renewable energy schemes (Department of the Environment 1993) and local development plans can be used in a pro-active manner by specifying those areas where renewable energy schemes could be regarded favorably (Kellett 1994b). Opportunities also exist through the building regulations, and local authorities are uniquely placed to assist the integration of planning, waste management, and transport policies (Kellett 1994a).

## Comments and Conclusions

Despite diverse national circumstances and policy frameworks, this basic comparison of experiences from a number of EU member states demonstrates that those who wish to promote the increased use of renewable energy technologies can achieve significant progress if they are sufficiently determined, committed, and innovative. Although a single common approach to the promotion of renewable energy technologies cannot be formulated, it is possible to identify certain important actions which can assist with this aspect of sustainable development.

First, clear aims and objectives for expanding the use of renewable energy technologies must be established in broad policy terms. This could include goals such as improving local air quality, decreasing reliance on fossil fuels and nuclear power, or reducing greenhouse gas emissions.

Second, political commitment and will is required to ensure that broad policy objectives can be translated into practical action and real developments. Once committed to the established aims, municipal authorities should ensure that the promotion of energy efficiency and renewable energy development is incorporated into local development plans. Where possible, they should integrate apparently separate policies in a complementary manner to achieve common goals. They should also assist the development of urban energy management and renewable energy schemes, either directly by forming appropriate agencies, or indirectly by coordinating networks of commercial companies and other relevant participants. It must be acknowledged that municipal authorities, commercial developers, and all other interested parties should be prepared to be innovative and learn from the experiences of other towns and cities, both nationally and internationally.

A third requirement is that local assessments of current and possible future energy supply and demand, including the prospects for energy efficiency improvements and the potential of renewable energy resources, be conducted and evaluated in terms of chosen policy objectives. Particular emphasis should be given to constructing appropriate energy systems in urban areas, especially district heating schemes which can incorporate a variety of different renewable energy sources.

Finally, the involvement of local people should be encouraged in every aspect of renewable energy development, especially financial ownership. Education through demonstration initiatives, information centers, and training facilities is therefore needed to foster public confidence in renewable energy technologies, especially those intended for use by individual households and small communities. All of these considerations are imperative in the movement toward sustainable energy planning and use, as demonstrated by the various partners in the CENET project. The need to consider all relevant factors, technology, economical feasibility, political and institutional frameworks, strategic planning, and public acceptability, is unequivocal, yet still remains the greatest challenge to achieving sustainability in cities.

# A RIVER OF TRAFFIC
## (AND ITS TRIBUTARIES)

# Part Six

# Assessing Our Progress

*The final section of our exploration of eco-city dimensions concerns how we assess our progress.* **Elizabeth Kline**, *Director of the Consortium for Regional Sustainability at Tufts University, near Boston, addresses the question of sustainable community indicators — what and how to measure progress. A sustainable community embodies four characteristics: economic security, ecological integrity, quality of life, and empowerment with responsibility. Kline describes each of these aspects separately and illustrates with examples from case studies developed to define and give some tangible meaning to the characteristics. In addition, she presents specific categories of what to measure for each characteristic. By understanding and using this framework, she argues, people can figure out for themselves what is wrong in their communities and what they want to do and have others do differently.*

*    **Jennie Moore**, *coordinator of Vancouver's Eco-city Network, has participated in developing local government vision statements, plans and policies to guide our communities toward a sustainable future. Why, she asks, do so many initiatives for sustainability fail to produce the type of changes necessary for a healthy community? To find out, she interviewed 51 citizens and officials familiar with Vancouver's highly regarded Clouds of Change Report to discover what barriers impeded implementation of the report's recommendations. Moore found three kinds of obstacles hinder eco-city change: perceptual or behavioral barriers, institutional or structural barriers, and economic or financial barriers. She concludes her chapter with strategies for overcoming these barriers.*

# 12

# Sustainable Community Indicators
## How to Measure Progress

### Elizabeth Kline

What motivates people in communities to change their economic strategies? Is it loss of jobs, out-migration of young adults, pollution and resulting health effects from certain industries, or insecurity from dependence on one major employer? What actions are taken to improve a community's environment? Are more wetlands or open spaces acquired, more health centers built in neighborhoods, or more incentives offered to businesses to prevent pollutants from being emitted into the air, water, or on the land?

How do people know if they are successful in their actions? Do they have more satisfying jobs, less violent crime on their streets, safer water to drink, or have more time to enjoy their families? The answers to these questions depend on the particular circumstances of each community, but they share a common focus on what and how to measure progress.

This chapter explains the value of developing and applying sustainable community indicators, describes what topic areas are most useful to measure, and suggests some specific indicators for each topic area to illustrate what people might choose to use in their own communities.

## The Value of Indicators

The most fundamental purpose for developing and applying sustainable community indicators is to help people in communities deal constructively with change. Communities vary considerably in terms of the influence of outside forces upon them and their ability to take control. No community is or can be self-sufficient, given today's economic, political, environmental, and social forces (Robinson and Tinker 1995).

Yet, through deliberate thought and actions people can become more self-reliant and can channel development to serve human and nonhuman interests both for the short and long term. Brendan Whittaker, Northern Forest Project director with the Vermont Natural Resources Council, expressed this sentiment in his article describing the predicament of people living in forested northern New England communities: "Like it or not, change is coming to the northern forest. Those of us who live here must help to guide it; otherwise the land that we love and our way of life will be swept aside in the rush, as has happened so tragically in other parts of the world" (Whittaker n.d.: 2).

Development of sustainable community indicators can provide a theoretical and practical framework for defining the meaning of a sustainable community and for measuring progress towards that goal (Hart 1995). People need a reality check to ensure that incremental steps are moving in desired directions and to hold and be held accountable for choices that individuals and collective entities make (Putnam 1994, 1995).

Sustainable community indicators can enable comparisons among communities, but are most valuable when measuring a community with itself over time (Oregon Progress Board 1992, Sustainable Seattle 1993). Indicators enable decision-makers and taxpayers to understand how well their investments are working and where changes are needed and desired.

Probably the greatest contribution of indicators is that hidden agendas, unanticipated consequences, successful efforts on undesired pathways, and inadequate sensitivity and responsiveness for concerns of all members of a community are revealed and can be addressed. The state of Minnesota discovered these lessons in developing its "Minnesota Milestones" in 1992. In its introduction entitled "Choosing our Future," the Minnesota Planning Department wrote, "Historically, government has done a poor job of measuring results. It does an excellent job of measuring how much activity occurs; how much money is spent, how many forms are filed, how many reports are prepared, how many permits are issued. But government is less successful at measuring results of those activities — whether they resulted in a safer or cleaner environment or a better life for Minnesota's citizens" (Minnesota Planning Board 1992:1).

In the development and choice of indicators people will discover what is important to them. Discussions about possible indicators and selection of priority indicators reflect the meaning of a community based on its values reflecting present, past, and future concerns of people and of other living things (Kemmis 1990, Craig 1995).

Articulating, understanding, and translating these values into actions necessitates a combination of clarity and certainty, as well as flexibility. A clear sense of direction, consistent and fair processes, and acceptable and measurable outcomes are ingredients which help provide a common understanding. Equally important are open-mindedness and an ability to respond to changes, diversity of perspectives and needs, and to the particulars of any community or place-based situation.

## What to Measure

The choice of *what* to target in measuring progress, deciding where to place investments, evaluating past accomplishments and identifying next steps, begins with understanding community people's key concerns — what are the passions, the fears, the controversies that attract people's attention, focus their energies, and provide the motivations for actions.

Examples from a recent evaluation of six sustainable community projects in northern New England illustrate what galvanized people's attention that led to constructive changes (Kline 1996). At least three things motivated people living in rural communities in Maine, Vermont, and New Hampshire to create and participate in committees and to develop and implement projects aimed at improving their economic viability, environmental soundness, and social/historical/cultural quality of life.

First, a sense of desperation drives people to invest in change in hopes that somehow their individual and collective lives will improve. For example, Hardwick, a community of 2,500 to 3,000 residents located in the Northeast Kingdom of Vermont, has gone through hard times. The once thriving granite industry long ago disappeared and a fire in the winter of 1992 destroyed three buildings on Main Street in the center of town. With the nearest interstate 25 miles away, there is a desire to create jobs locally. In this case, a desperate economic situation served as the impetus for and focus of the sustainable community project.

A second motivator for sustainable community actions is a desire to stay in a place. Being able to live in the town, city, or region where you grew up has meaning to many people. For example, many of the families living in the Cobscook Bay region of eastern Maine have lived there for generations despite significant economic hardships (Kline 1996). Given a long history of dependence on a natural resources-based economy (i.e., fishing, clamming, tipping, blueberry harvesting, and forestry), people's deep-rooted connections with nature and their preference for a rural quality of life, survival and enjoyment mean more than having a job.

A third motivating force which spurs some communities to shift directions and invest in change is a desire to improve people's quality of life. For example, in the Greater Farmington, Maine, sustainable community project, the group (Sustain Western Maine) adopted a vision statement which seeks to "preserve our prime assets: the natural beauty and the social values we hold dear." Their mission statement based on this vision is: "To help the region to utilize its natural, human, and technological resources to ensure that all members of present and future generations can attain a high degree of health and well-being, economic security, and a say in shaping their future while maintaining the integrity of the ecological systems on which all life and production depends" (Kline 1996).

The point of these examples is to illustrate that the choice of *what* to measure in evaluating progress, allocating resources, and/or holding people accountable depends on the values and interests of the affected persons in a community. What motivates some people may not resonate with others.

## A Framework for Considering What to Measure

Determining what to measure is a difficult task. To facilitate this process, a framework is suggested as a reference guide. It is not intended as a substitute for a community-derived process; rather, it can be a useful tool in helping people imagine and visualize aspects of a sustainable community which deserve their attention. This section draws on the reports "Defining a Sustainable Community" (October 1993) and "Defining Sustainable Community Indicators" (January 1995a) produced by, and available from, the author.

A more sustainable community embodies four characteristics: economic security, ecological integrity, quality of life, and empowerment with responsibility. Each of these aspects is described

separately and illustrated with examples from case studies developed
to define and give some tangible meaning to the characteristics. In
addition, specific categories of what to measure will be presented
for each characteristic.

## Economic Security

A more sustainable community includes a variety of businesses,
industries, and institutions which are environmentally sound
(in all aspects), financially viable, provide training, education,
and other forms of assistance to adjust to future needs, provide
jobs and spend money within a community, and enable
employees to have a voice in decisions which affect them. A
more sustainable community also is one in which residents'
money remains in the community.

A community whose economic base depends on the viability of
one or a few employers tends to be more vulnerable than one which
relies on many different sources of revenue and jobs. For example,
communities in the northeastern and northwestern regions of the
United States and parts of Canada which are heavily dependent on
natural resource-based economies, such as fishing and timber harvesting, are faced with severe economic and social hardships from
overharvesting of these resources. This circumstance applies similarly to communities depending on a single industry such as a
military base or a mill.

A case study of the St. John Valley region of Maine documented
the impact from closure of a military base on the affected communities. "The loss of an estimated 7,500 jobs will have a ripple effect
throughout the county, affecting everything from car dealerships
(several of which have already closed) to schools which will lose
the majority of their students, to retired military families that rely on
the base for services. Not only will the region's economy suffer, but
the significant loss in population translates into a loss of political
power as well" (Kline 1993:178).

Environmentally sound businesses, industries, and residences
provide economic security by improving competitiveness through
reduction in costs and increased worker productivity as well as by
improving the environmental and public health and safety of workers, visitors, and neighbors (Hawken 1993; Lovins/Rocky Mountain
Institute's publications; President's Council on Sustainable Development 1996).

On the community scale, an example of an environmentally sound business is Ragged Mountain in Conway, New Hampshire. This company produces outdoor sports wear made from recycled plastic bottles. From a survey conducted by the Mt. Washington Valley Economic Council (the organization funded through the Ford Foundation Northern New England Sustainable Community Project), people realized that the stitching work was done in another state because of a lack of trained stitchers and available machines. The Council helped purchase the stitching machines, arranged for an instructor from Ragged Mountain, and organized the first training session. The result is that the work — jobs and income — now remains in the region and the local businesses can hire trained local people.

Economic viability requires an ability to adapt to change, take advantage of opportunities and strengths, and identify and fulfill unmet needs. In a sustainable community context, economic viability often means finding the "niche" market. For example, people in Vermont and Quebec sell maple syrup. People in eastern Ohio Appalachia are creating microenterprises around producing specialty foods, ecologically sound knitwear, and garden tools for the elderly.[1]

Economic viability can mean the acceptance and nurturing of multiple part-time and seasonal jobs, lifestyles which depend on less consumptive habits, creative financing such as community-assisted agriculture or local currencies (i.e., "Ithaca Dollars"), and non-financial exchanges such as bartered trades. For example, Nancy and Gordon Gray are full-time dairy farmers in Groveton, New Hampshire. To make ends meet, they also sell vegetables at their farm stand, sell shares through a Community Supported Agriculture program, create compost from manure, food waste, cardboard, and town newspapers which they sell to other farmers, teach, and do carpentry.[2]

Investing in people through training and education helps ensure long term economic security. Economic forces such as globalization of firms, downsizing of companies, and technological communication changes will, inevitably, cause personal hardships and dislocations. Therefore, economic security does not mean job security. However, lifelong learning and training can enable people and communities to be resilient and adapt to those changes.

Two of the bottom lines in economic security are generating jobs and retaining more of the wealth within the community. In more sustainable communities, the concern is not only with job creation, but also with the nature of those jobs. A doubling of the number of jobs, for example, does not necessarily strengthen a community's economic base. If those jobs are primarily taken by people living outside of the community, then the local tax revenues are not increased. If they attract newcomers to the community, then the costs in public services to support these people may outweigh the economic benefits from the new jobs.

## Ecological Integrity

A more sustainable community is in harmony with natural systems by reducing and converting waste into nonharmful and beneficial products and by utilizing the natural ability of environmental resources for human needs without undermining their ability to function over time.

One of the goals of a sustainable community is to produce without polluting and without waste (Jelinski et al. 1992, Tibbs 1992; Hawken 1993). There will still be byproducts and end products, but each will have a beneficial use for some other purpose. For example, Jim Lovinsky created his Sylva Curl business by buying left-over small chunks of remainder poplar wood from a nearby mill and processing the chunks into shavings to make into dry bedding material for animals.[3]

Another example is a residential demonstration project in Cambridge, Massachusetts. The Centre for Sustainable Building and Technology is renovating a 1928 multi-family residential dwelling to illustrate how an ordinary house can reduce energy use, water consumption, and decrease household waste by using recycled materials such as cellulose insulation made from recycled newsprint; by using technologies such as heat recovery from kitchens, bathrooms, and laundry exhaust air and waste water; by recycling gray-water from bathroom sinks, showers, and washing machines for yard vegetation gardens, plant irrigation, and reuse; and by using efficiency measures such as water-saving showerheads, faucets, and toilets, compact fluorescent lighting, and use of passive solar design.[4]

This aspect of ecological integrity deals with reducing the risks and resulting impacts from human activities on natural resources. The second aspect focuses on understanding and acting within the ecological limits of those resources. Working to reduce adverse impacts and to prevent new emissions from harming water supplies or impairing people's breathing is a useful strategy, but how clean is clean? For example, how much waste water can be safely discharged into a vegetated wetland and still have the plants continue to absorb and process that pollution? How much water can be withdrawn from a pond or river stretch for water supply use without harming fish habitats? The answers lie in knowing their ecological health thresholds.

## Quality of Life

> A more sustainable community recognizes and supports people's evolving sense of well-being which includes a sense of belonging, a sense of place, a sense of self-worth, a sense of safety, and a sense of connection with nature, and provides goods and services which meet people's needs both as they define them and as they can be accommodated within the ecological integrity of natural systems.

This characteristic reflects many of the qualitative aspects of a community. Identifying people's perceptions, senses, and beliefs is more likely to come from interviews, observations, and surveys than it is from statistical analyses of data. Violent crime rates, for example, indicate a sense of safety, but do not necessarily incorporate people's fears about their safety. Whether a parent allows a child to play in the park nearby may have less to do with crime statistics than with the parent's perception of who else is likely to be in the park, what time of day or night the child wants to play, and even what experiences the parent had in playing in that park as a child.

Quality of life supports the notion that mental and spiritual well-being are as important as material well-being. "An extensive literature on various aspects of well-being defines the concept primarily in relation to the achievement of the aspirations that people hold for themselves, their families, and their communities." ... Well-being is defined as a process involving the articulation, pursuit, and achievement of personal aspirations; the development and exercise of human capacities; and the granting of recognition and support to individual aspirations, all within the context of equality (SPARC, 1993:3 and 18).

A sense of belonging and sense of place relate to attachments people feel towards their community. When people feel a sense of belonging, they also feel as if they have a stake in a place.

A sense of self-worth can be fostered and supported by a number of factors including achievement of one's goals and recognition by others. Micro-enterprise programs modeled after the Grameen Bank in Bangladesh, for example, recognize the importance of building the confidence of small-scale entrepreneurs through mentoring, self-training exercises, and peer lending support. An evaluation of Working Capital, a micro-enterprise assistance and development program serving Massachusetts, New Hampshire, Vermont, and Maine, found that 73 per cent of the people interviewed reported an increase in self-confidence, 43 per cent an increase in participation in social and civil affairs, and 32 per cent an improvement in family relationships.[5] These qualities are a constructive byproduct of an economic development strategy.

A connection to nature seems desirable for people living and working in cities as well as those in suburbs and rural areas. This reality is embedded in the city of Boston's 1993 Open Space Plan in its description of a vision of "a daily contact with nature, open space, recreational opportunities in one's own neighborhood. This vision weaves itself into the fabric of the community, renewing and strengthening each neighborhood both at a personal and a community level. Rather than the large regional parks, smaller spaces — community gardens, schoolyards, squares, and tree-lined residential and commercial streets, for example — impart a daily sign of hope to neighborhood residents who work toward livable communities" (Boston Parks and Recreation Department 1993: 13).

Creating satisfying links with other people and with nature is important, but not sufficient to improve people's quality of life. A community cannot survive without ensuring that basic human needs are provided. Adequate and appropriate housing, health care, transportation, and other human infrastructure needs must be met so that people can have the ability to be productive and enjoy life.

In the context of a sustainable or healthy community, some people are promoting the interconnections among these needs. For example, in its "Healthy Communities Handbook," the National Civic League asserts that "to address health in a meaningful way, we must start by redefining what health is and considering the relationship between wellness and key components of our living and working environments: quality education; adequate housing; availability of meaningful employment; access to job skills training and retraining; access to efficient public transportation; availability of recreational opportunities; healthy and clean physical environments; and access to health education and prevention services" (Norris 1993: vi).

## Empowerment with Responsibility

A more sustainable community enables people to feel empowered and take responsibility based on a shared vision, equal opportunity, ability to access expertise and knowledge for their own needs, and a capacity to affect the outcome of decisions which affect them.

An authoritarian community is not assumed to be a sustainable one because, eventually, people are driven by a desire and need for self-expression, self-determination, and an ability to influence decisions which affect their lives. Robert Bellah and the other authors of "The Good Society" claim that "the question is not just what should government do but how it can do it in a way that strengthens the initiative and participation of citizens, both as individuals and within their communities and associations, rather than reducing them to the status of clients" (Bellah et al. 1991: 17).

In order for people to feel and be more in control of their lives as individuals and collectively in communities, they need both to be empowered and to take responsibility. Empowerment — the opportunity and capacity for meaningful and effective participation — is important in shaping the future according to the needs and values of participants. Equal opportunity means that each member of the community, regardless of qualities such as race, gender, religious or political beliefs, economic status, or language be included in decision-making.

Without empowerment, communities can be buffeted and manipulated by forces outside their control. Even well-intentioned outsiders such as financial investors and technical assistants bring their own bias and self-interest to their contributions. Prerequisites for achieving empowerment include access to information and expertise, ability to process that information, i.e. to understand the problem or set of circumstances, and the ability to shape and have input into the decision-making process. Also important are self-esteem, a feeling of relevance, and respect for others.

Empowerment alone, however, does not produce effective and desired results. In addition, communities need to take responsibility for their own welfare and not rely on the goodwill, generosity, or self-interest of others to care for them.

## How to Measure

The previous section defined a more sustainable community as one which is economically secure, lives within ecological limits, and is socially just. This section focuses on how to measure whether people's decisions and the results of those choices are actually leading towards a more sustainable community. How do you know if the jobs created or the courses taught in high school in a community are the type that provide more economic security? How can you gauge the effectiveness of dollars approved by town meetings, city councils, state legislatures, and congress in helping or undermining the quality of life of communities? Are the environmental laws and regulations improving air and water quality not only in the short-term, but also over the longer time frame?

Again, a conceptual framework is presented to help people identify the particular indicators which may be most appropriate for their own community situations. This framework can guide people's choice of indicators by providing the reference points of what to measure in promoting economic security, ecological integrity, quality of life, and empowerment with responsibility. Knowing that economic security, for example, means diversity of economic sources, profitability, environmental soundness, lifelong education and training, employee satisfaction, and community investments and support does not immediately translate into a list of appropriate indicators. This translation requires another step —identification of generic categories, applicable to any community, for each characteristic that reflect the essential ingredients (i.e., the purposes, the values, the meaning). For example, economic security needs to measure four ingredients: disparities, environmentally sound utilization of natural systems, local wealth, and mutual assistance.

The table on the following page (Table 1) presents the four characteristics and their respective generic categories of what to measure.[6]

One example from each characteristic will be used to provide guidance on how these categories can be helpful in eliciting appropriate sustainable community indicators.

Economic security at a community scale can be measured, in part, by considering its "local wealth." Local wealth includes many aspects of wealth, both monetary and non-financial. The object is not only to measure economic activity transactions (i.e., the traditional eco-

| Table1: Indicators Matrix | | | |
|---|---|---|---|
| **Economic Security** | **Ecological Integrity** | **Quality of Life** | **Empowerment & Responsibility** |
| Disparities | Effectiveness of the Functional Capacity of Natural Systems | Respect for Self & Others | Reaching In |
| Environmentally Sound Utilization of Natural Systems | Environmentally Sound Utilization of Natural Systems | Caring | Equity/Fair Playing Field |
| Local Wealth | | Connectedness | Capacity |
| Mutual Assistance | | Basic Coverage | Accountability |

nomic indicator — gross domestic product), but also to measure economic values such as social, human, and natural resources capital (Daly and Cobb 1989; Cairncross 1992; Krishnan et al. 1995).

Exchanges and investments can be measured in dollars, in bartered trades, and in voluntary contributions. An assumption is made that the more a community retains its wealth, the more sustainable it is. However, like all systems, some resources come from outside the community and others flow from the community to the outside. Sustainability, therefore, is not synonymous with self-sufficiency, but is closer to the notion of self-reliance.

Potential indicators which seek to measure a community's local wealth include: percentage of residents owning local businesses (or shares in businesses); percentage of large-sized businesses entirely owned locally as compared with branch operations owned by outsiders; percentage of products and services which local businesses purchase from other local businesses; percentage of residents' purchases made locally; number of firms offering or the number of hours provided for skills development and training for new employment opportunities; and percentage of community-generated taxes kept locally, versus transmitted to state and federal governments.

Information and data for many of these indicators may not be easily accessible now. So, initially, the primary utility of these indicators may be to establish and monitor "strategic directions" rather than to quantify successes.

Measuring ecological integrity is more difficult than measuring economic security. Many indicators, including those adopted through sustainable community indicators projects, focus on meeting environmental standards, calculating the number of acres of a natural resource (i.e., wetlands, open spaces, forests) that are purchased or destroyed or quantifying the amount of water or energy consumed. These type of measurements do not evaluate the health of the natural resource systems. For example, knowing the number of gallons of water a community consumes does not reveal if the aquifers or watersheds are adequately replenished.

More important ingredients to measure are the functional capacities of natural resources and environmentally sound utilization of natural systems. The latter is also an ingredient of economic security since the message is how to create a sound economy which is designed to improve the environmental infrastructure. Possible relevant indicators include percentage of energy used in a community generated by facilities using renewable energy resources; percentage and volume of waste material converted into beneficial uses; replacement of virgin (raw) material by recycled products; percentage of products returned in a product take-back program; number or percentage of acres in a watershed managed using sustainable forestry practices; percentage of food in a community which is imported; and daily vehicle miles traveled (VMT) per person per year in fossil-fuel powered single occupancy vehicles as compared with VMT in electric and alternatively fueled vehicles.

The third characteristic, quality of life, is likely to be measured in qualitative, as well as quantitative, terms. For example, if a community wants to measure its "basic coverage" (i.e., provision of basic services) it can measure access by proximity of facilities — how many people are in walking distance to a library or health care center. However, such measurements do not reveal whether or not people are actually getting the service. Are non-English speaking persons taking books out of the library? Are children from poorer families getting inoculations to prevent diseases? The significance between these two different approaches to measuring basic coverage can be important. For example, a university survey revealed that approximately ten per cent of the respondents in Cambridge, Massachusetts, felt that their health care needs were not being met, even though the city provides extensive coverage through neighborhood health care centers. Once city health care officials discovered this finding, they responded by targeting some funds to hire "outreach" staff to conduct home visits (Kline 1995b: 31).

The fourth aspect of a community, empowerment with responsibility, hones in on the degree to which people feel that they have control over their lives. Articles and books on the decline of American democracy (Berry et al. 1993, Putnam 1994,1995) proclaim the lack of public involvement, citing statistics such as the lower number of voters in elections, the smaller number of people joining charitable organizations, and the reduced volunteer hours performed.

These authors rely on indicators and data which can be analyzed for long-term trends. However, are voting tallies or dollars contributed to the Red Cross really measuring whether and how people's voices are being heard and reflected in decisions? Moreover, is the critical consideration how many people participated in a public hearing or whether the outcome benefits the expressed desires of the public?

In trying to evaluate progress in this realm, four ingredients can be considered: "reaching into" a community, equity/fair playing field, capacity, and accountability. Because of its unusual nature, the first one will be explained and illustrated. "Reaching out" is a common concept which denotes the search for allies to support someone or some group's idea. "Reaching in," on the other hand, is a continuous engagement process predicated on no predetermined solution. Its focus is on connecting to and bringing in more people and ideas to a process so that decisions made along the way can reflect a variety of viewpoints and meet a diversity of needs. It expresses the idea of examining to what extent communities are broadening the base of participation, hearing new voices, tapping into unused or underutilized resources, and engaging citizens to express their own concerns and to devise their own responses.

Indicators aim to measure the results of a "reaching in" process. Some indicators focus on the opening up process itself by measuring the number of new participants over time or the number of languages translated at public meetings or the use of facilitators. Another type of indicator measures the source of ideas/recommendations (e.g., from the consultant, the government regulator, the neighborhood group). A third evaluates the outcome of participation (e.g., the number of community gardens created over a specified time period). Although difficult to quantify initially, these indicators strive to encourage a process which constantly seeks more people's involvement, listens attentively to ideas, and responds to recommendations from the people being served or otherwise participating.

## Conclusions

Many people say that they want to live in communities (whether defined as households, neighborhoods, organizations, cities, or ecosystems) which are environmentally healthy, economically secure, democratic, and offer a high quality of life for themselves and their children. Yet, oftentimes, they make decisions or defer to others to act on their behalf without knowing, tracking, or evaluating whether these individual choices build towards this vision of a better life.

This chapter describes the fundamental aspects of a more sustainable community and how all of us can begin to make incremental improvements along those pathways. The act of identifying and applying sustainability indicators can help guide our choices, encourage people to work together and help each other, and hold ourselves and others accountable for actions taken or overlooked.

The use of the specific characteristics mentioned — economic security, ecological integrity, quality of life, and empowerment with responsibility — can help people move beyond current ways of thinking and acting. This blueprint is intended to help people who care about their communities, but are angry, frustrated, or restless with what is happening to them. By understanding and using this framework, people can figure out what is wrong and what they want to do and have others do differently.

The goal of community sustainability is to improve, rather than to reach an end point. Communities are at different stages of community-building and, therefore, what strategies, indicators, and results work for some may not work for others. Communities in early phases of community building need to focus more on jump-starting a process or expanding their core base of interest and support. Those which are more mature can expand their identities and ties within a region to steer more of the forces which influence their communities. And those most sophisticated communities will be able to garner the attention and resources of outside partners who have independent agendas and capabilities, and who want to gain value for themselves through collaboration (Kline 1996).

# 13

# Inertia and Resistance on the Path to Healthy Communities

## Jennie Moore

Many local governments have been busy generating vision statements, plans, and policies to guide our communities towards a sustainable future. Citizens have devoted countless hours to participating in these processes, and one such notable example is the City of Vancouver's *Clouds of Change* report (1990). In response to growing concerns about global climate change and worsening regional air quality, the mayor of Vancouver, B.C., initiated the Task Force on Atmospheric Change consisting of locally appointed scientists, medical doctors, academics, and business people. The task force was charged with identifying actions that the city could take to reduce its contribution to global climate change. Recognizing that day-to-day activities of urban residents and businesses are the root cause of global atmospheric problems and recognizing that municipalities are constricted by scarce resources, the task force generated thirty-five recommendations that could be acted on immediately to transform Vancouver into a healthier and more sustainable urban community. The *Clouds of Change* report was the result of the task force's efforts. It makes recommendations to:

> phase out all uses of ozone depleting chemicals;
> reduce carbon dioxide emissions through vehicle trip reduction ordinances, improved bicycling infrastructure, and road pricing systems that favor public transit;

> institute energy efficient land use patterns that reduce the need for motor vehicle travel;
> shift away from dependence on fossil fuels for municipal fleet operations; and
> define a leadership role for Vancouver in networking with other municipalities and lobbying senior governments for their cooperation.

The report received unanimous council support and was lauded as a template for creating a "Green City." So why has *Clouds of Change*, like so many initiatives for sustainability, failed to produce the types of changes necessary for a healthy community?

To find out, city councillors, municipal employees, task force members who wrote the report, and citizens who participated in *Clouds of Change* public processes were asked to identify in their own words what barriers impeded implementation of the recommendations.

Fifty-six people were interviewed with the following representation from each group: six councillors, twenty-one civic staff, eleven task force members, eighteen citizens.[1] Their responses reveal that even when there is agreement at the local level as to which direction society should take and what needs to be done, obstacles hinder progress towards achieving change. For the most part, the types of barriers encountered fell into three categories: i) perceptual/behavioral, ii) institutional/structural, and iii) economic/ financial. The existence of barriers reveals a common oversight in our approach to dealing with sustainability. It is that knowledge is not directly translated into action (Figure 1). Other factors operate in the space that exists between knowledge and action which interfere with our ability to make real progress towards achieving our goals for healthy communities and a healthy planet. Therefore, interviewees were also asked to make suggestions regarding what strategies would help overcome the barriers they encountered.

Knowledge ⟶ □ Action

Figure 1: A Space Exists Between Knowledge and Action in which Barriers Operate

## Barriers to Policy Implementation

**Perceptual/Behavioral Barriers** Perceptions condition our beliefs and guide our actions. Perceptual/behavioral barriers are primarily visible at the level of the individual, but they can also reverberate through an entire society. Examples include lack of understanding about the issues related to sustainability, perceived disempowerment, competing issues, lack of civic staff "buy-in," differences in perception, overwhelming complexity, and uncertainty. Citizens reported feeling frustrated and alienated by government sponsored public participation processes and in government. Beliefs prevailed that i) ability to affect consumptive behavior is limited because it is entrenched in cultural values, ii) the city is able to implement symbolic measures, but actions that will result in meaningful change can only be implemented by senior levels of government, and iii) political attempts to bring about change are secondary in impact to those of technological improvement.

Furthermore, effort to take action on some recommendations was undermined by citizens who feared the economic and/or social consequences implementation would have on them. This observation introduces additional perceptual/behavioral barriers that deal with perceived inequity, lack of choices, and disjunction between verbal support and willingness to take action. There is a tendency to verbally support sustainability initiatives without taking into consideration what will personally be required to implement them. Because values tend to sound good and noble, people can claim to uphold certain values even though they have no impact on their behavior (Hultman 1979: 29). Most often, people's behavior is only partly due to their values and is heavily influenced by contextual setting and tradition (Michaelis 1996). A world that historically has been designed for unsustainable living leaves little opportunity for individuals to make alternative choices. When such choices are possible, action which supports sustainability may still not be adopted if it is perceived that the personal sacrifices are greater than the benefits both to the community at large and to the individual. If one feels that one's own sacrifice will be taken advantage of by someone else, thereby nullifying any possible benefits, motivation to act diminishes. In a society where cultural norms inherited from past decades of sanctified consumption continue to define the aspirations of many citizens, the perception that individual efforts will not produce change seems validated. This becomes a rationale for abdicating personal and civic responsibility to behave in a way that supports sustainability.

**Institutional/Structural Barriers** Dimensions of institutional/structural barriers include elements of perception, as in fear of losing constituent support and fear of losing control or power. Institutional/structural barriers affect the organizational operations of public institutions. Barriers in this category include limitation of jurisdiction, conflicting regulations, weak links between government and constituents, weak linkages among the policies of civic and senior levels of government, and inappropriate structure of government. The city is an urban ecosystem: the relationships among human actions, infrastructure management, and ecological impacts are closely related. However, the civic departments are highly segregated. This creates difficulties in organizing interdepartmental initiatives, scheduling meetings, arranging funding, and coordinating activities.

A general perception among councillors and civic staff was that the city was making progress on most of the recommendations except those which lay outside its jurisdiction. Also, municipal initiatives were sometimes undermined by the activities of other government agencies pursuing incompatible objectives. This problem replicates itself at the regional level, where efforts to reduce the number of vehicles arriving in the city center are frustrated by provincial highway improvement projects. Yet, even within the municipality, debates arose in council over conflicting policies. One policy calls for keeping costs to a minimum, others call for increased expenditures on environmental initiatives such as *Clouds of Change*. Lack of an environmental nongovernment organization to pressure government to include environmental values in its decision-making was cited as an additional barrier in cases where decisions had to be made between competing issues.

Citizens looking to create solutions that support sustainability often find their efforts thwarted by permit restrictions and regulations which force compliance to the status quo — unsustainable building and land use patterns. Examples include low density zoning bylaws which regulate number of units per lot or acre, instead of the amount of square footage of the built area; minimum parking space requirements which often exceed the needs or wants of residents; and mandatory connection to water and sewer which precludes the introduction of alternative technologies such as composting toilets or solar aquatic sewage treatment systems which treat wastes on site. In theory, alternative technologies are permitted if a fail-safe, backup system is in place, e.g., sewer. However, the cost of providing both systems in the same project is prohibitive. Therefore, despite the availability of alternative technologies, their introduction into mainstream use continues to be impeded.

**Economic/Financial Barriers** Both individuals and governments operate in a context where financial considerations and economic realities influence perceptions of what is, and perhaps more importantly what is not, feasible. Examples of economic/financial barriers include inadequate funds, existing funds pre-allocated to ongoing programs, motives for financial gain, failure to guarantee results, marginal pricing and economic valuation, lack of a prioritizing mechanism, unwillingness to pay more taxes, and fear of disadvantaging the poor.

Limited municipal resources force councillors and civic staff to make value-based decisions on which issues are the most important to address. It is difficult to balance the urgency of a broad spectrum of issues such as housing, crime, drinking water, etc., in addition to global issues such as atmospheric change, particularly if a system for prioritizing these issues has not been established. Councillors reported that the general economy, housing pressures, and zoning changes are issues that receive their attention first. Accommodating new policy initiatives requires trade-offs that affect existing programs. Unless the benefits of re-allocating money from existing programs to new initiatives are clearly visible, there is little incentive to do it.

The constant pressure of limited fiscal resources makes councillors resist implementing initiatives which might negatively impact income-generating activities for the city. In the past, technologies such as the automobile, which now poses a threat to sustainability, became inextricably tied to work practices. Unknowingly, society began to trade sustainability for productivity. As long as this pattern persists, efforts to change remain limited to those means which do not inhibit production. Restricting the ease with which employees commute to work and increasing the cost of goods' movement within the city, e.g., through application of a carbon tax, were among the top concerns with respect to negative impacts on business as a result of *Clouds of Change* implementation. There was a fear that implementation of these initiatives would encourage businesses to relocate outside of Vancouver, thereby reducing the municipal tax base.

**Knowledge and Action** By reviewing the barriers that hindered implementation of *Clouds of Change,* one begins to sense that knowledge is not always directly translated into action. Other factors are also at work. Many social change theorists believe that action is primarily motivated by our desire to meet our personal needs. Therefore, at the heart of social change is the individual. Understanding how individuals form perceptions about which needs are to be met and what priority they should take becomes crucial to understanding larger social patterns. Our perceptions determine our consent to operate within existing political and institutional structures that appear to meet our needs, and they condition our acceptance of the economic constructs which heavily influence the operations of corporations and public institutions. However, many cultural values, government regulations, and financial accounting systems ignore the importance of taking responsibility for the social and environmental consequences of our activities. As a result, they contribute to a society structured to encourage actions that do not support sustainability and a population which demonstrates emergent behavior patterns that are not conducive to its own long-term survival.

Perhaps it is fair to argue that all three categories of barriers are themselves couched in the one problematic barrier of perception. Because our beliefs are based on fragmentary knowledge, they may not correctly reflect the way the world truly is, in all its complexity. Beliefs are a product of our experiences, which include the lessons we are taught about how to perceive the world. From experience, we form our perceptions about the world, how it works, what is right and wrong, good and bad (Hultman 1979: 9). The formation of our beliefs is an inductive process. However, when we place so much confidence in our perceptions that we forget the degree to which they have been abstracted from the world's incredibly complex reality, we succumb to the fallacy of misplaced concreteness (Daly and Cobb 1989: 25). As a result, we are vulnerable to unforeseen circumstances that may interfere with our ability to meet even the most basic needs on an ongoing basis in the future.

We must therefore be adaptive, constantly adjusting to new information and changing circumstances. The more sensitive we can be as individuals, anticipating and preparing for change based on incoming information, the better our chances for survival. However, opportunities to recognize changing circumstances are not always readily available. With the introduction of increasingly sophisticated technology and globalization of world markets, it is becoming difficult to detect the ecological and social consequences of our actions. Impacts may only be felt in the long-term future, or they may occur in a remote geographic area. For example, we hear stories about the decimation of rainforest habitat in South America which is driven by our demands for cheap beef and other cash crop products such as coffee and soybean-based foods. Destruction of rainforests is predicted to accelerate climatic change; however, we do not notice any immediate climatic effects. Furthermore, extinction of species and disruption of indigenous people's way of life is not visible from our vantage point, thousands of kilometres to the north. Thus, we continue to demand cheap foods and delicious coffee. Our lives go on as they always have.

The separation of consequence from action creates what is referred to as an incomplete feedback loop. A feedback loop exists when an individual is i) capable of assessing an initial state, ii) taking action, and iii) sensing the consequences of that action and its effects on the initial state. Such feedback may be positive, encouraging further action, or negative, suppressing further action. However, an incomplete feedback loop means that the connection between cause and effect is disrupted and there is no feedback whatsoever. Because modern society is characterized by incomplete feedback loops, the consequences of an individual's actions are not always explicit. A person may not be aware of certain impacts, or a person may be aware but not forced to take responsibility for them. Unless decision-makers choose to complete the loop by virtue of their conscience, there is no stimulant to forgo an action which meets one's personal needs at the expense of undermining global sustainability. Hence, when incomplete feedback loops exist, knowledge alone is not always sufficient to modify behavior. Thus, knowledge is not successfully turned into action.

## Strategies for Overcoming Barriers

By recognizing how barriers prevent action, it is possible to devise strategies for successful implementation of policy initiatives. When asked to present strategies for overcoming the barriers that worked against the recommendations in *Clouds of Change,* interviewees provided the following suggestions.

To address perceptual/behavioral barriers, ideas were put forward to pursue implementation of the three most important recommendations until they were done and then move on to those remaining; to improve communication mechanisms between governments and their constituents; to focus on raising awareness about the relationship between an individual's actions and impacts on the ecosphere; to examine other successful campaigns, such as the nonsmoking campaign; and to promote self-help. This last point bears further explanation. A result of the urbanizing process is that citizens' needs for goods and services are increasingly fulfilled by others, where once much of the work was done by oneself. As a result, citizens seem to have grown accustomed to looking to government for solutions to problems. Success in creating healthy communities requires that citizens become aware of their own responsibility to bring about the changes they desire. Citizens have more rights and freedom to act than a municipality; therefore, they can initiate more experiments and local community projects. Often, as local initiatives proceed through various steps of implementation, municipal regulatory barriers arise. By confronting these restrictions and working with councillors to have them removed, the process of changing our communities into healthier and more sustainable places begins.

Additional strategies for overcoming perceptual/behavioral barriers were: expand communication links with other cities who have successfully implemented environmental initiatives, and develop programs that improve the choices available to citizens who want to lead lifestyles that support sustainability. The suggestion of providing more choice is a crucial one. Many policy initiatives fail despite their inherent logic because they assume that citizens are in a position to exercise more choice than perhaps is really the case from the citizen's perspective. A particular model of behavioral change makes this point explicit (Figure 2). It identifies problem awareness as only the first step in a series of changes that lead to a desired behavior. Raising awareness is not enough. Providing opportunities for experimentation with alternatives and providing a variety of choices which enable citizens to tailor particular alternatives to meet their own needs and situations are fundamental elements in bridging the gap that exists between knowledge and action.

**Figure 2: A Process of Behavior Change**

Strategies for overcoming institutional/structural barriers included suggestions to improve networking and cooperation among nongovernment organizations; to create opportunities for partnerships among local governments, businesses, community associations, and nongovernment organizations; to institute a citizen review board or use an existing body such as a citizen's advisory commission to monitor implementation of each recommendation; to establish standards to measure progress; and identify lead agencies to be held accountable for the coordination of policies and related activities of the other government agencies whose cooperation is required for implementation success. Improved coordination of activities by all sectors, be they private or public, was a commonly suggested strategy. To this end, networking becomes an extremely powerful tool. In order to be effective agents for change, individuals working in government, nongovernment, and private sectors must identify each other and work together to realize progress towards a sustainable society.

Strategies were also put forward to adapt government structures so that they include mechanisms for addressing issues based on long term planning horizons. Suggested examples included the introduction of community councils or round tables which would act as auxiliaries to the existing government. To compensate for the problems that result from segregated municipal departments, the introduction of new goals for the city must follow a process that brings the various departments on-side. Workshops that include councillors, department heads, and some staff should always be a part of the policy recommendation process. Unless those charged with implementation believe in an initiative's worth and attainability, motivation to do the work will be lacking.

Strategies for overcoming economic/financial barriers focused on demonstrating the financial advantages of implementing initiatives, highlighting how initiatives could simultaneously meet a multiplicity of municipal objectives, and indicating how negative impacts on the financially disadvantaged members of the community could be avoided. There are tremendous cost savings in terms of reduced expenditures on infrastructure, safety, and health care that can be achieved by implementing policies that support sustainability. Understanding how these savings will be achieved helps decision-makers rationalize the initial expenditures required to support the initiatives. Furthermore, because the benefits may only become visible over the long term, it is helpful to point out how implementation of specific initiatives can help meet other municipal goals. For instance, efforts to provide intermodal transportation, such as accommodating bicycles on public transit and creating pedestrian-oriented communities which reduce automobile dependency, also benefit those who would otherwise find it financially burdensome to own a vehicle.

Additional recommendations focused on finding ways to include externalized costs in market pricing systems and encouraging government agencies to demonstrate their commitment to ecological sustainability through their purchasing choices and conservation efforts.

## Conclusion

Understanding how barriers operate reveals opportunities for overcoming them. The concepts associated with creating sustainable communities are not difficult; it is the process of bringing them to fruition that is challenging. Nevertheless, bit by bit, individuals are working in their communities to change what is unhealthy and replace it with sustainable alternatives. This type of civic responsibility is perhaps at the heart of the change process. In a national study about what factors contributed to effective regional government in Italy, the degree of civic participation in a region was found to be the leading contributor above education level, economic development, and demographic characteristics (Putnam 1993: 118).

A civic community is marked by a high degree of participation in daily community life. It can be measured by assessing such things as the level of newspaper readership; the density of social networks; or the number of sport clubs, social clubs, volunteer organizations, business associations, etc. which encourage individuals to participate in activities where they meet other members of the community and discuss common interests and concerns.

Civic communities encourage individuals to act cooperatively. They provide the contextual situation to act according to conscience despite economic and immediate, need-meeting motivations which encourage one to do otherwise. Thus, civic participation provides a means for completing the feedback loops which today, in their incomplete state, contribute to the inertia and resistance which impede progress towards achieving sustainability. In this manner, civic participation becomes a powerful tool in overcoming the barriers to implementation of policies that support sustainability.

Citizen activists in Vancouver realized the importance of networking and cooperating with one another to achieve their visions for a Green City and as a result, Vancouver's Eco-city Network was born.[2] The network focuses on improving communication and cooperation among the various community and non-governmental organizations in the city. A primary focus is enhancing awareness of the linkages between issues of urban ecology, social justice, and community economic development. By working together, groups from a diversity of backgrounds gain momentum in their efforts to achieve common goals that not only benefit the environment, but improve living conditions for the poor and create more opportunities for social betterment for all members of the community.

When groups from a particular sector, such as the environmental sector, lobby council regarding an issue, it is very easy for them to become marginalized by council as "special interest groups." However, when groups from a diversity of backgrounds such as social health and welfare, youth, ratepayers, business, and the environment all start going to council asking for the same things, then these groups can no longer be dismissed as "special interest." Their diversity begins to resemble the diversity of people in any given community. They begin to represent the interests of the "average citizen."

With this recognition in hand, members of the Vancouver Eco-city Network set about trying to determine the most appropriate way to improve networking amongst the various organizations in the city while simultaneously enhancing awareness of the often overlooked linkages among issues of environment, social justice, and economic development. After a lengthy process of participatory democracy, it was decided that hosting a series of forums would be the most appropriate way to go. Forums were always accompanied by potluck dinners or desserts which gave people an opportunity to get to know each other and provided an incentive for people to bring guests who might not otherwise be active participants in community life.

After a year of hosting such forums, members of the network reflected on their achievements and the following conclusions were reached. By diligently sticking to a participatory decision-making process at the outset, in which members tried to reach consensus, agreement was made on the most benign means of proceeding, i.e., holding public forums. Although everyone could agree to this, those ready and willing to do more soon lost interest in the network. By catering to the more placid majority, we may have lost an opportunity to do more dynamic things to raise public awareness, and we certainly lost the energy of a significant group of people. A lesson to be learned from this experience is that whenever possible, people should be encouraged to pursue their interests and every effort should be made to include or accommodate diverse activities.

Nevertheless, those who persisted and participated in the forums felt that they had come to know a significant number of community activists from all walks of life and that creation of this social fabric was invaluable to their personal morale and improved their effectiveness in their community work. Thus, the forums, and perhaps more importantly the social events which accompanied them, may have created the fertile ground for even greater changes which are still to come. Indeed, a growing restlessness was beginning to brew amongst network members. Although we had all come to know each other better, had we really changed anything in terms of moving Vancouver towards a Green City future?

Longing for more concrete change, members of the network set a new objective for the following year. Forums were still important and one or two would be held, but in addition, the network decided to focus on particular issues or activities that were pivotal to creating a Green City. These issues included addressing the need for improved transportation options, promoting the creation of a model sustainable community in a particular part of the city, protecting low income housing, and establishing a volunteer directory which linked individuals and organizations together. Interestingly enough, the first two issues coincide with *Clouds of Change* recommendations which the City of Vancouver is still pursuing. For each of the four issues chosen, members of the network went out to the organizations who were already working in these areas and asked what would help them improve their efforts towards realizing their goals. Network members then worked to assist the various organizations in whatever capacity they could. Much of this work to date has involved identifying and bringing together the various groups who are working on the same issue to discuss their work, share experiences, and strategize around cooperative initiatives. Future opportunities to reflect on this most recent network approach are bound to reveal new insights as Eco-city members continue to participate in the greening of their city.

Opportunities to increase the civic capacity of our own communities exist at almost every turn. Simply saying "hi" to a neighbor begins to create a social relationship. Working cooperatively with other individuals or organizations on joint projects helps build the kinds of networks that strengthen the social fabric of a community. Engaging in local politics, or at least knowing who the local politicians are, increases opportunities for community self-determination. By engaging in these sorts of activities, each of us becomes a catalyst for change.

# 14

# Epilogue

# Some Notes on Eco-city Culture

## Mark Roseland

As I put this book, and myself, to bed, I sense there's a dimension missing from these *Eco-city Dimensions*. It was not my intention, as mentioned in the preface, for this book to be comprehensive. But the question that often nags me when I think about ecological social change is this: what (besides this book, of course) will it take for these ideas to catch on? How can we make issues like eco-city planning and green economic development "cool" or "sexy" to a wider public? What, in other words, is the *cultural* dimension of eco-cities?

I don't have the space or expertise to address the entire cultural dimension of eco-cities, but I can provide a few musical notes on the subject. About a year before this book was published, I was walking through my Vancouver neighborhood when I noticed some unusual graffiti. Someone had posted a homemade sign on a telephone pole that read simply "Imagine No Cars." Feeling very task-oriented that day, I added it to my list and went about my business. Later that evening I sat down and tried to "imagine no cars." I scribbled down a few thoughts, then wrote the lyrics below to the tune of John Lennon's song "Imagine."

I brought my guitar to the next meeting of Vancouver's Eco-city Network, and had the audience join in on the chorus while I sang my "No Cars" version of "Imagine." A member of the Vancouver Bicycle Choir was there; he asked for the lyrics and soon they were performing it.

A month later I was speaking at a national conference on sustainable transportation in Vancouver. I was the final speaker on the closing panel. I told the assembled suits that while it was great to see them hosting conferences and writing reports about sustainable transportation, we cannot build popular support for these ideas unless we address the cultural dimension of sustainability. I had "Imagine ... No Cars!" put up on the overhead, a woman from the Bicycle Choir leaped out of the audience with a guitar, and the somewhat astonished plenary sang along.

The rest, as they say, is history. The lyrics have been photocopied, faxed, e-mailed and published in more places than I can keep track of.[1]

End of story — almost. Included in the "Green Communities" issue of *Alternatives* (Roseland 1996b) was a short piece by Michael Torreiter entitled, "Song Cycles: Choir on Bikes," about a group of Toronto-area cyclists who perform bike-oriented adaptations of popular vocal music *while riding around the streets* of Toronto. Excerpts from their bicyclized versions of "Day-o" and Beethoven's "Ode to Joy" also appear below.

You may not be able to convince everyone you know to read this book right now, but you may be able to get them singing. In the long run, that might be more important.

**Imagine ... No Cars!**
*words by Mark Roseland*
(sing to the tune of "Imagine" by John Lennon)


Imagine there's no cars, it's easy if you try
Nothing to honk or curse at, above us clear blue sky
Imagine all the people walking down the streets


Imagine no more freeways, it isn't hard to do
No need to pave the planet, so much quieter, too
Imagine all the people on bicycles in the streets

Chorus:
You may say that I'm a dreamer, and I'm not the only one
I hope someday you'll join us, and the world will be more fun


Imagine there's no traffic — that's sort of hard to do
No more obnoxious drivers, including me and (especially) you
No more stressed out people, racing around in a ton of steel


Imagine public transit, that takes you where you go
In cities built for people, instead of the auto
Imagine all the rollerblades, skateboards, and wheelchairs
sharing all the streets


Chorus:
You may say that I'm a dreamer, and I'm not the only one
I hope someday you'll join us, and the world will be more fun


Imagine you could get there, that "there" was not that far
No need to use up fossil fuels, fill our lungs with toxic tar
Imagine all the music streets could have, if not for cars


Chorus:
You may say that I'm a dreamer, and I'm not the only one
I hope someday you'll join us, and the world will be more fun


◎

Bells are ringing, hearts are singing, songs of bikes and two-wheeled modes

Lights are shining, wheels are turning in our minds and on the roads

— *from "Ode to Joy" by Ludwig van Beethoven, bicyclized by Song Cycles*

◎

Way-o, way-ay-ay-o
    Freeway not the only way home!
Freeway goes like the crow flies — straight —
    Freeway not the only way home!
Bike route twist like a mean rattlesnake —
    Freeway not the only way home!
Come, traffic planners, now, look at all the choices —
    Freeway is not the only way home!
Come, traffic planners, now, look at all the choices —
    Freeway is not the only way home!

— *music from "The Banana Boat Song" (Day-O) composed by Erik Darling, Bob Carey, and Alan Arkin, with lyrics recycled by Song Cycles*

# Notes

## Chapter 1: Dimensions of the Future

1. Register (1987) cites seven key biological/bioregional principles for ecologically rebuilding cities: 1) diversity is healthy; 2) fairly large areas are required for natural species to develop diversity of population; 3) land has a limit (carrying capacity) to the quantity of biological material it can naturally support in a particular climate; 4) there is a green hierarchy in sustainable community planning (e.g., native and useful plants before lawns and ornamentals); 5) make wastes into new resources; 6) biological pest controls and nutrients are generally preferable to chemicals; and 7) species and habitat protection is a regional problem, not simply an urban one (e.g., fences, forest management, long commutes).

2. Register is no longer with Urban Ecology. He now works with another Berkeley organization, Eco-city Builders, which aspires to build model projects that demonstrate shifting development patterns from sprawl to ecologically healthy "cities of walkable centers."

3. These include, for example, Ebenezer Howard (1902); Patrick Geddes (1915); Paul and Percival Goodman (1947); Lewis Mumford (1964); Ian McHarg (1969); Christopher Alexander (1977); and Anne Whiston Spirn (1984).

4. Space permitting, other paradigms which could also be discussed here include environmental justice, ecological economics, the steady state, ecofeminism, deep ecology, the conserver society, new physics, and the Gaia hypothesis.

5. An earlier version of parts of this survey appeared in Gardner and Roseland (1989).

6. Also known as alternative, renewable, soft, intermediate, radical, liberatory, and human-scale technology.

7. This definition is based on the founding report for the Centre, written by David Ross and George McRobie in 1987. McRobie was a colleague of E. F. Schumacher. His *Small Is Possible* (1981) was

inspired by Schumacher's *Small Is Beautiful.*

8. Social ecology is a term with various meanings in various places, e.g., a branch of urban sociology. The social ecology referred to here, however, is focused primarily around the writings of Murray Bookchin.

9. Greens in the U.S. have generally expanded this list to include an explicit emphasis on decentralization (see, e.g., Tokar 1987).

10. Tokar (1987) adds freedom, equality, and democracy to the list.

11. Elements of bioregionalism can be traced back to the writings of, for example, Kropotkin, Geddes, and Mumford.

12. I wish to thank Dr. Julia Gardner for this discussion of native world views.

13. For a fuller discussion of this literature, see Roseland 1995.

14. A similar argument could be made for some of the other terms discussed here, in particular Sustainable Communities (e.g., Roseland 1992a), Sustainable Cities (e.g., Haughton and Hunter 1994), and Local Sustainability Initiatives (e.g., ICLEI 1993).

15. Another approach to the challenge of defining sustainable communities is to specify *necessary conditions* for sustainable communities. For example, I have developed the argument (Roseland 1992b) that efficient use of urban space, reduction of resource consumption, improvement of community livability, and administration for sustainability are necessary conditions for sustainable community development.

## Chapter 3: Putting Cities in their Place

1. Much of this paper is based on Ray Tomalty, Robert B. Gibson, Donald H. M. Alexander, and John Fisher, *Ecosystem Planning for Canadian Urban Regions* (Toronto: ICURR, 1994), a study funded by, undertaken for, and available from the Intergovernmental Committee on Urban and Regional Research, 150 Eglinton Avenue East, Suite 301, Toronto, Ontario M4P 1E8, Canada.

   The monograph examines the concept of ecosystem planning, surveys initial application of this approach in 13 Canadian cases (plus two from the United States) and reviews 11 movements and methods that share features with the ecosystem approach but are carried out in different contexts or for different purposes. It concludes with discussion of a five-step framework for applying an ecosystem planning approach to urban-centered regions in Canada.

   The authors of this paper note especially the research and analysis of our colleague John Fisher, who carried out the review of the 15 ecosystem planning initiatives.

2. See Tomalty et al., *Ecosystem Planning for Canadian Urban Regions*, Chapter 2, especially the discussion of the Fraser River Estuary Management Program, the Fraser Basin Management Board, and the Georgia Basin Initiative in British Columbia, the Meewasin Valley Authority in Saskatchewan, and the St. Lawrence Action Plan in Quebec.

3. For details, see Tomalty et al., *Ecosystem Planning for Canadian Urban Regions*, Chapter 4.

## Chapter 4: Healthy Sustainable Communities

1. A longer version of this chapter was presented at the International Healthy and Ecological Cities Conference in Madrid, March 22-25, 1995 and has been summarized in a series of four columns in *New City Magazine* 16:1, 16:2, 16:3 and 16:4 (1995-96).

2. In presenting the report of the World Commission on Environment and Development to the World Health Assembly in 1988, Gro Harlem Brundtland observed that "ultimately, the whole report is about health." Others have been more explicit in stressing that social resources and the social environment likewise have to be sustained (see, for example, Osberg 1990).

3. The value of such a shift has been recognized by many authoritative bodies in recent years. For example, before it was abolished by the new Conservative government in the fall of 1995, the Premier's Council in Ontario had been working to develop strategic goals for the province that integrate social well-being, environmental quality and economic vitality (The Premier's Council, 1991).

4. Phil Ferguson and Don Houston have proposed measuring some of these factors through both an environmental quality index that measures the environmental quality within a community and an environmental sustainability index that measures the community's regional and global impact. See Ferguson and Houston 1993.

5. See Marmot 1994. Other papers in *Daedalus*, 123:4, a special edition on Health and Wealth, also address this matter.

6. Assessment of such impacts can be assisted by using what Ferguson and Houston (1993) refer to as an environmental sustainability index, or the "ecological footprint" approach developed by Rees and Wackernagel (1992).

7. The planning profession in Canada has, nonetheless, already contributed significantly to thinking about the integration of health, equity, and sustainability. The Canadian Institute of Plan-

ners (CIP) has been a sponsor and base for the Canadian Healthy Communities Project, which between 1988 and 1991 spurred the creation of healthy community projects across Canada. (The other sponsors were the Federation of Canadian Municipalities and the Canadian Public Health Association). As well the CIP has encouraged a lively debate about more holistic planning in the planning literature — see *Plan Canada,* 24:9 (1989), special issue on healthy communities — and has itself published reports advocating pursuit of sustainability as "the intent and central operating principle of planning" and a concept with social and cultural dimensions to be implemented with "full regard for issues of social equity" (CIP 1990).

8. There is a clear distinction between government and governance. According to Osborne and Gaebler, in their introduction to *Re-inventing Government* (1991), "Governance is the process by which we collectively solve our problems and meet our society's needs. Government is the instrument we use." Actually, government is *one* of the instruments, perhaps the main one we use, but the distinction between government and governance is important. Governance involves many players; in fact the community as a whole (at least in theory) should be involved in the process of governance.

9. For a more detailed discussion of possible changes in the structure of government, see Hancock 1994.

10. For example, ensuring an adequate, affordable, nutritious, and ecologically produced food supply for people in communities requires the involvement of many stakeholders, not just provincial authorities in a Ministry of Agriculture. Local food policies and local food systems are being addressed by new structures such as the Toronto Food Policy Council (see TFPC 1994).

11. One example of a more involving form of ownership and living is cohousing; see McCamant and Durrett (1988).

## Chapter 5: Enhancing Community Health Promotion with Local Currencies

The research for this chapter was supported by a grant from the National Research and Development Program of Health Canada.

1. See, e.g., Epp 1986; Evans 1987; Mustard 1993; Podborski et al. 1987; Premier's Council of Ontario 1991; Spassoff, 1987; WHO 1986.

2. LETS in various communities around the world have been called "Local exchange trading systems," "local energy transfer," etc. In French, they are called REEL, (Réseaux d'échange et d'emploi

local), or SEL (Systèmes d'échange locaux) in which the local currencies are called *grains de sel* (grains of salt).

3. Because LETS is a very recent phenomenon, having been developed for the first time in 1983, gaining widespread use only since 1990, there is very little research data in existence. Therefore, this analysis is mostly theoretical, supported with what empirical evidence is available. I use the following as theoretical bases for situating LETS as a health promotion strategy: Health Canada document, "Achieving Health for All: A Framework for Health Promotion" (Epp 1986), "The Ottawa Charter for Health Promotion" (WHO 1986), and the models of healthy communities proposed by Labonté (1993) and Hancock (1993). I have used the latter in this analysis because they are ecological and bring an inclusive concept of environmental sustainability to the discussion of the determinants of health.

4. Greco (1994) quoting the U.S. Federal Reserve, points out that conventional money is deliberately made into a scarce commodity in order to maintain its value. Scarce commodity currency encourages debt, which by means of interest and the need for collateral maintains a continual flow of wealth from poor to rich (Kennedy 1988).

5. Since LETS are often started unannounced by small, unofficial, community groups, the exact number of systems, even within one's local area, may be difficult to determine.

6. It is not essential to the creation of local money that something actually be exchanged; one might credit another's account just to express appreciation, for example.

7. In the regular economy, too, a large amount of national currency is issued not by the Bank of Canada or the Federal Reserve of the United States, but by the commercial banks when they issue loans, effectively creating money out of nothing (Greco 1994: 18-21).

8. Since green dollars are backed up by an individual's commitment to return a service at some point to the community, for municipalities or other institutions to issue green dollars, they, too, must back up the money they issue with service, either by taking local taxes in green dollars, or by green dollar sales. Even a tiny percentage of municipal taxes in local currency would inject a huge amount of nonconvertible local currency into the local economy.

9. Indeed, without such networks, the current strain on the welfare system may cause social programs to fail, forcing yet more idle capacity and unused resources (Rotstein and Duncan 1991: 431,

Lerner 1994).

10. In contrast, national currencies, which are structured as scarce commodities in order to maintain international confidence (Greco 1994), by their very structure as scarce commodities · induce inequities that often negate their use as a medium of exchange (Paul 1990; Rotstein and Duncan 1991). Dobson (1993: 37) points out that it is the structure of national currencies which ensures that the net flow of wealth be from poor to rich, be it at the level of individuals or communities. The LETS paradigm addresses the structurally induced inequities locally without affecting the value of the currency globally.

11. A lively international debate is being carried on electronically between those for whom LETS is simply an economic tool and those for whom it is a vehicle for social intervention.

12. There are at the moment several LETS research projects underway. Our study of LETS in Toronto, funded by Health Canada, is in the early data-gathering stage, and two students are completing PhD theses on LETS in the U.K.

13. A nonrepresentative survey done in Toronto in 1995 revealed that the great majority of respondents were highly educated, with at least some college or university, with low incomes, almost all earning under $20,000 per year.

## Chapter 6: Economic Development as a Path to Sustainability

1. This information is based on reports from City of Berkeley Energy Office, City of Berkeley Budget, and personal conversations with City of Berkeley staff.

2. This information is based on personal knowledge from visits to each community and from discussions with local officials in each community.

## Chapter 8: Urban Density and Ecological Footprints

1. This chapter is based in part on Walker's Master's thesis in the School of Community and Regional Planning at the University of British Columbia. The financial support of the Natural Sciences and Engineering Research Council in the preparation of the thesis is gratefully acknowledged.

2. Note that humanity's ecological deficit and accumulated debt may be more critical to survival that our fiscal deficits and debts, yet the former are totally ignored in the current frenzy to reduce the latter in many countries.

3. In fact, our calculations to date do not even tell the whole *consumption* story. Only major categories of consumption have

been included and we are only beginning to examine the land area implications of waste discharges other than carbon dioxide. This means that our current footprint calculations are almost certainly significant *underestimates* of actual ecosystem appropriations.

4. To simplify the calculations, density was assumed not to influence the consumption of food, consumer goods, and services, or the transportation of goods.

5. This is the "pull." A "push" might come from full cost accounting, including changes in taxes and other economic incentives that would make low density alternatives less affordable.

## Chapter 9: Ecology and Community Design

1. As defined below, "ecological communities" is a broader concept than, for example, the "neotraditional" development model (e.g., Seaside, in Florida) that has received considerable attention recently in North America.

2. During my site visits, which ranged from three days to five weeks, I interviewed the architects and planners to acquire general facts and to determine the limitations and problems confronting designers wishing to put their ecological principles into practice, undertook an extensive photo documentation, made field notes and sketches, discussed aspects of the community with members, and in some cases talked with neighbors. In Vallersund Gård, Norway, I designed and supervised a construction project over a period of five weeks, which presented me with an opportunity to get an insider's view of an ecological community.

3. Arguably, planning for the long term is more feasible in these countries than in North America where people move more frequently.

## Chapter 10: Cultural Dynamics in Waitakere City

A version of this chapter appeared in *Cities* Vol.13, No.5, 1996.

The author wishes to thank Taotahi Pihama, Manager, Maori Issues Unit, and Wallace Paki, Maori Issues Coordinator, for information and perspectives. Comments on earlier drafts and information from Greg George, Principal Planner, Waitakere City, are greatly appreciated.

1. The other key action platforms are: urban development options, economic development, infrastructure, environmental quality, city image and town center upgrading, communtiy service, leisure activities and recreation, asset management and development, and financial strategy (Waitakere City Council, 1993c).

## Chapter 11: Municipal Initiatives for Promoting the Use of Renewable Energy

The authors would like to thank the following people for their assistance in preparing this chapter: Ms. A. E. Baumann and Ms. A. R. Wilshaw of the Newcastle Photovoltaics Applications Centre, University of Northumbria, Newcastle-upon-Tyne, United Kingdom; Mr. H. Beeck and Mr. T. Breitkreuz, Consulectra Unternehmensberatung GmbH, Hamburg, Germany; Mr. H. Darrah, Southampton Environment Centre, Southampton, United Kingdom; Mr. N. Fleming, Richmond Walker Associates, Southampton, United Kingdom; Dr.-Ing. H.-P. Grimm and Dr. M. Sthr, CENET, Munich, Germany; Prof. T. KjJr, Roskilde University Centre, Roskilde, Denmark; Mr. B. Rasmussen, StorstrÀm amt, Nykobing F., Denmark; Ing. G. Zamboni, AGSM, Verona, Italy.

## Chapter 12: Sustainable Community Indicators

1. "New Directions for Micro-enterprise Development" by the Appalachian Centre for Economic Networks in Athens, Ohio (1993).

2. "STA-NORTH Region, New Hampshire: A Community Getting Plugged In". Unpublished evaluation report by Elizabeth Kline for the Ford Foundation. January, 1996, p. 2.

3. Interview on site in East Hardwick, Vermont (October 27, 1995).

4. "The Sustainable Housing Demonstration Project: Cambridge, Massachusetts" by the Centre for Sustainable Building and Technology, Inc. 1753 Massachusetts Avenue. Cambridge, MA 02140. Tel: 617/491-5757. Fax: 617/491-5858.

5. "Working Capital and Its Impact on Self-Employed Businesses and the Community: Preliminary Analysis of a Survey of 137 Loan Group Members" by Jeffrey Ashe (July, 1993), p. 6.

6. This Indicators' Matrix appears in and is more fully explained in "Defining Sustainable Community Indicators" by Elizabeth Kline (January, 1995).

## Chapter 13: Inertia and Resistance on the Path to Healthy Communities

1. This chapter is based in part on the author's Master's thesis for the School of Community and Regional Planning at the University of British Columbia.

2. The Vancouver-based Eco-city Network was established in May, 1994 at the Greening Our Cities Conference, which generated a tremendous amount of energy and enthusiasm for achieving Green City objectives in the Greater Vancouver area.

## Chapter 14: Epilogue

1. Although this book is protected by copyright, permission is hereby granted to freely reproduce the song lyrics to "Imagine ... No Cars!" Please send the author a copy of any new songs you discover or write!

# Access Information

*Alternatives Journal: Environmental Thought, Policy, and Action*
  Faculty of Environmental Studies
  University of Waterloo
  Waterloo, Ontario  N2L 3G1, Canada
  Tel: (519) 888-4567, ext. 6783; Fax: (519) 746-0292
  e-mail: alternat@fes.uwaterloo.ca
  home page: http://www.fes.uwaterloo.ca/Research/Alternatives/

*Local Environment*
  Carfax Publishing Company
  P.O. Box 25, Abingdon, Oxfordshire  OX14 3UE, UK, or
  875-81 Massachusetts Avenue, Cambridge, MA, 02139, U.S.A., or
  P.O. Box 352, Cammeray, N.S.W.  2062, Australia
  1-800-354-1420 (U.S.A. and Canada)
  +44 (0) 1235 521154 (worldwide, 24 hours, 7 days/week)

*The Urban Ecologist*
  Urban Ecology
  405 14th Street, Suite 701
  Oakland, CA  94612, U.S.A.
  Tel: (510) 251-6330; Fax: (510) 251-2117
  e-mail: urbanecology@igc.apc.org


  ECOCITY: Sustainable Urban Development
  <ECOCITY@SEGATE.SUNET.SE>
  LISTSERV address: LISTSERVE@SEGATE.SUNET.SE
  archives: http://segate.sunet.se/archives/ECOCITY.html

# Bibliography

Aberley, D., *Boundaries of Home: Mapping for Local Empowerment* (Gabriola Island, B.C.: New Society Publishers, 1993).

Aberley, D., ed., *Futures By Design: The Practice of Ecological Planning* (Gabriola Island, B.C.: New Society Publishers, 1994).

Adams, H., *Prison of Grass: Canada from a Native Point of View* (Saskatoon: Fifth House Publishers, 1987).

Agarwal, A., and S. Narain, *Towards Green Villages: A Strategy for Environmentally Sound and Participatory Rural Development* (New Delhi, India: Centre for Science and Environment, 1989).

Alden-Branch, M., "The State of Sustainability," in *Progressive Architecture* (March 1993) 79.

Alexander, C., et al., *A Pattern Language: Towns, Buildings, Construction* (New York: Oxford University Press, 1977).

Alexander, C., *The Timeless Way of Building* (New York: Oxford University Press, 1979).

Alexander, C., *et al., A New Theory of Urban Design* (Oxford: Oxford University Press, 1987).

Ashe, J., "Microenterprise Assistance and Development: Working Capital and Its Impact on Self-Employed Businesses and the Community," in *Working Capital.* July 1993. .

Baines, J., J. Wright, C. Taylor, K. Leathers, and C. O'Fallon, "The sustainability of natural and physical resources - interpreting the concept," Studies in Resource Management No. 5 (Lincoln College, Canterbury: Centre for Resource Management, 1988, NZP 333.7 S964).

Ballantyne, B. and N. Sutherland, "Fuzzy Boundaries and Maori Land in Otago: A Proposal Full of Potential and Pitfalls." Presented at the Sixth Colloquium of the Spatial Information Research Center, University of Otago, Dunedin, New Zealand, May 17-19, 1994.

Barlow, C., *Tikanga Whakaaro: Key Concepts in Maori Culture* (Oxford: Oxford University Press, 1993).

Bellah, R. N., R. Madsen, W. M. Sullivan, A. Swidler, and S. Tipton, *The Good Society* (New York: Vantage Books, 1991).

Berg, P., *et al, A Green City Program for San Francisco Bay Area Cities and Towns* (San Francisco, CA: Planet Drum Books, 1989).

Berry, J. M., K. Portney, and K. Thomson, *The Rebirth of Urban Democracy* (Washington, D.C: The Brookings Institute, 1993).

Berry, T., *The Dream of the Earth* (San Francisco: Sierra Club Books, 1988).

Bishop, N., *Natural History of New Zealand* (Auckland: Hodder and Stoughton, 1992).

Bookchin, M., *The Rise of Urbanization and the Decline of Citizenship* (San Francisco: Sierra Club, 1987).

Boothroyd, P., "Community Economic Development: An Introduction for Planners" (Vancouver: UBS Centre for Human Settlements, 1991).

Boston Parks and Recreation Department, "Open Space Plan for Boston." Boston, MA: Planning and Department Division, Boston Parks and Recreation Department, 1993.

Boutelier, M., S. Cleverly, C. Marz, L. Sage, and R. Badgley, "Community Action and Health Promotion," Presented at the Annual Conference of the Ontario Public Health Association, Toronto, November 17, 1992.

Brenner, M. H. and A. Mooney, "Unemployment and health in the context of economic change," *Social Science and Medicine*. 17:1125-1138 (1983).

British Columbia Round Table on the Environment and the Economy (BCRTEE), Commission on Resources and the Environment, Fraser Basin Management Program and National Round Table, *Local Round Tables - Realizing Their Potential* (Victoria: Queen's Printer for British Columbia, 1994).

British Columbia Energy Council, "Planning Today for Tomorrow's Energy - An Energy Strategy for British Columbia" (Vancouver, B.C.: B.C. Energy Council, 1994).

Brown, L. R., H. Kane, and E. Ayres, *Vital Signs 1993* (Washington, D.C.: Worldwatch Institute, 1993).

Brown, L.R. et al., *State of the World 1996* (Washington, D.C.: Worldwatch Institute, 1996).

Bucht, E., "Green Spaces in Urban Structure," *Management and Implementation of Ecological Measures in Human Settlements,* a report from an ECE Research Colloquium in Copenhagen, September 1991, Ivor Amrose and Ulf Christiansen, eds. (Copenhagen: Danish Building Research Institute Housing and Urban Planning Division, 1991).

Buhrs, T and R. Bartlett, *Environmental Policy in New Zealand: The Politics of Clean and Green?* (Auckland: Oxford University Press, 1993).

Burby, R., J. Higgins, E. Kaiser, C. Matthews, and M. Stanco, "Saving Energy in Residential Development: A Report for Local Government." (Chapel Hill: Centre of Urban and Regional Studies, University of North Carolina, 1982).

Cahn, E. and J. Rowe, *Time Dollars* (Emmaus, PA: Rodale Press, 1992).

Cairncross, F., *Costing the Earth: The Challenge for Governments, The Opportunities for Business* (Cambridge, MA: Harvard Business School Press, 1992).

Callicott, J. B., "Traditional American Indian and Western European Attitudes Toward Nature: an Overview," *Environmental Ethics* 4:293-318 (1982).

Calthorpe, P., *The Next American Metropolis: Ecology, Community, and the American Dream* (New York: Princeton Architectural Press, 1993).

Campbell, R. M., and P. W. G. Newman, "Local Government and Transport Energy Conservation," *Planning and Administration,* 1 (1989), 68-75.

Canadian Institute of Planners (CIP), *Reflections on Sustainable Planning*

(Ottawa: Canadian Institute of Planners, 1990).

Canadian Public Health Association (CPHA), *Human and Ecosystem Health: Health Implications of the Ecological Crisis* (Ottawa: Canadian Public Health Association, 1991).

Capra, F. and C. Spretnak, *Green Politics: The Global Promise* (New York: E. P. Dutton, 1984).

City of London, *London Strategic Plan, Final Report* (London, Ontario: City of London, October 1994).

City of Oakland, Office of Economic Development and Employment, "1994 Annual Report on the Oakland/Berkeley Recycling Market Development Zone" (Oakland, CA: City of Oakland, 1994).

City of Parksville, Healthy Communities Parksville, *Community Visions* (City of Parksville, Box 1390, Parksville, BC V9P 2H3, 1993).

City of Toronto, *Healthy Toronto 2000* (Toronto: Toronto Board of Health, 1988).

City of Toronto, *Goals and Principles for a New Official Plan* (Toronto: Cityplan '91 Task Force, 1990).

City of Toronto, *Health Inequalities in the City of Toronto, Report of the Community Health Information Section* (Toronto: City of Toronto Department of Public Health, 1991).

City of Vancouver, *Clouds of Change: Final Report of the City of Vancouver Task Force on Atmospheric Change* (Vancouver: City of Vancouver, June 1990).

Community Economic Development Centre, Simon Fraser University (1996), World Wide Web site http://www.sfu.ca/cedc/

Consortium for Regional Sustainability, "Market-Based Initiatives for Controlling Emissions from Motor Vehicles." (Boston, MA: Northeast States for Coordinated Air Use Management, 1993).

Cook, P., *Back to the Future: Modernity, Postmodernity, and Locality* (London: Unwin Hyman, 1990).

Costanza, R. and H. Daly, "Natural Capital and Sustainable Development," *Conservation Biology* 1:37-45 (1992).

Cotman, D., "The Sustainable Housing Demonstration Project." (Cambridge, MA, Centre for Sustainable Building & Technology, n.d.).

Craig, D.,"State of the Community: South Puget Sound." (Olympia, WA: Sustainable Community Roundtable, April 1995).

Daly, H. E. and J. B. Cobb, *For the Common Good: Redirecting the Economy Toward Community, the Environment and a Sustainable Future* (Boston: Beacon Press, 1989).

D'Amour, D., "Towards an Investigation of Sustainable Housing." Sustainable Development and Housing Research Paper No. 2. Prepared for Canada Mortgage and Housing Corporation (Ottawa: CMHC, 1993).

Darrow, K., et al., *Appropriate Technology Sourcebook* (Stanford: Volunteers in Asia, 1981).

Dauncey, G., "A harbour in a storm," in *After the Crash: The Emergence of the Rainbow Economy* (Basingstoke, UK: Green Print, 1988) 50-69.

Della Costa, J.,*Working Wisdom: The Ultimate Value in the New Economy* (Toronto: Stoddart, 1995).

Department of the Environment, Planning Policy Guidance Note 22: Renewable Energy, Her Majesty's Stationery Office, London, United Kingdom, 1993.

DeWalt, B., "Using Indigenous Knowledge to Improve Agricultural and Natural Resource Management," *Human Organization* 53(2): 123-131 (1994).

Dobson, V. G., *Bringing the Economy Home from the Market* (Montréal: Black Rose Books, 1993).

Dodge, J., "Living by Life: Some Bioregional Theory and Practice," in *CoEvolution Quarterly*, No. 32 (Winter, 1981) 6-12.

Doering, R., "Sustainable Communities: Progress, Problems and Potential," *National Round Table Review*, special issue on sustainable communities (Spring 1994).

Draper, R. "Making equity policy," *Health Promotion.* 4: 91-95 (1989).

Drucker, P. F., *Post-Capitalist Society* (New York: HarperCollins, 1993).

Ekins, P., ed, *The Living Economy: A New Economics in the Making* (London: Routledge, 1986).

Ellul, J., *The Technological Society* (Toronto: Random House of Canada, 1964).

Engwicht, D., *Towards an Eco-city: Calming the Traffic* (Sydney, Australia: Envirobook, 1992).

Engwicht, D., *Reclaiming Our Cities and Towns: Better Living With Less Traffic* (Gabriola Island, B.C.: New Society Publishers, 1993).

Environment Canada, "The State of Canada's Environment - 1991" (Ottawa: Environment Canada, 1991).

Epp, J., "Achieving health for all: a framework for health promotion," *Canadian Journal of Public Health.* 77: 393-408 (1986).

Evans, J. R., *Toward a Shared Direction for Health in Ontario: Report of the Ontario Health Review Panel* (Toronto: The Queen's Printer for Ontario, 1987).

Ferguson, P., and D. Houston, "Indicators and Indices of Environmental Quality and Sustainability for the City of Toronto," unpublished background report for the *State of the City* Report (Toronto: Healthy City Office, City of Toronto, 1993).

Ferman, L. A., "Participation in the irregular economy," in Erikson, K. and S. P. Vallis, eds. *The Nature of Work: Sociological Perspectives* (New Haven: American Sociological Association, Presidential Series, 1990), 119-140.

Fordyce, M. W., "A review on the Happiness Measures: a sixty second index of happiness and mental health," *Social Indicators Research.* 20: 355-381 (1988).

Foster, T. W., "The Taoists and the Amish: Kindred Expressions of Eco-Anarchism," in *The Ecologist*, 17:1 (1987) 9-14.

Frank, J. E., "The Costs of Alternative Development Patterns" (Washington, D.C.: Urban Land Institute, 1989).

Freidson, E., "Labors of love in theory and practice: a prospectus," in Erikson, K. and S. P. Vallis, eds. *The Nature of Work: Sociological Perspectives* (New Haven: American Sociological Association, Presidential Series, 1990) 149-161.

Friend, G. et al, "Building An Environmental Economy: A Strategy for Environmental Business and Economic Development for the City of Berkeley," Consultant Report. Berkeley, CA, 1993.

Gagnon, L., "Energy and the Car-Bungalow-Suburb' Trilogy," cited in D. D'Amour, "Towards an Investigation of Sustainable Housing," (1993).

Galtung, J., "Towards a new economics: on the theory and practice of self-reliance," in Ekins, P., ed. *The Living Economy: A New Economics in the Making* (London: Routledge, 1986).

Gardell, B., "Reactions at work and their influence on non-work activities," *Human Relations*. 29: 885-904 (1976).

Gardner, J., and M. Roseland, "Acting Locally: Community Strategies for Equitable Sustainable Development," *Alternatives: Perspectives on Society, Technology and Environment,* October-November, 1989, 36-48.

Geddes, P., *Cities in Evolution* (London: Williams and Norgate, 1915).

Gehl, J., *Public Spaces and Public Life in Perth* (Perth: Department of Planning and Urban Development, 1994).

Gilman, D., and R. Gilman, eds., *Eco-Villages and Sustainable Communities* (Context Institute: Bainbridge Island, Washington, 1991).

Girardet, H., *The Gaia Atlas of Cities: New Directions for Sustainable Urban Living* (New York: Doubleday/Anchor Books, 1992).

Girouard, M., *Cities and People* (New Haven: Yale University Press, 1985).

Glaser, B. and A. Strauss, *The Discovery of Grounded Theory.* (Chicago: Aldine, n.d.).

Glover, P., " Strength of hour grows while value of dollar declines," *Ithica Money.* 1:3:1 (1992).

Glover, P., Personal communication and "econ-lets" internet conference. (1995)

Goodman, L., "The prevalence of abuse among homeless and housed poor mothers: a comparison study," *American Journal of Orthopsychiatry.* 61:489-500 (1991).

Goodman, P., and P. Goodman, *Communitas: Means of Livelihood and Ways of Life* (New York: Vintage, 1960; originally published in 1947).

Gordon, D., *Green Cities: Ecologically Sound Approaches to Urban Space* (Montreal/New York: Black Rose Books, 1990).

Grant, J. F., Kellett, J. E., and Mortimer, N. D., Regional Renewable Energy Resources: The Potential Contribution to Energy Demand, 25th Annual Conference of the Regional Science Association International British and Irish Section, Dublin, Eire, 14-16 September 1994.

Gratz, R. B., *The Living City* (New York: Simon and Schuster, 1989).

Greco, T. H., News from LETSonoma, electronic communication on WEB network (1993). April 14, 1993.

Greco, T. H., *New Money for Health Communities* (Tucson, AZ: self-published, 1994).

Haanen, A., "Geographic Data for Regional Resource Management in New Zealand," unpublished master's thesis (Dunedin: University of Otago Library, 1992).

Hagen, T., and L. Rose, " Learning by Doing? Experimental Programs as a Tool for Public Policy Formation in Norway," *Scandinavian Housing and Planning Research,* 6 (1989) 17-30.

Hahn , E., and U. E. Simonis, "Ecological Urban Restructuring," *Ekistics,* 348 (May/June 1991) 199-209.

Hall, P., *Cities of Tomorrow* (Berkeley: Berkeley University Press, 1987).

Hancock, T., "Health, Human Development, and the Community Ecosystem: Three Ecological Models," *Health Promotion International,* 8:1 (1993) 41-47.

Hancock, T., "A Healthy and Sustainable Community: The View From 2020," in C. Chu and R. Simpson, eds., *The Ecological Public Health: From Vision to Practice,* (Toronto: Centre for Health Promotion, University of Toronto, 1994) 245-253.

Hancock, T., "Creating Healthy and Sustainable Communities: The Challenge of Governance," *Proceedings: Conference on Health and the Urban Environment,* David Britt, ed. (Manchester: The British Council, 1995).

Hancock, T. and L. Duhl, "Promoting Health in the Urban Context". WHO Healthy Cities Paper No 1. (Copenhagen: FADL for the WHO Healthy Cities Project Office, WHO Regional Office for Europe, 1988).

Handy, S., "How Land Use Patterns Affect Travel Patterns: A Bibliography," Council of Planning Librarians Bibliography 279. (Chicago: Council of Planning Librarians, 1992)

Hanson, T., *The New Zealand Green Dollar Management Guide: How to Set up and Run a Green Dollar Local Exchange and Trading System* (Taranaki, N.Z.: mimeo, 1991).

Hart, M., "Guide to Sustainable Community Indicators" (Ipswich, MA: Quebec Labrador Foundation/Atlantic Centre for the Environment, 1995).

Haughton, G., and C. Hunter, *Sustainable Cities* (London: Jessica Kingsley, Regional Policy and Development Series 7, 1994).

Hawken, P., *The Ecology of Commerce* (New York: HarperCollins, 1993).

Hodge, G., *Planning Canadian Communities: An Introduction to the Principles, Practices, and Participants.* (Scarborough, Ontario: Nelson Canada, 1991).

Holley, J., "New Directions for Micro-enterprise Development," (Athens, Ohio: Appalachian Centre for Economic Networks, 1993).

Hough, M., *City Form and Natural Process* (London: Croom Helm, 1984).

Hough, M., *Out of Place: Restoring Identity to the Regional Landscape* (New Haven: Yale University Press, 1990).

Howard, E., *Garden Cities of Tomorrow* (London: Faber and Faber, 1902).

Hultman, K., *The Path of Least Resistance: Preparing Employees for Change* (Austin, Texas: Learning Concept Publishers, 1979).

Industry Canada and Environment Canada, *A Strategy for the Canadian Environmental Industry* (Ottawa: Minister of Supply and Services Canada, 1994)

International Council for Local Environmental Initiatives, "The Local Agenda 21 Initiative: ICLEI Guidelines for Local and National Local Agenda 21 Campaigns" (Toronto: ICLEI 1993).

Isin, E., and R. Tomalty, "Resettling Cities: Canadian Residential Intensification Initiatives: Main Report." Prepared for Canada Mortgage and Housing Corporation (Ottawa: CMHC, 1993).

Jackson, M., *LETS and Sustainability - a study in human geography,* PhD dissertation proposal. (Department of Social Sciences, LaTrobe University College of Northern Victoria, Australia, 1993)

Jacobs, J., *The Death and Life of Great American Cities* (New York: Vintage Press, 1961).

Jacobs, J., *Cities and the Wealth of Nations* (New York: Random House, 1984).

James, C., *New Territory: The Transformation of New Zealand 1984-1992,* (*Wellington: Bridget Williams Books, 1992).*

Jelinski, L. W., T. E. Graedel, R. A. Laudise, D. W. McCall, and C. K. N. Patel, "Industrial Ecology: Concepts and Approaches" in *Proceedings of National Academy of Sciences,* Vol 89 pp793-797 (1992).

Jessup, P., H. Hamm, and J. Fraser. *Saving the Climate, Saving Cities: Briefing Book on Climate Change and the Urban Environment* (International Council for Local Environmental Initiatives, Toronto, Canada, 1993).

Kareoja, P., "360 Degrees of Architecture," *The Finnish Review of Architecture* (March 1993) 15.

Katz, P., *The New Urbanism* (New York: McGraw-Hill, Inc., 1994).

Kellett, J. E., The Organization of the Land Use Planning System in England and Wales and its Implications for Renewable Energy Developments, Report No. SCP8/5, Resources Research Unit, Sheffield Hallam University, United Kingdom, January 1994a.

Kellett, J. E., The Role of the Municipality in the Integration of Renewable Energy Schemes in the United Kingdom, Report No. SCP8/10, Resources Research Unit, Sheffield Hallam University, United Kingdom, September 1994b.

Kemeny, J., "Community-based Home and Neighborhood Building: An Interview With John Turner," *Scandinavian Housing and Planning Research,* 6 (1989) 157-64.

Kemmis, D., *Community and The Politics of Place* (Norman, OK: University of Oklahoma Press, 1990).

Kennedy, M., *Interest Free Money* (Steryerberg, Germany: Permakultur InstituteV, 1988).

Kickbush, I., WHO Healthy Cities Project. (Geneva: WHO, 1988).

King, A. D., "Exporting Planning: The Colonial and Neo-Colonial Experience," *Urbanism Past and Present,* 5 (1978) 12-22.

King, S., et al., *Co-Design: A Process of Design Participation* (Scarborough, Ontario: Nelson Canada, 1988).

Kline, E., "Defining a Sustainable Community," (Medford, MA: Tufts University, October 1993).

Kline, E., "Defining Sustainable Community Indicators," (Medford, MA: Tufts University, January 1995a).

Kline, E., "Defining Sustainable Community Indicators: Examples from Cambridge, MA," (Medford, MA: Tufts University, February 1995b).

Kline, E., "Northern New England Sustainable Communities Implementation Project," for the Ford Foundation, the New Hampshire Charitable Foundation, the Vermont Community Foundation, and the Maine Community Foundation (January 24, 1996). Unpublished report.

Kostoff, F., *The City Shaped: Urban Patterns and Meanings Through History* (London: Thames and Hudson, 1991) 83.

Krishnan, R., J. M. Harris, and N. R. Goodwin, *A Survey of Ecological Economics* (Washington, D.C., Island Press, 1995).

Labonté, R., "A Holosphere of Healthy and Sustainable Communities," #2 in Lectures in Health Promotion Series (Toronto: Centre for Health Promotion and Participaction, 1993).

Labonté, R., "Health Promotion and Empowerment: Practice Framework," #3 in Issues in Health Promotion Series (Toronto: Centre for Health Promotion and Participaction 1994).

Laitner, S., for The American Council for An Energy Efficient Economy, "Energy Efficiency and Job Creation: The Employment and Income Benefits from Investing in Energy Conserving Technologies." Berkeley, CA: n.d.

Laituri, M. and C. Cocklin, "The regional resource evaluation project: a New Zealand contribution to GIS methodology and application." Proceedings of Australasian Urban and Regional Information System (AURISA), Adelaide, Australia, 23-26 November 1993.

Lang, P., *LETS Work: Rebuilding the Local Economy* (London: Grover Books, 1994).

Lang, R., "Energy and Density." Prepared for Canada Mortgage and Housing Corporation (Ottawa: CMHC, 1985).

Lappe, F. M. and P. M. DuBois, *The Quickening of America: Rebuilding Our Nation, Remaking Our Lives* (San Francisco, CA: Jossey-Bass, 1994).

Lemkow, L., "Equity: the state of the art," *Health Promotion.* 4:103-108 (1989).

Lerner, S., "The future of work in North America: good jobs, bad jobs, beyond jobs," *Futures.* Vol. 26, No.2 (March 1994).

Linton, M., personal communication, May 28, 1993.

Linton, M., personal communication, April 30, 1993.

Linton, M., *Local Currencies* (Courtenay, B.C.: Landsman Community Services, 1989).

Linton, M. and T. Greco, "The local employment and trading system," *Whole Earth Review* Summer: 104-109 (1987).

Lovins, A. B. and L. H. Lovins, "Reinventing the Wheels," *The Atlantic Monthly* 276:75-86 (1995).

Lovins, H., and A. Lovins, Many documents are published and distributed by their Rocky Mountain Institute, 1739 Snowmass Creek Road, Snowmass, Colorado 81654-9199.

Lyons, A., "Housing Improvement, Public Health, and the Local Economy," in *Our Cities, Our Futures.* (Copenhagen: WHO Europe, 1996.)

MacGill, G., and J. Dawkins, "Fremantle: An Urban Conservation Success Story," in P. Newman, S. Neville and L. Duxbury, eds., *Case Studies in Environmental Hope* (Western Australia: Environmental Protection

Authority for the Western Australian State Conservation Strategy, 1988).

MacGillivray, A. and S. Zadek, "Accounting for Change: Indicators for Sustainable Development," (London: The New Economics Foundation, October 1995).

———. (ed), "Accounting for Change: Papers from an International Seminar at Toynbee Hall," (London: The New Economics Foundation, October 1994).

MacRae, M., "Realizing the Benefits of Community Integrated Energy Systems. Study No. 45" (Calgary, Alberta: Canadian Energy Research Institute, 1992).

McCamant, K., and C. Durrett, *Cohousing: A Contemporary Approach to Housing Ourselves* (Berkeley: Habitat Press, 1988).

McChesney, I., "The Brundtland Report and sustainable development in New Zealand," (Centre for Resource Management, Lincoln University and University of Canterbury, February, Information Paper No. 25, 1991).

McHarg, I., *Design With Nature* (Garden City, NY: Natural History Press, 1969, reprinted in 1992 by John Wiley).

McNeeley, J.A., and D. Pitt, eds., *Culture and Conservation: the Human Dimension in Environmental Planning* (New York: Croom Helm, 1985).

McRobie, G., *Small is Possible* (London: Cape, 1981).

Maori Issues Unit, 1995a, Memo: Maori Issues Unit: Responsibilities.

Maori Issues Unit, 1995b, Management Workshop: Identification of Issues.

Marbach, C., "The client role in staff burn-out," *Journal of Social Issues* 34:111-124 (1978).

Marmot, M., "Social Differentials in Health Within and Between Populations," *Daedalus,* 123:4 (1994) 97-215.

Marshall Macklin Monaghan Ltd., "Estimating Energy Consumption for New Development," Prepared for the Ontario Ministry of Energy. Toronto, 1982.

Mechanic, D., "Socioeconomic status and health: an examination of underlying processes," in Bunker, J., D. Gomby, and B. Kehrer, eds. *Pathways to Health: The Role of Social Factors* (Menlo Pk., CA: Henry J. Kaiser Family Foundation, 1989).

Meyer, P. B., "Bioregions as econo-regions," *The Planet Drum Review.* 11 (1986).

Michaelis, L., "Greenhouse Gas Abatement in the Transportation Sector" (presented at the International OECD Conference, *Towards Sustainable Transportation,* Vancouver, B.C., March 26, 1996).

Minnesota Planning Board, "Minnesota Milestones," (St. Paul, MN: Minnesota Planning, December 1992).

Mitlin, D., and D. Satterthwaite, "Cities and Sustainable Development," Background Paper prepared for "Global Forum '94," Manchester, 24-28 June 1994 (London: International Institute for Environment and Development, 1994).

Mollison, B., *Permaculture One* and *Two* (Winters, CA: International Tree Crops Institute, 1978, 1979).

Mumford, L., *The Highway and the City* (New York: New American Library,

1964).

Mustard, J.F., *The Determinants of Health* (Toronto: Canadian Institute for Advanced Research, 1993).

Natural Resources Unit, "Maori Values and Environmental Management" (Wellington: Natural Resources Unit, Manatu, 1991).

Newcastle City Council, *Energy and the Urban Environment: Strategy for a Major Urban Centre*, Volumes 1 and 2 (Newcastle-upon-Tyne, United Kingdom, 1992).

New Zealand Planning Council. "Who gets what? The distribution of income and wealth in New Zealand," (Wellington: New Zealand Planning Council. November 1990).

Newman, P., "An Ecological Model for City Structure and Development," *Ekistics,* 40:239 (1975).

Newman , P. W. G., and T. L. F. Hogan, "A Review of Urban Density Models: Towards a Resolution of the Conflict Between Populace and Planner," *Human Ecology*, 9:3 (1981) 269-304.

Newman, P., and J. Kenworthy, *Cities and Automobile Dependence: An International Sourcebook* (Brookfield, VT: Gower Technical, 1989).

Newman, P., J. Kenworthy, and T. Lyons, *Transport Energy Conservation Policies for Australian Cities - Strategies for Reducing Automobile Dependence* (Western Australia: Murdoch University, 1990).

Newman, P., J. Kenworthy and L. Robinson, *Winning Back The Cities: A Choice Guide* (Sydney: Australian Consumer's Association, 1992).

Newman, P. W. G., and M. Mouritz, "Principles and Planning Opportunities for Community Scale Water and Waste Management," *Desalination* (in press 1996).

Norris, T., *The Healthy Communities Handbook* (Denver, CO: National Civic League, 1993).

Nozick, M., *No Place Like Home: Building Sustainable Communities* (Ottawa: Canadian Council on Social Development, 1992).

Offe, C. and R. Heinze, *Beyond Employment: Time, Work and the Informal Economy* (Cambridge: Polity, 1992).

Olkowski, H., et al., *The Integral Urban House: Self-Reliant Living in the City* (San Francisco: Sierra Club Books, 1979).

O'Neill, M., "La sélection d'indicateurs pour évaluer villes et villages en santé: éléments de problématique," Summary of symposium on healthy cities indicators (Université Laval, Québec, 1992).

Oregon Progress Board, "Oregon Benchmarks: Standards for Measuring Statewide Progress and Government Performance," (Salem, OR: Oregon Progress Board, 1992).

Organization for Economic Cooperation and Development, *Urban Energy Handbook — Good Local Practice* (Paris: OECD, 1995).

Osberg, Lars, Sustainable Social Development (Halifax: Department of Economics, Dalhousie University, 1990), mimeo.

Osborne, R., and T. Gaebler, *Reinventing Government* (Reading, Massachusetts: Addison-Wesley, 1991).

Owens, S., *Energy, Planning, and Urban Form* (London, England: Pion Publishing, 1986).

Parr, D., *The Climate Resolution: A Guide to Local Authority Action to Take the Heat Off the Planet*, Friends of the Earth (London, United Kingdom, January 1994).

Patterson, J., *Exploring Maori Values* (Dunmore Press, 1992).

Paul, D., "Economic injustice: is it built into the future already?" Presented to the 41st Pugwash Conference (United Kingdom, 1990).

Perks, W., and D. Van Vliet, *Assessment of Built Projects for Sustainable Communities* (Calgary: Faculty of Environmental Design, The University of Calgary and Ottawa: Canada Mortgage and Housing Corporation, 1993).

PLEBS, *The New Zealand Green Dollar Quarterly* (Christchurch, N.Z.: Plains Exchange Barter System. Winter issue, 1992).

Podborski, S., A. Pipe, M. Jette, N. Shosenberg et al., *Health Promotion Matters in Ontario: A Report of the Minister's Advisory Group* (Toronto: The Queen's Printer for Ontario, 1987).

Premier's Council on Health, Well-being, and Social Justice, The Healthy Public Policy Committee, *Nurturing Health: A Framework on the Determinants of Health* (Toronto, Ontario: Government Bookstore, 1991).

President's Council on Sustainable Development, "Sustainable America: A New Consensus" (Washington, D.C.: PCSD, 1996).

Putnam, R., R. Leonardi and R. Nanetti, *Making Democracy Work: Civic Traditions in Modern Italy* (Princeton, NJ: Princeton University Press, 1993).

Putnam, R., "Bowling Alone: Democracy in America at the End of the Twentieth Century," Nobel Symposium, 27-30 August 1994, Uppsala, Sweden.

Putnam, R., "Tuning In, Tuning Out: The Strange Disappearance of Social Capital in America." The 1995 Ithiel de Sola Pool Lecture in Political Science & Politics. December 1995, pp. 664-682.

Racey, D., *For Greens: A Common Focus* (Unpublished manuscript disseminated electronically on WEB, 1990).

Raeburn, J., "Health promotion research with heart: keeping a people perspective," *Canadian Journal of Public Health* 83 Supp.1:S20-24 (1992).

RAIN, *Knowing Home: Studies for a Possible Portland* (Portland: Rain Umbrella, 1981).

Rees, W. E., "More Jobs, Less Damage: A Framework for Sustainability, Growth and Employment." *Alternatives* 21: 4:24-30 (1995).

Rees, W. E., "Revisiting Carrying Capacity: Area-based Indicators of Sustainability." *Population and Environment* 17:3:195-215 (1996).

Rees, W., and M. Wackernagel, in "Ecological Footprints and Appropriated Carrying Capacity: Measuring the Natural Capital Requirements of the Human Economy," in A. M. Jansson, M. Hammer, C. Folke and R. Costanza, eds., *Investing in Natural Capital:The Ecological Economics Approach to Sustainability* (Washington DC: Island Press, 1992).

Rees, W. E., and M. Wackernagel, "Urban Ecological Footprints: Why Cities Cannot be Sustainable (and Why They are a Key to Sustainability)," *EIA Review* (in press, 1996).

Regional Roundtable on Recycling and Community Economic Development, "Jobs in California's Recovered Materials Economy," Issue Paper #1. Oakland, CA: 1994.

Register, R., *Eco-city Berkeley: Building Cities for a Healthy Future* (Berkeley, CA: North Atlantic Books, 1987).

Register, R., "Eco-Cities: Rebuilding Civilization, Restoring Nature," in Aberley, D., Editor, *Futures By Design: The Practice of Ecological Planning* (Gabriola Island, B.C.: New Society Publishers, 1994).

Remschmidt, H., M. H. Schmidt, and P. Strunk, *Causes and prevention of violence*. Report on the work of the Violence Commission of the federal government. Zeitschrift Fur Kinder - Und Jugendpsychiatrie 18:99-106 (1990).

"Resource Management Act," (Wellington: New Zealand Government Press, 1991).

Revenue Canada, Interpretation Bulletin, subject: Income Tax Act, Barter Transactions, No. IT-490, Reference: sections 3, 9, 69 (Ottawa: Deputy Minister of National Revenue for Taxation, 1982).

Riggle, D., "Welcome Signs for Green Business," *Business* January/February 1995, 20-24.

Roberts, J., *Changed Travel — Better World? A Study of Travel Patterns in Milton Keynes and Almere* (London: TEST, 1992).

Roberts, W. and S. Brandum, *Get a Life! How to Make a Good Buck, Dance Around the Dinosaurs and Save the World While You Are at it* (Toronto: Get-a-Life Publishers, 1995).

Robinson, J. and J. Tinker, "Reconciling Ecological, Economic, and Social Imperatives: Towards an Analytical Framework," SDRI Discussion Paper Series 95-1 (Vancouver, B.C.: Sustainable Development Research Institute, University of British Columbia, 1995).

Rootman, I., "Health Promotion: Past, Present and Future," #3 in Lectures in Health Promotion Series (Toronto: Centre for Health Promotion and Participaction, 1993).

Rootman, I., et al., Development of an Approach and Instrument Package to Measure Quality of Life of Persons with Developmental Disabilities (Toronto: Centre for Health Promotion, 1992).

Roseland, M., *Toward Sustainable Communities: A Resource Book for Municipal and Local Governments* (Ottawa: National Round Table on the Environment and the Economy, 1992a).

Roseland, M., *Toward Sustainable Communities: A Planning Framework for Municipal and Local Governments* (Vancouver: School of Community & Regional Planning, University of British Columbia, 1992b).

Roseland, M., "Sustainable Communities: An Examination of the Literature," in *Sustainable Communities Resource Package* (Toronto: Ontario Round Table on the Environment and the Economy), April 1995.

Roseland, M., Guest Editor (D. M. Duffy and T. I. Gunton, Co-Editors), "Shared Decision-Making and Natural Resource Planning: Canadian Insights," Special Issue of *Environments* Journal, Faculty of Environmental Studies, University of Waterloo, Waterloo, Ontario. Vol. 23(2), 1996a.

Roseland, M., Guest Editor, "Green Communities" issue, *Alternatives Journal: Environmental Thought, Policy and Action*, Vol 22, No. 2, April/May 1996b.

Rotstein, A. and C. A. M. Duncan, "For a second economy," in Drache, D. and M.S. Gertler, eds. *The New Era of Global Competition: State Policy and Market Power* (Montreal & Kingston: McGill- Queen's University Press, 1991), 415-434.

Royal Commission on the Future of the Toronto Waterfront (RCFTW), David Crombie, chair, *Regeneration: Toronto's Waterfront and the Sustainable City — Final Report* (Toronto: Minister of Supply and Services Canada/Queen's Printer for Ontario, 1992).

Ryan, P., *The Revised Dictionary of Modern Maori* (Auckland: Heinemann Education, 1989).

Sale, K., *Dwellers in the Land: The Bioregional Vision* (San Francisco: Sierra Club, 1985).

Salutin, R., "Hello? Is there anyone left living in the real world?," *The Globe and Mail* June 7, 1996.

Schneider, K. R., *On the Nature of Cities: Towards Enduring and Creative Human Environments* (San Francisco: Jossey Bass, 1979).

Schumacher, E. F., *Small is Beautiful: A Study of Economics as if People Mattered* (New York: Harper & Row, 1973).

Seligman, M. E. P., *Learned optimism* (New York: Knopf, 1991).

Seyfang, G. J., *The Local Exchange Trading System: Political Economy and Social Audit*, MSc thesis. (School of Environmental Studies, University of East Anglia, U.K., 1994).

Shenker, B., *Intentional Communities* (London: Routledge and Kegan Paul, 1986).

Sheppard, L., Personal communication with Liz Sheppard, founder of LETS Link, U.K.

Smith, E. J., "A Perspective from a Nuu-chah-nulth on Planning Sustainable Communities," in W. E. Rees, ed., *Planning for Sustainable Development: A Resource Book* (Vancouver: UBC Centre for Human Settlements, 1989) 127-129.

Smothers, R., "Study Finds Environmental and Economic Health Compatible." *New York Times* Oct. 19, 1994

Snohomish County Transportation Authority, "Creating Transportation Choices Through Zoning: A Guide for Snohomish County Communities" (Lynwood, Washington: Snohomish County Transportation Authority, 1994).

Social Planning and Research Council, "Well-Being: A Conceptual Framework and Three Literature Reviews," (Vancouver, B.C.: Social Planning and Research Council of B.C., 1993).

Spassoff, R., *Health for all Ontario*, Report of the panel on health goals for Ontario (Toronto, 1987).

Spirn, A. W., *The Granite Garden: Urban Nature and Human Design* (New York: Basic Books, 1984).

Statistics Canada, "Environmental Perspectives, 1993 Studies and Statistics," Catalogue 11-528E. (Ottawa: Statistics Canada, 1993a).

Statistics Canada, "Family Expenditure in Canada 1992," Catalogue 62-555. (Ottawa: Statistics Canada, 1993b).

Statistics NZ, Supermap 2 Census figures, 1991.

Stevenson, H. M. and M. Burke, "Bureaucratic logic in new social movement clothing: the limits of health promotion research," *Health Promotion International* 6:281-289 (1991).

Stevenson, M., "Selected Healthy City Indicators: A Research Agenda," Final report to the Healthy City Office, City of Toronto (Toronto: York University Centre for Health Studies, 1990).

Strasser, H., and S. Randall, *An Introduction to Theories of Social Change* (London: Routledge and Kegan Paul, 1981).

Strategy and Development Unit, "Background Paper 1: The Coast" (Waitakere City: Waitakere City Council, August, 1993a).

Strategy and Development Unit, "Background Paper 3: The Countryside" (Waitakere City: Waitakere City Council, August, 1993b).

Strategy and Development Unit, "Background Paper 5: Heritage" (Waitakere City: Waitakere City Council, August, 1993c).

Strategy and Development Unit, "Background Paper 7: Streams" (Waitakere City: Waitakere City Council, August, 1993d).

Strategy and Development Unit, "Waitakere City update" (Waitakere City: Waitakere City Council, 1994).

Stren, R., R. White, and J. Whitney, eds., *Sustainable Cities* (Boulder, Colorado: Westview Press, 1992).

Surface Transportation Policy Project (STPP), *A Citizens Guide to Transportation Planning and Livable Communities* (New York: STPP, 1994).

Surpin, R., and T. Bettridge, "Refocusing Community Economic Development," *Economic Development & Law Centre Report*, Spring, 1986, pp. 36-42.

Sustainable Seattle, "Indicators of Sustainable Community: A Report to Citizens on Long-Term Trends in Our Community," (Seattle, WA: Sustainable Seattle, 1993).

Swift, R., "What If The Greens Achieved Power?" in *New Internationalist*, May 1987 reprinted in *Utne Reader* 23, (Sept/Oct 1987) 32-33.

Take It Back Foundation and The Institute for Local Self-Reliance, "Recycling as Economic Development" (Washington, DC: ILSR 1993).

Tibbs, H. B. C., "Industrial Ecology: An Environmental Agenda for Industry," *Whole Earth Review*, Winter 1992, pp. 4-10.

Tokar, B., *The Green Alternative* (San Pedro: R. & E. Miles, 1987).

Tomalty, R., R. B. Gibson, D. H. M. Alexander, and J. Fisher, *Ecosystem Planning for Canadian Urban Regions* (Toronto: ICURR, 1994).

Toronto Food Policy Council (TFPC), *Reducing Urban Hunger in Ontario: Policy Responses to Support the Transition from Food Charity to Food Security*, Discussion Paper #1 (Toronto: Toronto Food Policy Council, 1994).

Towers, G., *Building Democracy: Community Architecture in the Inner Cities* (London: UCL Press, 1995).

Tsouros, A., ed., *The WHO Healthy Cities Project: A Project Becomes a*

*Movement* (Copenhagen: WHO Europe, 1990).

Turner, L., "Berkeley Emerges as A Leader In Environmental Business Promotion," *Nation's Cities Weekly* (National League of Cities), Jan. 1995, p 3.

United Nations Conference on Environment and Development, "Outcomes of the Conference" (Rio de Janiero, Brazil: UNCED Agenda 21, June, 1992).

United Nations Development Program (UNDP), *Human Development Report 1994* (Oxford: Oxford University Press, 1994).

United States Department of Energy, "The Jobs Connection: Energy Use and Local Economic Development," in *Tomorrow's Energy Today for Cities and Counties*, pamphlet series (Washington, DC: US DOE, 1994).

United Way, *Listening to London II* (London, Ontario: United Way, 1994).

Urban Ecology, *Eco-city Conference 1990 Report* (Berkeley, CA: Urban Ecology, 1990).

Urban Ecology, "Mission Statement and Accomplishments," World Wide Web site (1996)

Urban Ecology, *The Urban Ecologist* (quarterly). [See Access Information.]

Urban Ore Inc. and The Centre for Neighborhood Technology, "Reuse, Recycling, Refuse and the Local Economy: A Case Study of the Berkeley Serial MRF" (Berkeley and Chicago: Urban Ore and CNT, 1993).

Wackernagel, M., and W. E. Rees, *Our Ecological Footprint: Reducing Human Impact on the Earth* (Gabriola Island, BC: New Society, 1995).

Waitakere City Council, "Environmental issues: an overview," August 1993a.

Waitakere City Council, "City futures: strategic directions," 1993b.

Waitakere City Council, Annual plan 1994/95, 1994a.

Waitakere City Council, Draft Waitakere City Greenprint, 1994b.

Walker, L., "The Influence of Dwelling Type and Residential Density on the Appropriated Carrying Capacity of Canadian Households," M.Sc. (Planning) Thesis, School of Community and Regional Planning, University of British Columbia, 1995.

Wates, N., and C. Knevitt, *Community Architecture* (London: Penguin, 1987).

Welbank, M., *Planning for the Planet: Sustainable Development Policy for Local and Strategic Plans*, Friends of the Earth (London, United Kingdom, June 1994).

Whittaker, B., "Change Is Coming, and We Can Guide It," *Vermont's Northern Forests: A Resource for the Future Newsletter* (Montpelier, VT: Vermont Natural Resources Council, n.d.).

Willapa Alliance and Ecotrust, "Willapa Indicators for a Sustainable Community," (South Bend, WA: Willapa Alliance, 1995).

Williams, C. C., "Informal sector solutions to unemployment and social exclusion: the case of Local Exchange Trading Systems (LETS)," in Hardy, S., G. Lloyd, and I. Cundell, eds., *Tackling Unemployment and Social Exclusion: Problems for Regions, Solutions for People* (London: Regional Studies Association, 1994) 87-90.

Williams, C. C., *Informal sector responses to unemployment: an evaluation of the potential of Local Exchange Trading Systems (LETS)*, *Work, Employment and Society* (forthcoming, 1996a).

Williams, C. C., "*The New Barter Economy: A Preliminary Appraisal of Local Exchange and Trading Systems (LETS)*," Working Paper no. 22. (Leeds: Centre for Urban and Environmental Management, Leeds Metropolitan University, 1996b).

Willams, C. C. and J. Windbank, "Spacial variations in the informal sector: a review of evidence from the European Union," *Regional Studies* 28:819-825 (1994).

Willoughby, K., "The Local Milieu' of Knowledge Based Industries," in J. Brotchie, P. Newman, P. Hall, E. Blakeley and M. Battie, eds.,*Cities in Competition* (Melbourne: Cheshire, 1994).

Wilkinson, R., "The Epidemiological Transition: From Material Scarcity to Social Disadvantage," *Daedalus,* 123:4 (1994), pp. 61-70.

Woodroffe, A., "Optimal Urban Population Density: A Case Study in Minimizing Energy Use in Transport and Buildings," (Murdoch: Murdoch University Institute for Science and Technology Policy, ISTP Occasional Paper 1/94, 1994).

World Commission on Environment and Development (WCED), *Our Common Future,* The Brundtland Report, United Nations (New York: Oxford University Press, 1987).

World Health Organization (WHO), *Health Promotion: A Discussion Paper on Concepts and Principles*(Copenhagen: WHO European Office, 1984).

World Health Organization (WHO), Health and Welfare Canada, and the Canadian Public Health Association, "Ottawa Charter for Health Promotion," *Canadian Journal of Public Health* 77: 425-427 (1986).

WHO Europe, *The Ottawa Charter for Health Promotion* (Copenhagen: World Health Organization (WHO) Europe, 1986).

WHO Europe, *Healthy Cities Project: Workshop in Indicators,* Summary report. (ICP/HSR 619, Barcelona, 1987).

WHO Europe, *Our Cities, Our Future* (Copenhagen: World Health Organization (WHO) Europe, 1996).

Zachary, J., "Sustainable Community Indicators: Guideposts for Local Planning," (Santa Barbara, CA: Community Environmental Council of the Gildea Resource Centre, 1995).

**THE SWARM**